NEW VISIONS

Henie Onstad Kunstsenter

Published on the occasion of the exhibition

NEW VISIONS: THE HENIE ONSTAD TRIENNIAL FOR PHOTOGRAPHY AND NEW MEDIA

Henie Onstad Kunstsenter
April 14–September 17, 2023

Editor	Susanne Østby Sæther
Managing editor	Karen Monica Reini and Susanne Østby Sæther
Copy editor	Brian Sholis
Editorial assistance	Żaneta Kruszelnicka and Tiril Erdal
Texts	Inga Lāce, Eglė Rindzevičiūtė, Reem Shadid, and Susanne Østby Sæther
Artist presentations	Inga Lāce, Reem Shadid, and Susanne Østby Sæther in collaboration with artists
Design	Håkon Stensholt, ANTI
Typefaces	Neue Haas Grotesk Text Pro by Christian Schwartz, FreightText Pro by Joshua Darden, PicNic by Velvetyne, Purple Haze by Font Spectrum
Paper	150 gsm Munken Kristall and 150 gsm Magno Gloss
Printed by	die Keure Printing, Brugge, Belgium
Published by	Henie Onstad Kunstsenter and Mousse Publishing Henie Onstad Kunstsenter Sonja Henies vei 31 1311 Høvikodden, Norge hok.no Mousse Publishing Contrappunto s.r.l. Via Pier Candido Decembrio 28, 20137, Milan–Italy
Distributed by	Mousse Publishing
Available through	Mousse Publishing, Milan moussemagazine.it DAP | Distributed Art Publishers, New York artbook.com Les presses du réel, Dijon lespressesdureel.com Antenne Books, London antennebooks.com
First edition	2023
Price	€ 35 / $ 40
ISBN	978-8-86-749572-6

REITAN RETAIL · Aars · ABG SUNDAL COLLIER · SAHA · ifa Institut für Auslandsbeziehungen

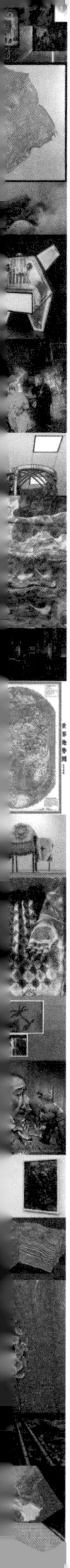

FOREWORD

Caroline Ugelstad
Director of exhibitions and collections and chief curator

Henie Onstad Kunstsenter is proud to present the second edition of *New Visions: The Henie Onstad Triennial for Photography and New Media*. The inaugural triennial opened in 2020 and brought together recent works by thirty-one international artists. This was the first major international presentation in Norway foregrounding contemporary artists who work experimentally with camera-based practices.

In the second edition of *New Visions*, Henie Onstad directs its lens toward artists and practices associated with Eastern Europe, Central Asia, and the Middle East. In its program, Henie Onstad is concerned with the freedom of expression and experimentation of artists and cultural workers. The artistic cultures of Eastern Europe, Central Asia, and the Middle East offer both rich traditions and exciting new scenes focused upon experimental film, photography, and media art. By drawing upon experiences specific to those histories and today's cultural, social, and geopolitical arrangements, these artists offer new insights into these regions – and into how we are all connected. The triennial includes sculptures, textiles, and monumental wall and video installations from twenty-two international artists and features eight new commissions. Its central themes are energy production and distribution, the extraction of natural and man-made resources and, by extension, the ecological, social, and political consequences of these ventures.

In Norway, Henie Onstad was one of the first institutions to treat photography seriously as an independent artistic form. Since 2017, the art center has sought to re-establish this position. The institution has developed a program centering on photography and new media, presenting solo exhibitions with significant Norwegian and international photographers and extensive group exhibitions in addition to the talent program *Young Photographers*. The flagship of this venture, which is unique in a Nordic context, is *New Visions*. We will continue to build and promote the triennial to ensure Henie Onstad remains at the forefront of contemporary art and new media. This is in keeping with the institution's tradition of embracing the avant-garde.

Henie Onstad would like to extend a big thank you to the two curators who worked on this year's triennial in close collaboration with Susanne Østby Sæther, Henie Onstad's curator of photography and new media. Inga Lāce and Reem Shadid have brought new knowledge and new perspectives to Henie Onstad and we are extremely grateful for their dedication to the project. Fritt Ord has been an important contributor to the conversation program Henie Onstad launched in advance of the triennial, called *New Visions in Conversation*, which aimed to support Ukrainian artists and to strengthen awareness and knowledge of Russia's full-scale invasion of Ukraine as seen through artists' perspectives. Henie Onstad also extends a big thank you to our important collaborators on the photo program. Aars has enabled a special commissioned work for the triennial, called the Aars Commission, which in 2023 has been awarded to Farah Al Qasimi. Our other supporters, ABG and Reitan Retail, also make the photo program at Henie Onstad possible. Furthermore, Henie Onstad thanks the contributors to the catalog, the artists' galleries, and, most importantly, the artists for their voices, independence, and insights.

NEW VISIONS 2023

Inga Lāce, Reem Shadid,
and Susanne Østby Sæther

Daily life has changed drastically over the past three years: many of our interactions were funneled through screens; news of the world became more immediately accessible and more contested than ever; in-person interactions and environments have become optional; and when we *have* ventured out into that world, we've done so warily and with precautions in place. Collaborating to curate *New Visions 2023*, from multiple homes in multiple time zones, has been a challenge – but also would have been impossible not too long ago. In the past year, we have worked from Oslo, Riga, Beirut, Palestine, and New York – sometimes amid quickly changing conditions. Toward the end of 2022, in Oslo, an energy crisis meant people were suddenly debating nuclear power sources. In Riga, the war in Ukraine had brought solidarity, but also fear of a potential Russian invasion; it also elevated nationalist tendencies and ethnic tensions to levels unseen since the 1990s, and those factors strained the most recent election. For two years, Beirut has been suffering under a total state collapse, with an unimaginable energy crisis at its center. Connecting these places and others, weaving them into a network of shared pasts and futures, physical infrastructures and digital networks, this exhibition focuses on subjects like energy production and distribution, the extraction of natural and human-made resources, and, by extension, the ecological, social, and political consequences of these ventures.

The second edition of *New Visions: The Henie Onstad Triennial for Photography and New Media* brings together works by artists that tackle these themes through experimental approaches to photography and other processes of automated image making. "New Visions," the title of the triennial, references László Moholy-Nagy's 1932 manifesto "A New Instrument of Vision" and its impact on twentieth-century experimental photography. We believe that, just as photography was a tool for new perceptions and conceptions of an increasingly mechanized world in the early twentieth century, so artists today use photography to explore our increasing entanglements with machines and processes of automation and extraction. In doing so, they bring forth novel forms of affective, social, and political engagement.

Significantly, photography is understood here in an expanded sense. It is a porous practice that constantly leaks into and entwines with adjacent mediums, materials, and entities and a continuum that extends from its chemical and analogue origins to its coded and digital state. Scholars, artists, and critics have given this transformed understanding of photography many designations, most of which turn on notions of instability: the contemporary photographic image is said to be "flexible," it is "fluid and malleable," "polymorphic," "versatile," "modular," and "soft, not only infinitely malleable but merged with software."[1] Thus conceived, *photography* here also encompasses time-based practices such as film, video, and VR, and – in line with Moholy-Nagy's appreciation of machines – extends to images produced by virtual cameras, machine vision, and artificial-intelligence software. In line with this inclusion of images that are not generated by a human subject, photography is also seen as distributed across human and non-human actors, entities, and systems. Joanna Zylinska's notion of *nonhuman photography* resonates here.[2] For Zylinska, nonhuman photography encompasses photographs made *by* nonhumans, but also photographs *of* nonhuman spaces and photographs *made for* nonhumans. Her book calls for acknowledging the ever-present nonhuman elements of photography, since it is here "that photography's creative, or world-making, side can be identified."[3] It is in this sense that many of the artists presented here explore the nonhuman dimensions of photography.

More recently, the concept of "synthetic images," referring to images generated by artificial intelligence and more specifically by so-called generative adversarial networks (or GANs), has gained traction. While such images are not photographic in the sense that they are "drawn with light," as the etymology of the term *photography* indicates, they are frequently photorealistic and thus are often mistaken for and treated as photographs. Moreover, as with other digital images enmeshed in networks of data transmission and storage that require immense amounts of energy, synthetic images are powered by what the environmental historian Alfred W. Crosby has called "fossilized sunshine," his term used to describe petroleum and other fossil fuels.[4] In *this* sense, synthetic images are also "drawn with light."

From its start, photography has been deeply entwined with practices of extraction. In the well-researched catalogue text accompanying the 2022 exhibition *Mining Photography: The Ecological Footprint of Image Production*, curators Boaz Levin and Esther Ruelfs point out that "fossil energy and photography [...] were intimately linked from their advent, developing concomitantly and in close proximity."[5] William Henry Fox Talbot, developer of the calotype – a photographic negative from which multiple prints could be made – was invested in a silver mining business and helped develop the use of animal-derived gelatin in early printing processes.[6] Moreover, several of photography's (historically shifting) material components result from resource extraction. Copper was utilized in the industrially produced copperplates that in the 1840s and '50s were photography's first image support. Silver is still a basic component of much black-and-white photography through the silver gelatin printing method and has been so since the 1870s.[7] Both metals arrived in photographers' hands through colonial networks of extraction. Indeed, throughout its history, the development and dispersion of photography has been powered by fossil fuels, colonial expansion, and exploitative resource extraction.

Material extraction

Extractive economies also connect Eastern Europe, Central Asia, the Middle East (through Arabian Gulf countries), and Norway, among other places. The end of the 1960s and beginning of the '70s saw an oil-industry boom across these regions.[8] This economic dependence on oil and gas helped bring into view the various political and economic relationships between them. *New Visions 2023* attempts to excavate how some of those relations and networks are guided by parallel practices, common interests, and resonant struggles.

By the mid-'70s, following the Six-Day War between Egypt and the Zionist occupation forces in Palestine, the Soviet Union switched its strategic alliance from Egypt to Syria to better achieve its goals in the Middle East.[9] The effects can still be witnessed today in what has become overlapping proxy wars following the Arab Spring. These wars are part of a larger history that connects Lebanon, the (Arabian) Gulf Cooperation Council region, and, inadvertently, Syria, Palestine, Egypt, and Jordan to the Kremlin via ex–Soviet bloc territories. By way of technological advancements and political and economic desires, those connections extend further to Central, Northern, and Western Europe. This relationship is encapsulated primarily in the extraction of power – be it energy like electricity, water, and oil or immaterial matters such as cultural, data, or demographic dominance.

Details of the Soviets' inextricable network of profit and extraction are laid out by Giorgi Gago Gagoshidze and Tekla Aslanishvili in their work *Stone of Hell* (2021). In this experimental essay-film they excavate how manganese ore extracted in the village of Chiatura, Georgia, was sold to the German company Krupp by the Soviet regime. Manganese is used in steel production, and Krupp utilized it in the manufacturing of weapons used by combatants in both world wars. Krupp also invested in the early development of photography. Photography's material entwinement with the military-industrial complex is here brought to the fore, along with the ecological and social exploitation in Chiatura enforced by the Soviet regime and continued as part of the globalized, neoliberal market economy.

Long before the Soviet Union took control of Central Asia, cotton – also known as "white gold" – was grown in the region. Its production tended to be centered in small workshops weaving cloth for domestic consumption. In the 1960s, the Soviet administration did something many considered extreme, starting a major water-diversion project on the arid plains of Kazakhstan, Uzbekistan, and Turkmenistan. The region's two major rivers – the Syr Darya and the Amu Darya, fed by snowmelt and precipitation in faraway mountains – were used to transform the desert into farms for cotton and other crops. This massive act of geoengineering caused the slow disappearance of the Aral Sea that these rivers once fed. The slow violence manifested not only toward the lake and its surroundings, but also toward the people inhabiting nearby lands.

Even though cotton has been critical to the development of Uzbekistan's economy and the country is one of the largest cotton producers in the world, it has also been the cause of environmental destruction and systemic forced labor. How can that story, an invisible part of both Western clothing and traditional Uzbek garments, be re-read today? Can we look at the material without seeing the violence of its making? Artist Dilyara Kaipova, in her series *Curse of Cotton* (2022), has printed the photos of cotton flower symbols found across the country upon traditional cotton robes called *chapans*. In doing so, the artist amplifies the tension inscribed in the cotton flower. On the one hand, it is an economic backbone and the symbolic icon of the country; on the other, it is a stand-in for the quiet exploitation of Uzbekistan's raw materials and human resources.

Slow agricultural violence also resonates in the work of artist and photographer Seif Kousmate, which refers to the once agriculturally rich and now-abandoned Akka Oasis in Morocco. With one of the world's largest phosphate reserves in Morocco, mining started as early as the 1920s and has played a key role in geopolitics ever since. A century of phosphate extraction has had devastating environmental effects on the nation's farmlands, poisoning water sources and polluting the air, leaving many in mining regions with cancers. Kousmate, in his series *Waha* (2020–), photographs Moroccan oases deserted and deteriorating because of this overexploitation and new agricultural practices. Where traditional family-based settlements once reigned, increasingly corporate farming has introduced agricultural methods that suck water away from native plants and endanger the oasis ecosystem itself. By burning the film and incorporating organic materials such as leaves or palm fronds in his prints, Kousmate insists on understanding what the environmental decay and economic power struggles have brought to us. Photographer Farah Al Qasimi treats such ruinous extraction more obliquely, as when she attends to the use of fresh water in the Gulf region, juxtaposing images of barren landscapes with lush floral motifs found across architecture and spaces of commerce in the United Arab Emirates. Fresh water is used to keep grass and flowers alive in public spaces, even though it's a region characterized by severe water stresses. Her layering of images also speaks to the blurred boundary between natural and artificial in the region, where infrastructure development continues without regard for the effects of rapid climate change in the region.

Wasteful agriculture also contributes to the slow destruction of the Baltic Sea's marine ecosystems, which figure literally in Kristina Õllek's photographs. The Baltic Sea is home to seven of the world's ten largest low-oxygen "dead sea" zones.[10] Excess fertilizer nutrients in the water, inadequate water treatment, and rising sea temperatures significantly affect the cyanobacterial community, leading to increasing toxic blue-green algae blooms that create these depleted, oxygen-starved areas. These dead zones have a major impact on marine ecology, and the sea's recovery capacity is very limited. More recently, in September 2022, a gas leak from the Russian Nord Stream 2 pipeline further damaged the Baltic Sea's ecology and created an additional tension in the global energy crisis. Through abstract-looking compositions, Õllek renders visible this slow violence. She has used sea salt, cyanobacteria, bioplastic, silicone, and other organic and inorganic materials to enhance her photographic works, suspending some of them in the air with chains, a nod to underwater anchors.

Pattern recognition

Another process of extraction undergirds image production in the twenty-first century: the abstracting of economic value facilitated by computational, networked photography. Each time a photograph is uploaded and shared on a social media platform such as Instagram, personal data is produced, captured, and commodified. Under these conditions – what social psychologist Shoshana Zuboff has called *surveillance capitalism* – abstraction is a process of extraction: the mining of data for which the photographic images on our screens frequently act as lure.[11] Data mining's effects perhaps most commonly surround us in the form of capitalist consumption. The algorithmic recognition of patterns (more precisely, identifying rules that describe specific patterns within the data)[12] is key to this process. The patterns that emerge from the mining of immense data sets affect our daily habits and relations with each other – how we feel, act, think, and live.

Neïl Beloufa's work taps into the algorithmic modulation of behavior and emotions with wit. His research-based practice often aims to expose mechanisms of control and power by excavating how digital interactions mediate contemporary society. With their cute appearance, the luminous robots in *New Visions 2023*, nicknamed *Yellow Host* and *Red Host*, appeal to our relational capacities. Yet their interactive features enmesh us in processes of data mining and content generation – and in the economic value production that ensues. Anna Ehrenstein also addresses the dissemination and circulation of culture and cultural goods across processes of algorithmic and human pattern recognition and extraction. In her ongoing body of work *A Lotus Is a Lotus* (2017–), she exhumes the desire for cultural difference across digital and physical realms. Heavily ornamented and patterned fake and folkloric objects – of a kind typically found in tourist markets of the former "Orient" – fill her photographic lenticular prints. In a video she further complicates notions of fake and original in a guide to the illegal backdoor Pearl Market in Beijing. *A Lotus Is a Lotus* continues Ehrenstein's longstanding exploration of who produces and judges cultural, economic, and aesthetic value and how the neocolonial conditions of the digital present uphold and upend these values.

Ketuta Alexi-Meskhishvili and Marat Dilman both use photography to explore how culturally coded and heritage patterns are repurposed for nation branding in mundane objects and surroundings.

In *Georgian Ornament* (2020–21), Meskhishvili uses plastic bags collected in her native Georgia as a point of departure for a series of semi-abstract photographs and textiles. Decorated with traditional motifs originally found in the architecture of byzantine churches, these bags are – like the objects that Ehrenstein photographs – made mainly for tourist consumption. Simplified into abstract, semi-ethnic form, they point to the time before the country's occupation by the Russian empire in the nineteenth century, an era that also fascinates the country's current conservative political leaders. Dilman shares Meskhishvili's eye for the politically imbued cycles of heritage reappropriation in post-Soviet states. His photographs are razor-sharp depictions of such ornaments in the visually hybrid landscapes of present-day Kazakhstan. Born in 1990, Dilman grew up in the newly independent, fossil-rich country, and his work captures in detail the juxtaposition of futurism and folklore that results from Kazakhstan's rapidly shifting socio-political, economic, and architectural identity.

Anthropologist Elizabeth Povinelli has written that "the nation-state remains as a place for and the source of an extraction of capital for those for whom the nation-state is an irrelevant or counterform of identity."[13] In this formulation, the nation-state is an extractive system through which the one percent pumps the resources out of the rest of the population. She illustrates this with a drawing of extractive pipes surrounding the earth and connecting various countries. This direct visualization of aggressive extraction makes us reconsider the "decorative" elements of international relations, from the rituals of cultural diplomacy to state and city branding. Are they just a cover? Can one reclaim the ornaments, and, with them, something true of national identities themselves?

Winners write national histories. Other narratives do not make the cut: alternative pasts, micro-histories, the everyday, the utopian, people's desires, and unrealized ideas. What if those came to the forefront? In his ongoing series *Someone Tried to Lock Up Time* (2018–), Basim Magdy asks this question through dream-like splinters of those lost stories. In Magdy's poetic juxtaposition of found photographs and his own text fragments, mounted onto color graded walls in pinks and yellows that evoke the cyclical movement of the sun, history from the perspective of the marginalized and forgotten blends with notions of deep time. Magdy's work conjures histories that escape the archive – that escape even the possibility of being recorded or stored.

This resonates with the work of Lesia Vasylchenko and her exploration of radically different temporal scales, the micro and the macro. In a new sculpture, synthetic aperture radar (SAR) imagery capturing sites of geological, human, and ecological precarity is embedded in a structure that includes soil from a Ukrainian grain field damaged by war, rocks obtained from an earthquake site, and simulation of glass made of refabricated nuclear waste. While SAR images operate at a temporal micro scale, these materials conjure the deep time of geology and the human impact on earth. Nuclear waste is one of the biggest ecological and logistical challenges of our time, since its half-life spans thousands of years. By using this material, Vasylchenko engages both our capacity for imagination and the responsibilities we have to future generations. Her research-based work explores how different timescales impact the earth through the data infrastructures that undergird today's observation and surveillance technologies.

In his 2020 book *The Good Ancestor*, Roman Krznaric suggests ways we can learn to think long-term in fast-paced and short term–focused societies. To expand our thinking about the future, he refers to the Seventh Generation Principle from Iroquois philosophy, which posits that decisions we make today should result in a sustainable world seven generations into the future. He also gives the example of the "cathedral thinking," which refers to projects that have taken more than a generation to finish.[14] In *RAKHNĖ* (2023), Emilija Škarnulyte's video installation commissioned for *New Visions 2023*, the artist envisions an undersea data storage infrastructure that points to the exponential growth of data and the need for novel means of storage, as well as to the general inaccessibility of that data. Škarnulytė speculates that these sites may, in decrepit form, one day be subject to archaeological research and to the myths and codices of a forgotten era.

Infrastructures of power

The camera has played drastically varied roles in social and civil movements. From being a weapon of the colonizer, used to document and segregate people, in the last thirty years photography has increasingly been repurposed as a tool for resistance and justice. During the Apartheid struggle in South Africa, photographic revelations of oppression played a key role in mounting pressure on the authoritarian political regime. It not only documented violence, but also demonstrated the strength and unity of the liberation movement. Photographic images also played a crucial role in the 2018 Hong Kong protests, during which protesters went to great lengths to stay anonymous. They used umbrellas, hats, masks, and face paint to evade facial-recognition tools and were cautious about how to transfer images and what communication tools they used to share data with each other. Later, when people could not gather on the streets due to COVID–19 lockdown restrictions, many used the online game *Animal Farm* to encode data through its different characters (until it was banned).

Generating images from various kinds of non-visual data has emerged as a strategy of subversion in concert with the more restrictive measures many authoritarian governments – from Hong Kong to Egypt, Iran to Kazakhstan – have enforced on protest and dissent. The war on (dis) information and an emphasis on exposure or revelation has become intrinsic to the fight against oppressive regimes that deploy reputational and information-focused tactics. Communication and representation are sites of struggle. Yet technology has also increasingly provided the means to reconstruct narratives, expose disinformation, and find channels of solidarity. In her work *AI Realism, Qantar 2022* (2022), Almagul Menlibayeva feeds the words of victims and eyewitnesses into text-to-image algorithms trained by the deep-learning model Transformer to construct images of the massive protests in Almaty in January 2022. These AI-generated images are, however, based on existing photographs that make up the datasets used to train the algorithms. The question arises: Can these images ever transgress the conditions that created them to offer alternative stories and imagine alternative futures?

With the increased automation and digitization of our struggles comes a corresponding need for the corporeal. Myriam Boulos, in her extensive project *What's Ours* (2019–), uses the camera as a reminder of the energy and intimacy of social unrest and uprisings against injustice. Images of collective and intimate moments during the Lebanese revolution of 2019–20 underscore the importance of the body, of tenderness and human connection. The series depicts moments of despair, love, death, shock, and harmony.

For those looking, there are more opportunities than ever to see the interconnected nature of the world. We can connect without disruption through video or voice calls, keep up with friends on social media, or learn about global events on the world wide web. Alongside this social interconnectedness, the global economy has never been as co-dependent. We witnessed the ramifications of the ship, Ever Given, that got stuck in the Suez

Canal in 2021, as well as the ongoing shortage of food supplies to Africa and the Middle East after Russia invaded Ukraine in February 2022. In their video installation *ONSET* (2023), Anna Engelhardt and Mark Cinkevich track Russian colonialism through its military bases. The work is reconstructed from CGI-generated and found imagery of the air bases Khmeimim, in Syria, Baranovich, in Belarus, and Saky, in Ukraine. Electricity is here used as a metaphor for the dependence of the possessing force on its host. To the south, Haig Aivazian delves into the history of using light as a tool for violence and torture, thereby contextualizing the current energy crises in Lebanon as part of a larger history of colonial and extractive endeavors. In his ongoing series of videos displayed on LED screens, Istvan Virag explores the relations between economics, the over-consumption of energy, and our environment. His latest video, *Pixel Pitch vol. 4* (2023), is a meditative visual examination of the oil industry and of alternative energy futures beyond fossil fuels and builds associative relationships between the viscous oil fueling capital flows and the hundreds of millions of years of sun-powered, compressed life that comprise it.

The networked character of our world was underscored in 1993 with the creation of the European Union, or more recently in the expansionist Belt and Road and Polar Silk Road initiatives. The latter is a new maritime route conceived by China that passes through the Russian waters of the slowly melting Arctic and terminates at newly built ports on the Arctic shores of Norway. It will connect Beijing to Asia and Europe through Russia and Norway with a network of logistics and transportation channels. Köken Ergun and Sahsa Azanova's research for their new collaborative work delves into the routes of the Polar Silk Road and outlines the geopolitical struggle over resources in the Arctic. The artists lay out the Polar Silk Road on Chinese cartographer Hao Xiaoguang's vertical maps that center the northern and southern hemispheres. A video supplements the maps with poetry, song, and stock imagery. Scrutinizing the role of infrastructure as soft power, the artists suggest that expansionism and extractivism go hand-in-hand as part of the redrawing of global cartographies.

Bringing together these twenty-two artists with ties to Eastern Europe, Central Asia, the Middle East, and Norway, *New Visions 2023* makes evident their shared interests in patterns of resource extraction and circulation across physical and digital infrastructures and across different time scales. With works created through altered chemical and digital photography, found footage, CGI, synthetic aperture radar, and other techniques, the exhibition and this volume present the experiments, outlooks, and imaginings – in short, the "new visions" – that arise from this diverse group of camera-based artists.

Pages 8–9
1. Artist and photographer Lucas Blalock has employed the term "flexible image" in *Objektiv Part I: The Flexible Image* (2016). http://www.objektiv.no/journal/2016/6/2/the-flexible-image-part-i. Accessed October 15, 2022. The notion of the "fluid and malleable image" is used, for example, by Andrew Dewdney. See his review "Nonhuman Photography," *New Formations* 94, 169. Alexandra Moschovi, Carol McKay, and Arabella Plouviez employed the term "versatile" in Moschovi, McKay, and Plouviez, eds., *The Versatile Image: Photography, Digital Technologies, and the Internet* (Leuven, Belgium: Leuven University Press, 2013): 11–32. Chantal Pontbriand, then curator of the Paris Photo fair, summarized the situation as follows: "The image becomes flexible, polymorph, more than ever temporal, but also corporeal." Quoted in Joanna Zylinska and Camilla Kuc, *Photomediations: A Reader* (London: Open Humanities Press, 2014): 11, http://openhumanitiespress.org/books/download/Kuc-Zylinska_2016_Photomediations-A-Reader.pdf. Accessed October 11, 2019. **2.** Joanna Zylinska, *Nonhuman Photography* (Cambridge, MA: MIT Press, 2017). **3.** Joanna Zylinska, "The Creative Potential of Nonhuman Photography," in *Photomediations: A Reader*, eds. Joannal Zylinska and Camilla Kuc, 207. **4.** As Boaz Levin and Esther Ruelfs point to, Nadia Bozak employs Crosby's term to describe photographic and cinematic images in her book *The Cinematic Footprint: Lights, Camera, Natural Resources* (New Brunswick, NJ: Rutgers University Press 2012), 30–31. Referenced in *Mining Photography: The Ecological Footprint of Image Production*, eds. Boaz Levin, Esther Ruelfs, Tulga Beyerle (Leipzig: Spector Books, 2022), 15–16. **5.** Boaz Levin and Esther Ruelfs, "Photography and Climate Change," in *Mining Photography: The Ecological Footprint of Image Production*, eds. Boaz Levin, Esther Ruelfs, Tulga Beyerle (Leipzig: Spector Books, 2022), 15. **6.** Ibid., 16. **7.** This method consists of an emulsion of silver salts in gelatin that creates a light-sensitive layer on top of a foundation of paper. A middle layer of baryta was introduced later. Following exposure of the negative and development in a chemical bath, the silver gelatin emulsion forms the image. **8.** "The history of oil in the region." *The Adelphi Papers* (1996), 36:300, 9–12, DOI: 10.1080/05679329608449344. In the post-Soviet countries significant oil production takes place in Russia, Ukraine, Azerbaijan, Kazakhstan, Uzbekistan. Until recently most of European countries were dependent on oil and gas from Russia, flowing through Ukraine; an entanglement that played its part in the current full scale Russian invasion in Ukraine. **9.** John C. Burch, *Background Issues Concerning Soviet Foreign Policy and Syrian Initiatives in the Middle East*, March 1986.

Pages 10–11
10. National Geographic Society, "Dead Zone," https://education.nationalgeographic.org/resource/dead-zone. Accessed January 22, 2023. **11.** Shoshana Zuboff, *The Age of Surveillance Capitalism: The Fight for a Human Future at the New Frontier of Power* (New York: Public Affairs, 2019). Abstraction in this sense obviously also relates to Karl Marx theory of alienation as the human and social implications of the abstraction and commercialization of labor. The notion of images as lure is put forth by Ingrid Hoelzl and Remi Marie in the short text "No Image, No Cry," where they describe the digital (photographic) image as a "lure for the actual processes of surveillance and control." https://generalhumanity.wordpress.com/2018/06/30/no-image-no-cry-by-ingrid-hoelzl/. Accessed October 12, 2022. **12.** *Encyclopedia Brittanica*, https://www.britannica.com/technology/data-mining/Pattern-mining. Accessed October 19, 2022.

Pages 12–13
13. Elizabeth A. Povinelli,, "What do White People Want?: Interest, Desire, and Affect in Late Liberalism," *E-Flux Conversations*, January 12, 2017, https://conversations.e-flux.com/t/elizabeth-a-povinelli-what-do-white-people-want-interest-desire-and-affect-in-late-liberalism/5845. Accessed October 8, 2022. **14.** Roman Krznaric, *The Good Ancestor. How to Think Long Term in a Short-Term World* (London: Penguin Books, 2021), 88, 94.

THE ATOMIC CONDITION

Eglė Rindzevičiūtė,
Kingston University London

When Russia invaded Ukraine in February 2022, one line of attack went through Chornobyl. Within a few days the Russian army captured Zaporizhzhia, the most powerful nuclear power plant in Europe. In addition to breaching the Geneva convention that prohibits military action in the vicinity of civil nuclear facilities, Putin threatened to deploy nuclear weapons to protect what he described as a Russian national interest in Ukraine. The Russian invasion has revived the seemingly long-relegated Cold War fear of a nuclear apocalypse.

However, in recent debates the nuclear risks are mostly defined in anthropocentric terms – how a nuclear attack would harm people. Few consider the terraforming impacts of nuclear explosions: the ways in which they can alter the very structure of the planet. When Paul Crutzen coined the term *Anthropocene*, he proposed dating it to the first nuclear explosions to produce isotopes that hitherto did not exist in nature.[1] Indeed, back in the early 1980s, Crutzen and his fellow atmospheric scientists warned leaders of the Soviet and Western blocs about the risk of nuclear winter – irreversible climate change as a consequence of a nuclear war.[2] In 2022, this Cold War lesson appears to have been forgotten; nuclear risks are not considered part of the global climate crisis, but a kind of competitor to it, as many fear that Russia's war will steer public attention away from the carbon fuel–driven apocalypse. Moreover, the ongoing energy crisis has spurred the nuclear power lobby to push small modular reactors as a helpful way to decarbonize the economy and bolster energy sovereignty. Finally, Finland and Sweden decided to join the nuclear-powered NATO alliance, in this way confirming the rationale of nuclear deterrence: a strategic belief that the countries equipped with equally powerful nuclear weapons are unlikely to wage war against each other, because doing this would risk "mutual assured destruction," a strategic concept nicknamed MAD by the American security analyst Donald Brennan in the 1960s.[3] However, although nuclear power has been questioned since the 1950s, in the twenty-first century the nuclear industry continues promoting it as a vital component of the solution for both climate change and national security. In this highly charged context, it is important to remember that the birth of nuclear power was entangled with colonial extractivism and attempts to weaponize geological systems in both liberal democratic and authoritarian regimes.[4]

Indeed, there was hardly ever a time when nuclear power was not controversial. Over the decades, both public and governmental attitudes toward nuclear power have oscillated between enthusiastic support, criticism, and indifference, as demonstrated in Vicki Lesley's 2019 documentary film *The Atom: A Love Affair*. Generations of scholars, creative practitioners, and activists have sought to keep nuclear power in the public focus. They questioned the arguments for nuclear power as a source of military and economic security, uncovered the societal impacts of its colonial roots and institutionalized secrecy, and called attention to the vast legacy of radioactive waste that will remain hazardous for hundreds of thousands of years. The rallying cry is that nuclear technology is neither merely technical nor is it simple. As the cultural theorist Anna Volkmar has noted, nuclear societies – societies that host any part of the nuclear cycle, such as uranium mining, the production of nuclear energy or nuclear weapons, or the storing of radioactive waste – continuously grow layers of complexity that render nuclear power fundamentally unknowable and ungovernable.[5]

I call this situation "the atomic condition," an assemblage of ways of life and physical environments that evolve with the nuclear industry. Like Volkmar and others, I posit that contemporary art has a role to play in the governance of nuclear power, not simply by giving the nuclear age visual representation, but also by contributing to the organization of the atomic condition, by opening the nuclear sector to greater public participation. This role, however, should not be regarded as a search for solutions, because, as Volkmar has written, a "solution is not what we seek."[6] Given the complexity of nuclear risks, what is sought is the enhancement of public accountability, openness, and responsibility.

Understanding the atomic condition

Experts, nuclear physicists, and engineers, working under a veil of great secrecy and deriving their authority from their narrowly technical expertise, brought the nuclear age into being. However, to understand the atomic condition is to go beyond the physics laboratory, the nuclear reactor, and the A-bomb and to engage with how colonial extraction on behalf of nuclear power has shaped the environment and society.[7] For example, producing nuclear energy often requires both the lands and the health of Indigenous populations. As the historian Gabrielle Hecht has noted, nuclearity – the categorization of materials and technologies as "nuclear" – is a matter of political negotiation that creates inequalities. For instance, since the 1960s, uranium mining has no longer been classified as part of the nuclear industry, making the uranium trade exempt from the nuclear non-proliferation treaty. Accordingly, safety standards that are applicable to the nuclear sector were not enforced, making the mining process cheaper and exposing mine workers to radioactive hazards.[8] Nuclear testing entailed land dispossession from Indigenous communities in, for instance, New Mexico, the Marshall Islands, the Novaya Zemlia archipelago, and Kazakhstan. Nuclear bombing, accidents, and contamination resulting from unsafe radioactive waste disposal contaminated the soil and water in Ukraine, Russia, and Japan.[9] Yet there have been few large public-health studies on the long-term impacts of low-level radiation.[10] The colonial and extractive roots of the atomic condition mean it is not that different from carbon regimes, particularly in terms of transforming the global biosphere, affecting the property rights of Indigenous communities, and creating new, human-made risks that are unequally distributed both geographically and socially.[11]

Like CO2-emitting industries, nuclear power has been part of the terraforming that characterizes the Anthropocene era.[12] Resonating with the modern notion of the boundless, transformative power of science and technology, the Cold War utopia of splitting the atom and moving the earth reminds us that the history of nuclear power is deeply entangled with geoengineering, as detailed in many environmental histories. For instance, US nuclear scientists, as Paul Josephson showed, initiated the project "Ploughshare," which entailed testing nuclear bombs for "peaceful purposes," such as building canals, tunnels, and mining, from the 1950s to the '70s. The Soviets also explored such uses for nuclear explosions: in addition to mining, the most prominent geoengineering project intended to redirect Siberian rivers to irrigate the land in Central Asian republics.[13] Thankfully, the river-redirection project was blocked by environmental scientists and not implemented. What remained, however, was the vast damage caused by uranium mining in the mountains and deserts of Central Asia, where the piles and ponds of radioactive uranium tailings mar the lives of locals and where the human cost of nuclear terraforming has not been fully accounted for, even in local histories.[14]

Despite the inherent diversity of the atomic condition, the public understanding of nuclear power tends to be confined to a particular set of objects: a nuclear reactor, an atomic bomb, and radioactive isotopes that can cause cancer. This is not surprising, because living with the atomic condition means dealing with extreme power inequities. The knowledge about nuclear technology the public can access, as the historian Alex Wellerstein has demonstrated, is limited because pervasive and systematic secrecy is inherent to the nuclear industry.[15] Given these constraints, there is no single privileged vantage point. That fact brings art practice and social and humanities scholarship on nuclear power closer together since they all seek to work around extremely limited access to sources. To study the atomic condition entails translation, re-assembling, improvisation, and adjustment, skills that are often credited to artists.

Beyond artistic representation

Since the 1940s, visual artists have experimented with nuclear imaginaries and reflected upon the atomic condition. For instance, the Italian group Art Nucleare, founded in 1951, turned away from abstract painting to art depicting distressed figures blending human and robotic features (as in Enrico Baj's *Fire! Fire!* [1963–64]). In response to the contamination of the land with uranium and plutonium in Andalusia, where US aircraft lost two hydrogen bombs, Jorge Castillo created the painting *Palomares* (1966), which uses organic, Surrealist shapes to reflect on the uncertainty around the impacts of radioactivity, an uncertainty amplified by the silence of political authorities.[16] On the other side of the Iron Curtain, artists explored the rational aesthetics of nuclear power, like Vladimir Yankilevsky in his pentaptych *Atomic Station* (1962).[17] Toward the end of the twentieth century, art interventions increasingly left the white cube of museums and galleries to shape a new political ecology that implies the political categorization of materials and technologies as "nuclear," what Hecht calls nuclearity, by entering public spaces and industrial and natural locations, and by increasing diversity and complexity through collaborative approaches.

The growing complexity of artistic responses to the atomic condition should not be underestimated; we should avoid mechanically classifying nuclear imaginaries into existing styles, genres, and periods. The British historian Jeff Hughes, for instance, critiqued reification of the nuclearity in "nuclear culture," deeming it "too general, too passive, too monolithic, too simplistic a category." For Hughes, the meaning of nuclearity lies in practices, specificities, and multiplicities.[18] In a similar vein, Volkmar and curator Ele Carpenter drew attention to the highly contextual ways that contemporary artists revisit and expand the visual regimes of nuclearity, going beyond the official iconography of the bomb, the mushroom cloud, and the cooling towers but also beyond the imagery produced by anti-nuclear movements.[19] Such critical and performative interventions often originate in response to the perception of lost control in this complex technosocial world.[20]

Materials

Going beyond visual representation, the artist and theorist Susan Schuppli suggests taking material agency seriously and recognizing "material witnesses," a term she coined in 2009 to refer to the imprints of a violent past on objects and materials.[21] Schuppli calls the early radiograms, also known as radioautographs, used by the US Army to measure the exposure of animals and plants to radioactivity "radiological events" – and not representations – because they constitute material evidence that can disclose repressed or secret knowledge.[22] Even stones leave a trace, as evidenced by Martin Howse's *Three Day Exposure Uraninite* (2016), for which he left a radioactive rock on orthochromatic film for three days in complete darkness. These imprints of radioactivity, according to Schuppli, make it evident just how entangled photography is in the assemblage of nuclearity. Reflecting on this entanglement, the artist Anaïs Tondeur has used irradiated plants to create captivating photograms. In these works, the rays of the sun, rather than ionizing radioactivity, produce the image, hinting at the importance of trust in the process to appreciate photography as a form of material witnessing.[23]

Indeed, it is precisely such chains of translation that, extending Schuppli's argument, the sociologist Andrew Barry suggests make material witnessing possible: it is linked into hybrid agencies and networks that combine technical and cognitive capacities to measure and interpret radiological events and to connect them back to their original contexts.[24] Material witnesses do not speak for themselves. Their messages need to be decoded and channeled through what Barry describes as "the apparatuses of translation": conceptual frameworks, devices, experts, and human witnesses. It is these apparatuses, argues Barry, that ultimately establish what exactly is at the heart of the matter – in a literal sense.

Regimes of secrecy therefore target material witnessing: for instance, the raw data contained in radioactive biosamples is highly valued and its circulation is closely guarded. Consider dendrochronology, a science that investigates deposits of CO2 and other chemicals in tree rings in order to date atmospheric and environmental events. During the Cold War, dendrochronology was securitized and entangled in the atomic condition: Soviet leadership strictly prohibited bringing tree samples outside the Soviet bloc because they could contain radioactive deposits that reveal the exact location of nuclear tests or accidents.[25] When the Russian army captured the Chornobyl nuclear power plant from February 24 to March 31, 2022, soldiers looted the Central Analytical Laboratory, stealing unique radioactive samples.[26] It is this vital witnessing of materiality that artists engaging with nuclear materials seek to amplify and make legible.

Visibility

The cultural theorist Alison Sperling interrogates the notion of exposure, where visibility and knowledge are entangled with ignorance and destruction, creating a *mangle* of nuclearity – to borrow Andrew Pickering's term, by which he refers to the nonlinear and not always rational way in which science and technology are created and produced.[27] This mangle of nuclearity makes it difficult to precisely establish the extent of damage and responsibility, especially where vulnerable populations are in question. For instance, should one situate the birth of the atomic bomb in the laboratories of the Manhattan Project (1939–46), the Trinity site in New Mexico (1945), Hiroshima and Nagasaki (1945), or the uranium mines in what was then the Belgian Congo, where the mining of exceptionally pure uranium started in the early 1940s? Or should the roots be traced to the expropriation of lands from Indigenous peoples near the Great Bear Lake in Canada that later became sites of uranium mines?[28]

This mangle is, as Ilona Jurkonyte argues, obscured rather than clarified by spectacular representations of nuclear testing. Blasts and mushroom clouds, she argues, became part of pop culture and a semiotic building block of the military-industrial complex.[29] Stunning atomic imagery and the artistic responses to it raise questions about ethics and responsibility that risk being erased by the captivating visuals. Consider, for example, film *CROSSROADS* (1976), created by the prominent American artist and experimental filmmaker Bruce Conner, who repurposed footage of the nuclear explosions in the Marshall Islands.[30] In contrast, Emilija Škarnulytė's films, such as *Energy Island* (2016) and the feature-length *Burial* (2022), tackle the mangle head-on, connecting the diverse, visible, and invisible origins of the atomic condition and hinting at the danger inherent to the technology's seductive glamour. In *Energy Island*, Škarnulytė's camera lens stalks the architecture of the Ignalina Nuclear Power Plant, including the chambers containing radioactive materials and the models with blinking control panels that seem like toys. In *Burial*, she starts and ends with geoengineering, tracing the underground parts of the nuclear cycle from uranium mines to deep radioactive-waste depositories, emphasizing the circumscribed character of nuclear knowledge and action.

Participation

Other artists, however, employ strategies outside the representational and visual when engaging directly with nuclear sites and themes. They seek to raise awareness, create new knowledge, and develop new circuits of power to enable vulnerable groups to assert their place in the hierarchical atomic world. Kevin Walby and Ben Davis developed a collaborative practice in Uranium City, a settlement in Canada that shrank from about 1,700 residents in the 1950s to just ninety in 2021. Walby and Davis taught residents the technique of tracing photographs through thin paper as a physical and cognitive engagement with nuclear landscapes.[31] Similarly, artists Alex Ressel and Kerri Meehan created sound work as well as workshops with aboriginal communities living with the contamination of uranium mining in Australia's Northern Territory.[32]

Artists also need time to engage with nuclear-engineering communities. The most prominent case in point, according to Carpenter, is the US sculptor James Acord, who spent fifteen years at the Hanford nuclear-production complex in Washington state, the crucible of American nuclear technology, where he received a license to handle radioactive materials and experiment with uranium and plutonium extraction.[33]

However, there is a risk of art practices being co-opted, particularly as community engagement is often required for obtaining funding.[34] And that funding often does not allow a sufficiently lengthy immersion in affected communities. As the art historian Kyveli Mavrokordopoulou has demonstrated, artists have questioned the political economy of cultural funding, raising the ethical importance of making long-term commitments to Indigenous communities. Atomic communities are saturated with visual cultures of their own and should not be regarded as wastelands to be enriched by professional artists. Instead, artistic strategies can radically situate knowledge to counteract a colonial, objectifying gaze of "the atomic locals."[35] In this way, artistic engagement can create circuits of transitional justice in the areas of fallout, disaster, and de-industrialization.

Crumbling of the Atom, Crumbling of the World?

Back in 1913, the pioneering abstract painter Wassily Kandinsky wrote:

> *The crumbling of the atom was to my soul like the crumbling of the whole world. Suddenly the heaviest walls toppled. Everything became uncertain, tottering and weak. I would not have been surprised if a stone*

had dissolved in the air in front of me and became invisible. Science seemed to me destroyed; its most important basis was only a delusion, an error of the learned, who did not build their godly structures stone by stone with a steady hand in transfigured light, but groped at random in the darkness for truth and blindly mistook one object for another.[36]

More than a century later, we are still learning to live in the atomic condition, to deal with the extremely relational and bounded nature of our nuclear knowledge. In addition to the modernist sense of destabilization inspired by nuclear physics and the Cold War fears of a nuclear holocaust, societies are facing the uncertain eternity of radioactive waste.[37] In this context, many artists seek to make the atomic condition tractable through the senses and through reflexive practices. In doing so, they expand and integrate the frames of relevance so that nuclear experts do not remain conveniently insulated but are systematically challenged to consider the many implications of nuclearity – in both space and time.[38] I would like to finish with the example of *Man and Elements* (1990), the last large public art work commissioned by the Ignalina nuclear power plant in Lithuania, the only plant in the European Union to feature Soviet-designed RBKM reactors. The work is a mosaic by the St. Petersburg artist Viktor Tatarenko installed on the side wall of a multistory apartment block.[39] Like Kandinsky at the beginning of the twentieth century, Tatarenko reflected on the human ability to partition what appeared to be indelible elements, depicting Icarus carrying symbols referring to water, earth, fire, and air. This whirlpool of ornaments coalesces into the figure of a broken atom, hinting at the Chornobyl disaster, a poignant reminder of the terraforming atomic condition.

Pages 16–17

1. Paul Crutzen, "Geology of Mankind," *Nature* 415:3 (2002), 23. **2.** Eglė Rindzevičiūtė, *The Will to Predict: Orchestrating the Future through Science* (Ithaca, New York: Cornell University Press, 2023). **3.** Robert Jervis, "Mutual Assured Destruction," *Foreign Policy* (November 2002), 40–42, 48. **4.** Jacob Darwin Hamblin, *Arming Mother Nature: The Birth of Catastrophic Environmentalism* (Oxford: Oxford University Press, 2013). **5.** Anna Volkmar, *Art and Nuclear Power: The Role of Culture in the Environmental Debate* (Lanham, MD: Lexington Books, 2022). Here Volkmar draws on the process-oriented notion of a "techno-human condition" proposed by Braden Allenby and Daniel Sarewitz, which aligns closely with my notion of the atomic condition. Braden R. Allenby and Daniel Sarewitz, *The Techno-Human Condition* (Cambridge: The MIT Press, 2011). **6.** Volkmar, 12. **7.** Svitlana Matviyenko, "Nuclear Cyberwar: From Energy Colonialism to Energy Terrorism." *E-flux Journal* 126 (April 2022), https://www.e-flux.com/journal/126/460842/nuclear-cyberwar-from-energy-colonialism-to-energy-terrorism. Accessed October 10, 2022. **8.** Gabrielle Hecht, *Being Nuclear: Africans and the Global Uranium Trade* (Cambridge, MA: The MIT Press, 2012). **9.** Robert Jacobs, *Nuclear Bodies: The Global Hibakusha* (New Haven, CT: Yale University Press, 2022); Susan Bauer and Tanja Penter, eds., *Tracing the Atom: Nuclear Legacies in Russia and Central Asia* (London: Routledge, 2022). **10.** Kate Brown, *Manual for Survival: A Chernobyl Guide for the Future* (New York: Penguin, 2020). **11.** Timothy Mitchell, *Carbon Democracy: Political Power in the Age of Oil* (London: Verso, 2013). **12.** Lawrence Badash, *A Nuclear Winter's Tale: Science and Politics in the 1980s* (Cambridge, MA: The MIT Press, 2009). **13.** Paul R. Josephson, "'Projects of the Century' in Soviet History: Large-Scale Technologies from Lenin to Gorbachev." *Technology and Culture* 36:3 (1995): 519–59.

Pages 18–19

14. Bauer and Penter, *Tracing the Atom.* **15.** Alex Wellerstein, *Restricted Data: The History of Nuclear Secrecy in the United States* (Chicago: The University of Chicago Press, 2021). **16.** Eduardo Subirats, "Palomares by Jorge Castillo," *Facing the Future: Art in Europe 1945–1968* (Brussels: BOZAR, 2016), 280–283. **17.** Daria Mille, "The Art of Exact Ideas: Impulses from Science in Unofficial Russian Art," *Facing the Future: Art in Europe 1945–1968* (Brussels: BOZAR, 2016), 378–395. **18.** Jeff Hughes, "What Is British Nuclear Culture? Understanding Uranium 235." *British Journal of History of Science* 45:4 (2012), 504–505. **19.** Ele Carpenter, "Shifting the Nuclear Imaginary: Art and the Flight from Nuclear Modernity," in *Cold War Legacies: Systems, Theory, Aesthetics*, eds. John Beck and Ryan Bishop (Edinburgh: Edinburgh University Press, 2016), 116–133. **20.** Anna Volkmar, *Art and Nuclear Power: The Role of Culture in the Environmental Debate* (Lanham, MD: Lexington Books, 2022). **21.** Susan Schuppli, *Material Witness: Media, Forensics, Evidence* (Cambridge, MA: The MIT Press, 2020). **22.** Schuppli, *Material Witness.* **23.** Michael Marder and Anais Tondeur, *The Chernobyl Herbarium: Fragments of an Exploded Consciousness* (London: Open Humanities Press, 2016). **24.** Andrew Barry, "Collective Empiricism and the Material Witness," *Journal of Visual Culture* 20:3 (2022), 491–505. **25.** Eglė Rindzevičiūtė, *The Power of Systems: How Policy Sciences Opened Up the Cold War World* (Ithaca, NY: Cornell University Press, 2016). **26.** Veronika Masenko, "My pugali russkikh radiatsiiei" [We scared the Russians with radiation], *The Village* (April 8, 2022); "Update 48—IAEA Director General Statement on Situation in Ukraine," IAEA (April 10, 2022), https://www.iaea.org/newscenter/pressreleases/update-48-iaea-director-general-statement-on-situation-in-ukraine. **27.** Alison Sperling, "Radiating Exposures," in *Weathering: Ecologies of Exposure*, eds. Christoph F. E. Holzhey and Arnd Wedemeyer (Berlin: ICI Berlin Press, 2020), 41–62. **28.** Laura Pitkanen and Matthew Farish, "Nuclear Landscapes," Progress in Human Geography 42:6 (2018): 862–880. **29.** Ilona Jurkonyte, *From Temperature of War to Descending Clouds: US Bomb Archive and the Marshall Islands*, unpublished PhD dissertation, Concordia University, 2022.

Pages 20–21

30. Maria Stavrinaki, "La Bombe: Bruce Conner, la guerre, la paix et les quatre éléments," *Les Cahiers du Mnam* 160 (2022): 4–32. **31.** Kevin Walby and Ben Davis, "Tailings and Tracings: Using Art and Social Science to Explore the Limits of Visual Methods at Mining and Industrial Ruins." *Visual Communication* (2022): 1–24, https://doi.org/10.1177/14703572211071117. **32.** http://m-a-r-s.online/sessions/decolonising-the-nuclear-public-lecture-and-research-workshop. **33.** James Acord, "Roundtable," *The Nuclear Culture Source Book*, ed. Ele Carpenter (London: Black Dog Publishing, 2016), 52–53. **34.** Leyla Jancovich, "The Participation Myth," *International Journal of Cultural Policy* 23:1 (2017): 107–121. **35.** Kyveli Mavrokordopoulou, "The Possibility of a Situated Nuclear Knowledge: Art in Contaminated Sites," *Toxic Immanence: Decolonizing Nuclear Futures and Legacies* (Montreal: McGill-Queen's University Press, 2022) **36.** Alwynne Mackie, "Kandinsky and the Problems of Abstraction," *Artforum*, November 1978, https://www.artforum.com/print/197809/kandinsky-and-problems-of-abstraction-35922. **37.** Ele Carpenter, *Perpetual Uncertainty. Art and Radioactivity*, exhibition at Malmö Konstmuseum, February 24–August 26 2018; Benoit Pelopidas, "The Birth of Nuclear Eternity," in *Futures*, eds. Sandra Kemp and Jenny Andersson (Oxford: Oxford University Press, 2021), 484–500. **38.** Carole Gallagher, "Making the Invisible Visible," *Bulletin of the Atomic Scientists* 69:6 (2013), 42–46. **39.** Linara Dovydaitytė, "(Re)Imagining the Nuclear in Lithuania Following the Shutdown of the Ignalina Nuclear Power Plant." *Journal of Baltic Studies* 53:3 (2022), 421.

ARTISTS IN THE EXHIBITION

HAIG AIVAZIAN

Haig Aivazian (b. 1980 in Beirut) **is an artist and writer based in Beirut who works across performance, video, drawings, installation, and sculpture**

Haig Aivazian's long-term artistic research centers on power and surveillance strategies in public spaces. He explores how these structures and apparatuses are embedded in our everyday lives and how they transform people, objects, animals, landscapes, and architecture.

In his video *All of Your Stars Are but Dust on My Shoes* (2021), Aivazian tracks the public administration of light and darkness as an essential policing tool. Composed of found footage and material from the artist's phone, the video moves among cities like New York and Paris, with his native Beirut setting the central pulse. By layering, splicing, and confronting disparate sounds and images, he creates an associative genealogy that ranges from whale-oil lamps to gas lanterns to LED bulbs and from blackouts to curfews. Aivazian generates a sensory meditation on how the fundamentals of human vision – light hitting the retina – have been mechanized and turned into tools that capture our movements, whether in everyday life or on-screen.

● **Biography** AIVAZIAN holds an MFA from Northwestern University, Chicago, and a BFA from Concordia University, Montréal. Between 2020 and 2022, he was artistic director of the Beirut Art Center, where he founded *The Derivative* (المشتق), an online publication. His work has been featured in solo and group exhibitions in institutions such as The Renaissance Society, Chicago; the Swiss Institute, New York; Ashkal Alwan, Beirut; Nottingham Contemporary, Nottingham, England; MAXXI, Rome; and Ming Contemporary Art Museum, Shanghai. Aivazian has also participated in biennials and triennials internationally, including the fifth New Museum Triennial, New York; the Yokohama Triennale, Yokohama; the 6th Marrakech Biennale, Marrakech; La Biennale de Montréal (BNLMTL); the 14th Istanbul Biennial; the National Pavilion of Armenia at the Venice Biennale; and Videobrasil, São Paulo.

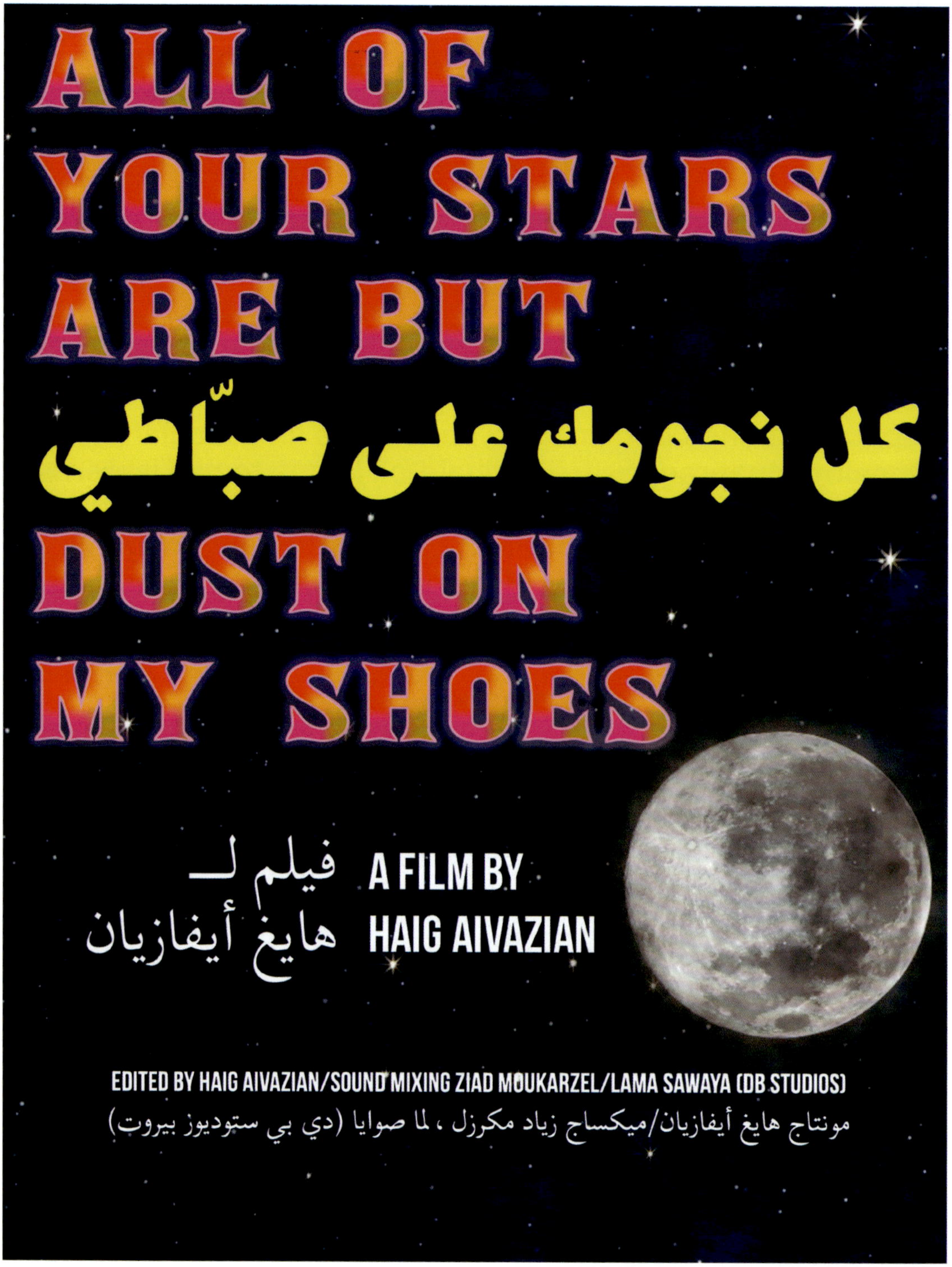

↑ Poster for *All of Your Stars Are but Dust on My Shoes*, 2021
↗ Stills from of *All of Your Stars Are but Dust on My Shoes*, 2021, single-channel video installation

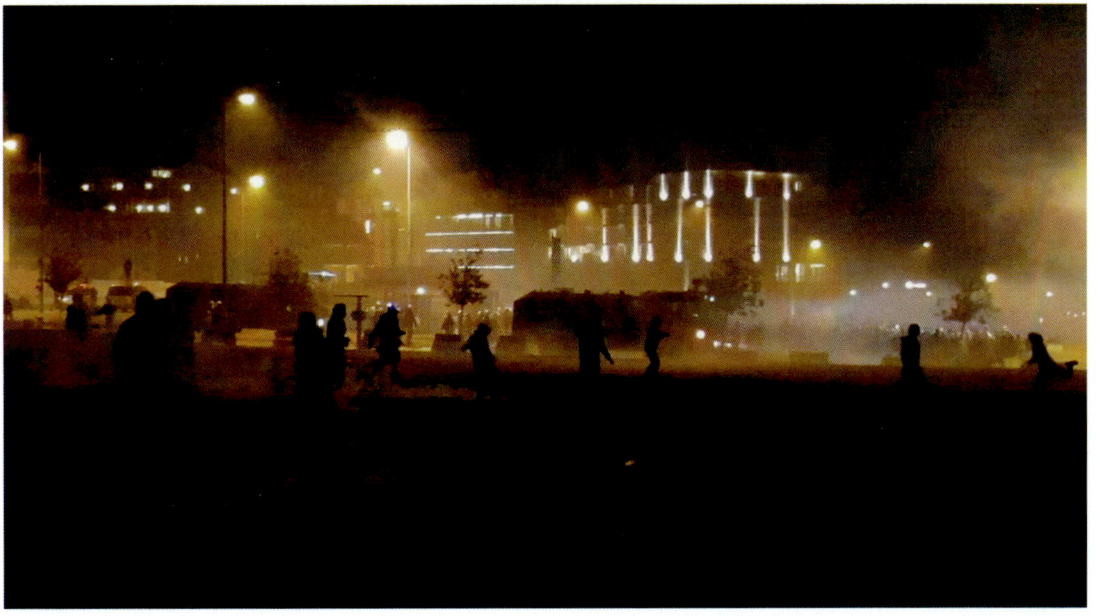

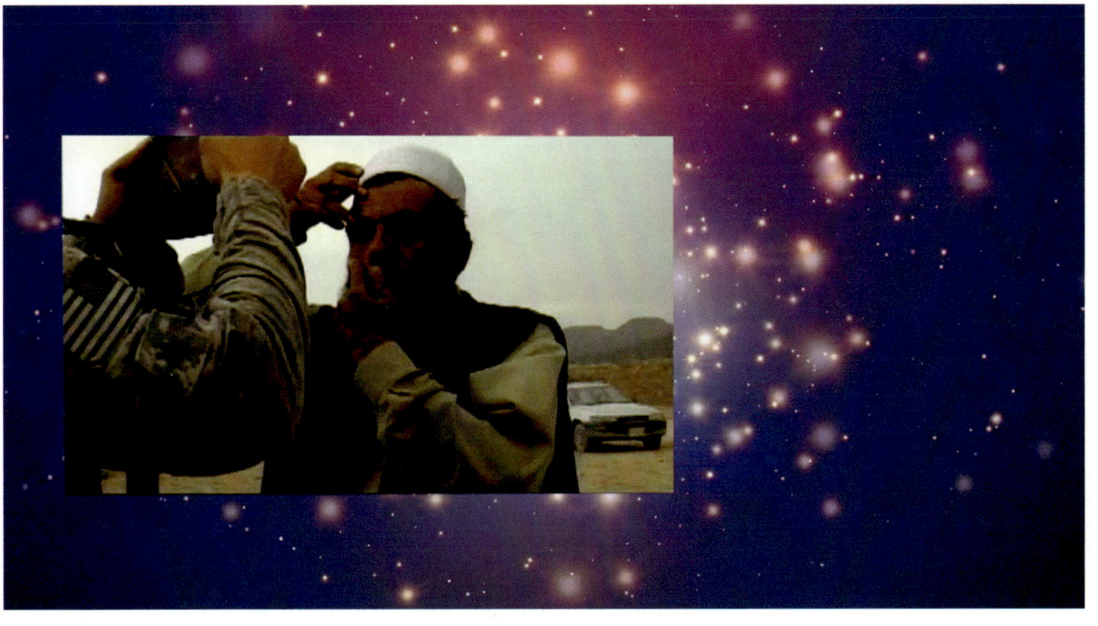

Haig Aivazian

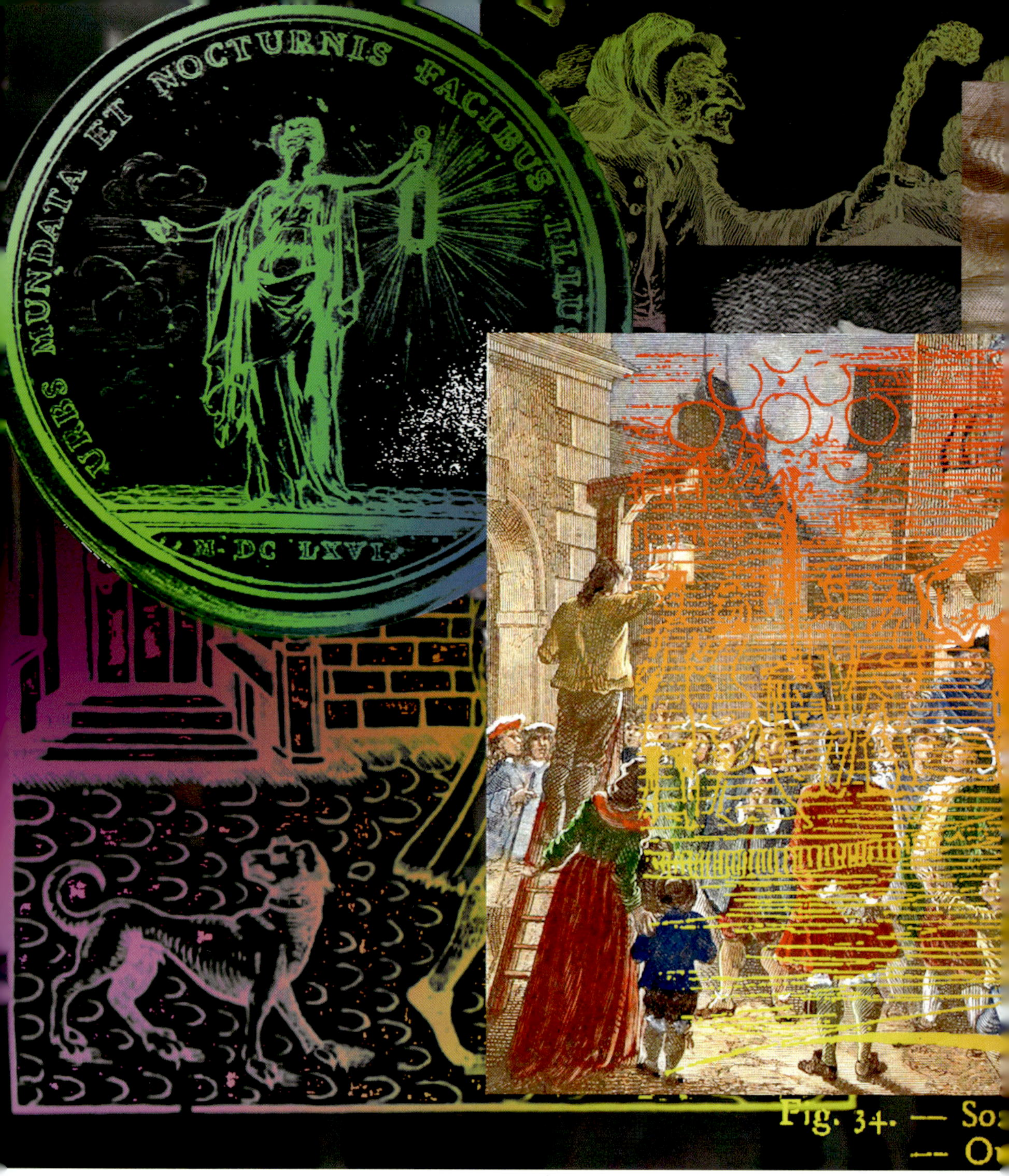

Still from *All of Your Stars Are but Dust on My Shoes*, 2021, single-channel video installation

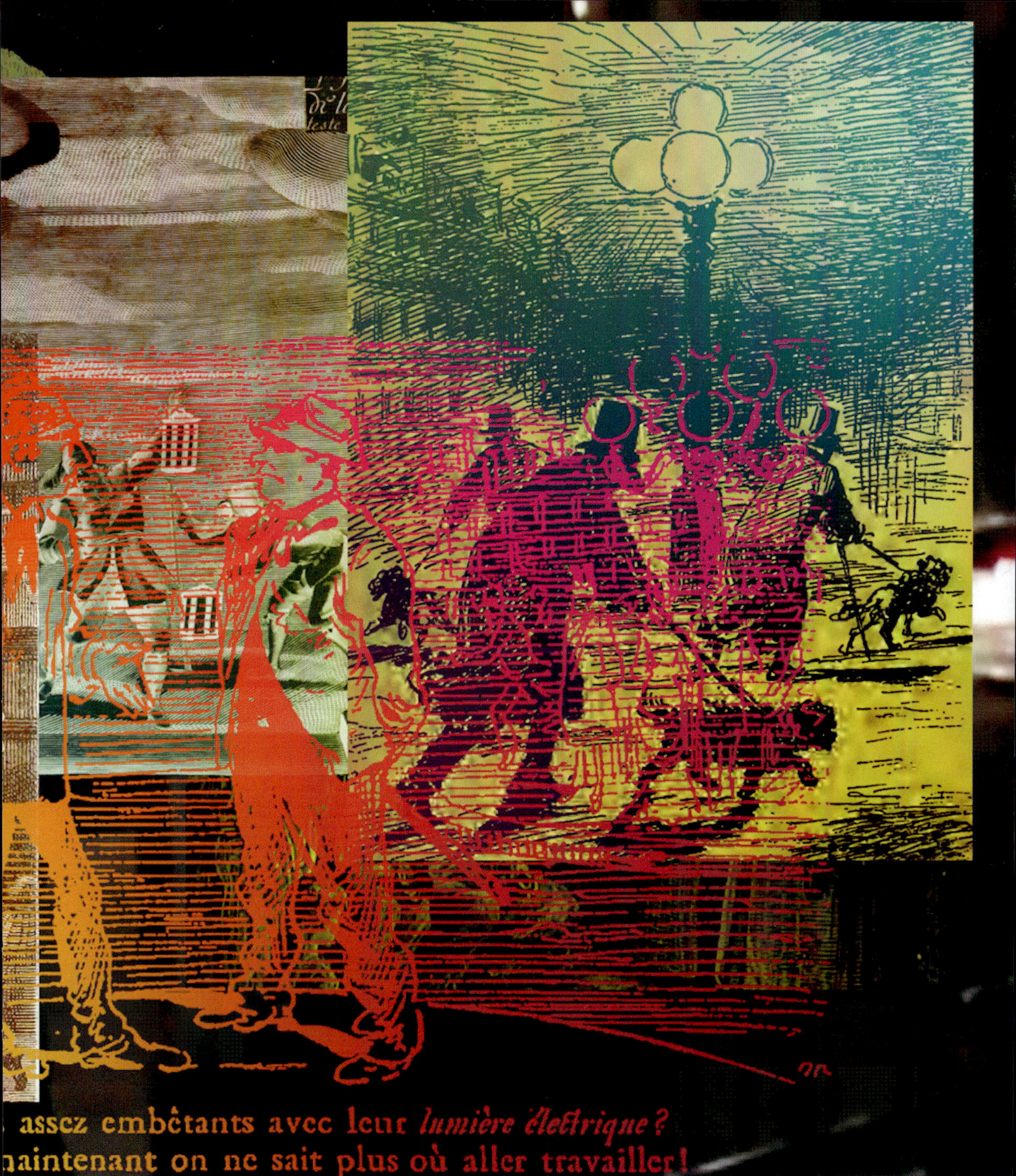

Haig Aivazian

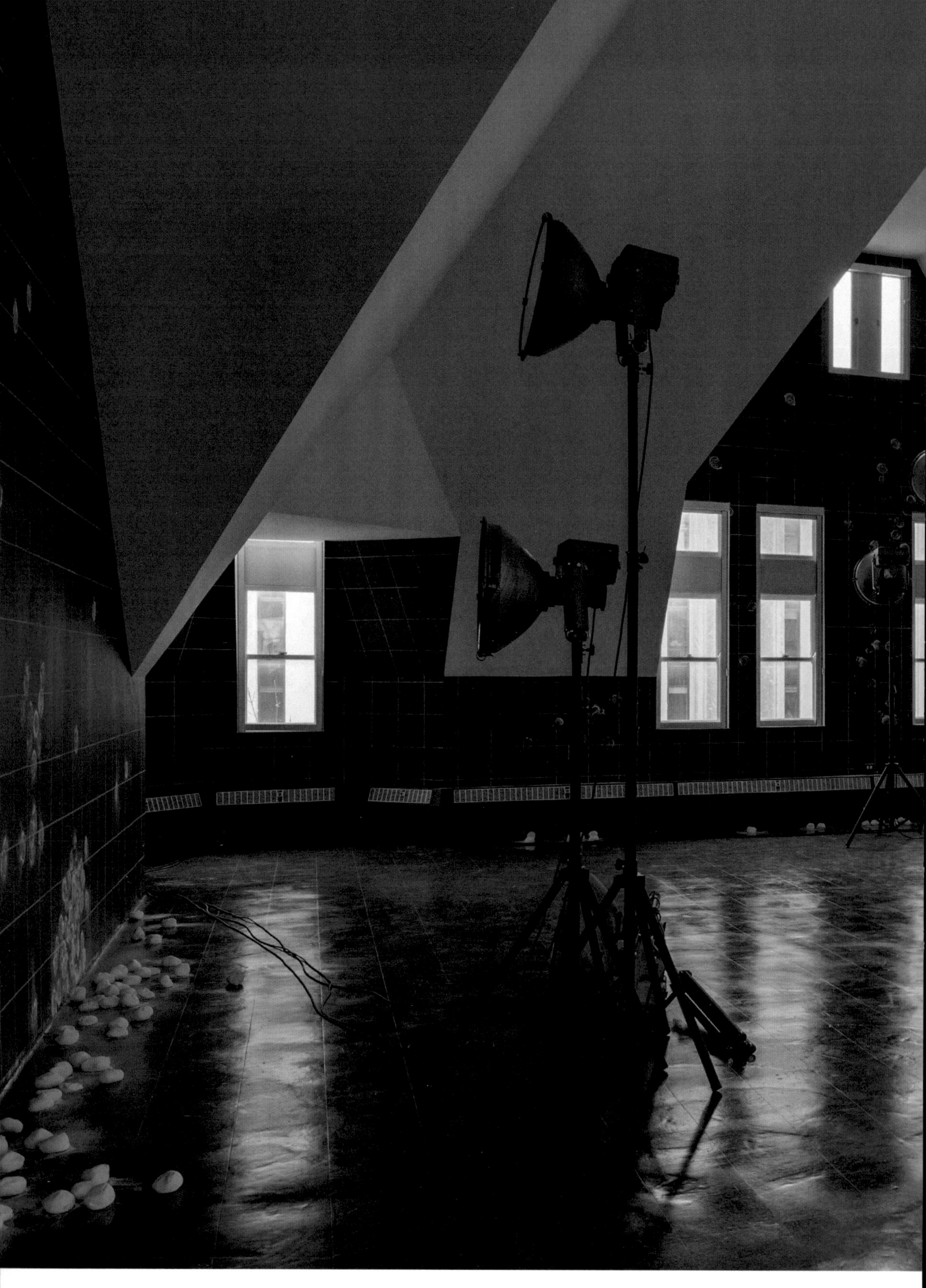

Installation view, *All of Your Stars Are but Dust On My Shoes*, The Renaissance Society, Chicago, 2021

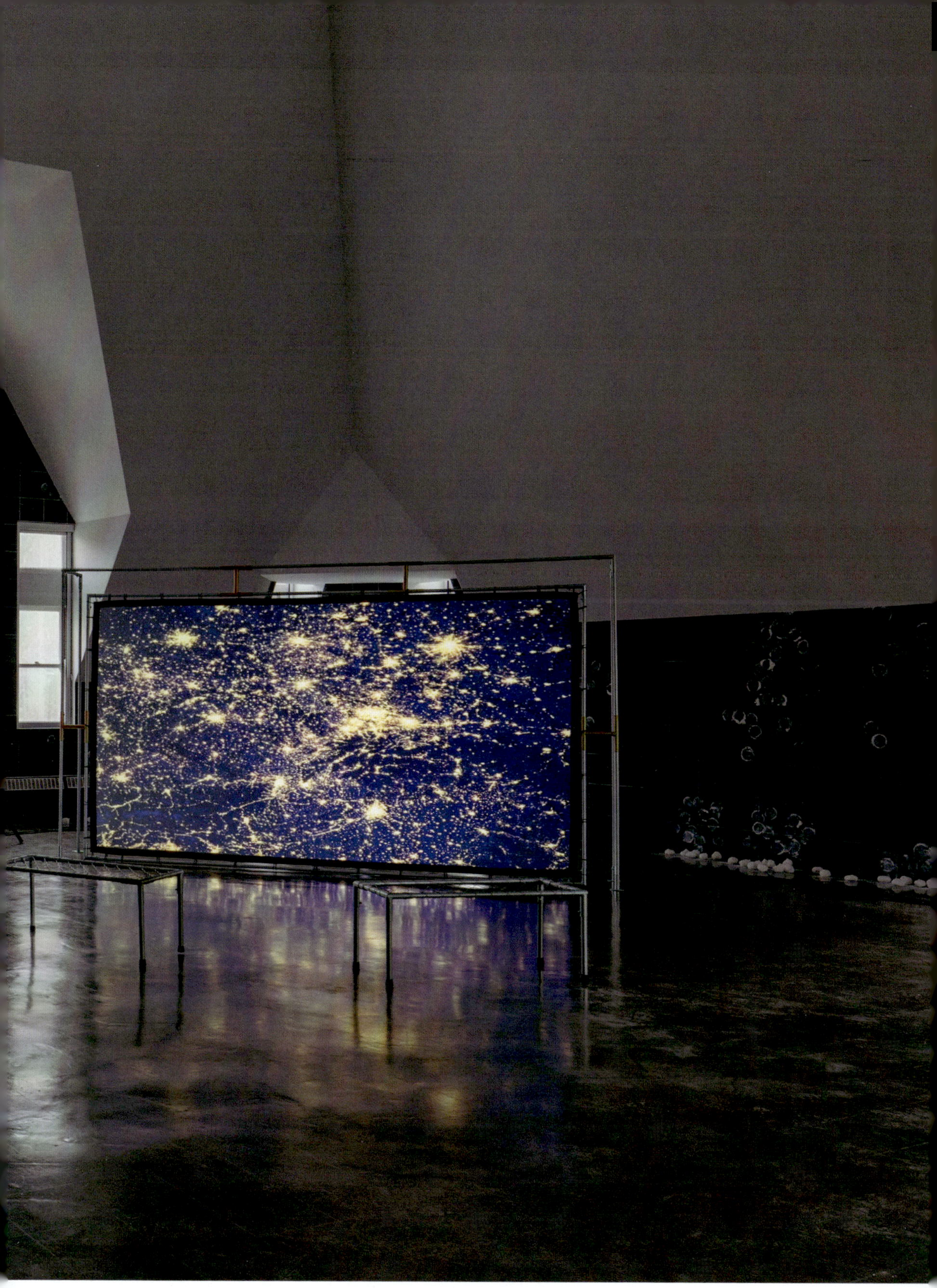

Haig Aivazian

KETUTA ALEXI-MESKHISVILI

Ketuta Alexi-Meskhishvili (b. 1979 in Tbilisi, Georgia) **is an artist and photographer based in Berlin**

For the past few years, Ketuta Alexi-Meskhishvili has been using plastic bags collected in her native Georgia to create *Georgian Ornament* (2020–21), a series of photographs and textile works. The bags, made mainly for tourist consumption, often include traditional motifs originally found in the architecture of Byzantine churches. Simplified into abstractions, these semi-ethnic forms represent a search for emancipatory transnational symbols from before Georgia's occupation by the Russian empire in the nineteenth century. However, just like the country's current retrograde and conservative political leadership, the ornaments reflect the past more than the present or the future. Plastic bags also present a paradox because they simultaneously project fragility (they can be torn) and endurance (they won't decompose for centuries). Alexi-Meskhishvili rightly calls them "future fossils."

To make *Georgian Ornament*, the artist has photographed the bags in her studio. In some cases, she has placed a semi-transparent plastic bag on top of a 4 × 5–inch color negative film, proceeding to expose the film using small finger lights originally meant for raving in night clubs. After developing and drum-scanning the negative, the artist has in some cases altered the image digitally before printing it as a photograph either on photographic paper or a textile. The translucent textile material and its drape emphasize the artist's interest in the play of transparency and light.

● **Biography** ALEXI-MESKHISHVILI studied photography at Bard College, Annandale, New York. She has had solo and group exhibitions at Galeire Molitor, Berlin; Les Rencontres de la photographie d'Arles, France; galerie frank elbaz, Paris; Sprengel Museum Hannover; Kölnischer Kunstverein, Cologne; and New Museum, New York. In 2023, she has an ongoing project titled Verkleidung at the Back Wall of Kunsthalle Basel and solo exhibitions at Helena Anrather, New York and LC Queisser, Tbilisi.

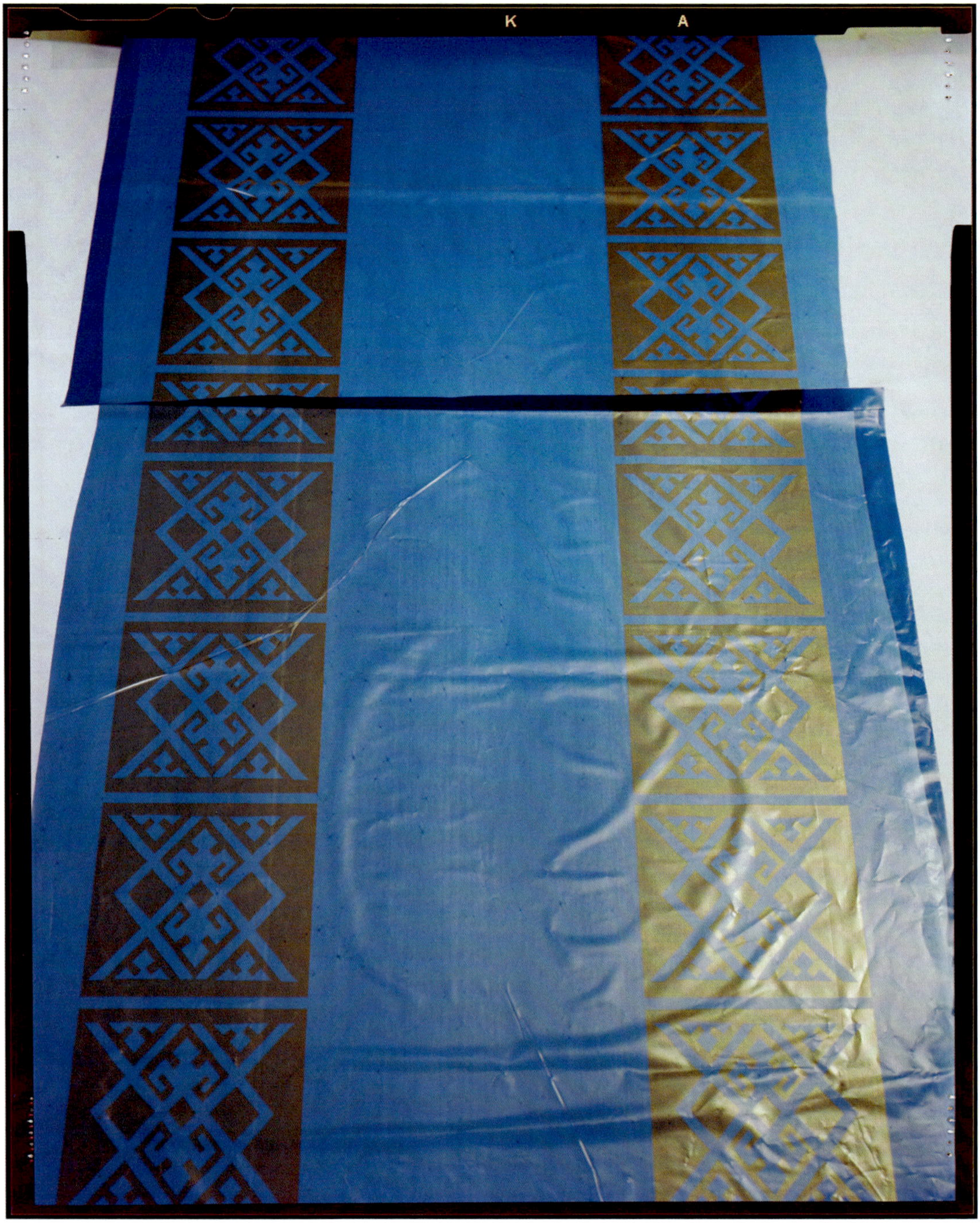

↑ *Braids*, 2021, archival pigment print
↗ *Braid*, 2021, archival pigment print

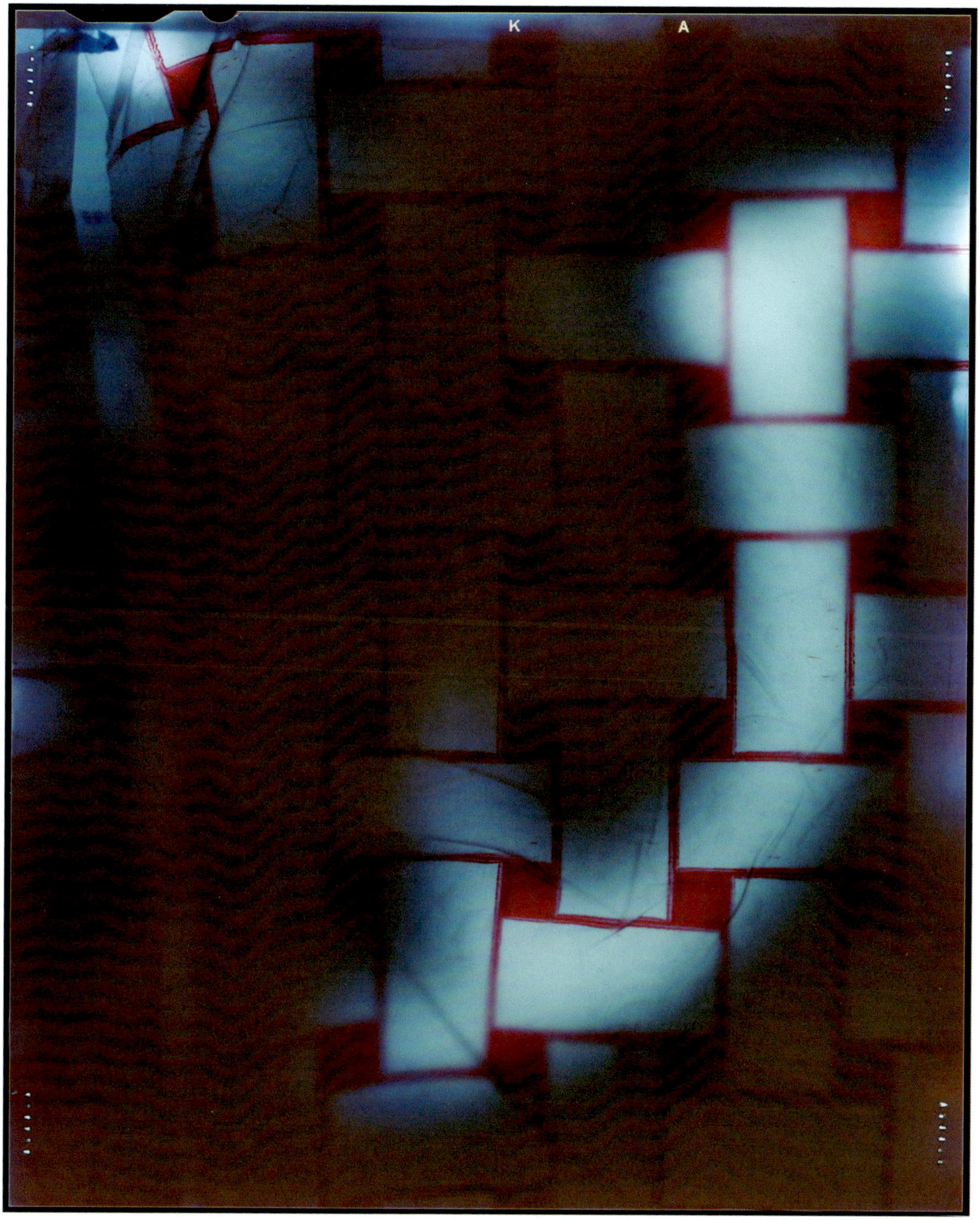

Ketuta Alexi-Meskhisvili

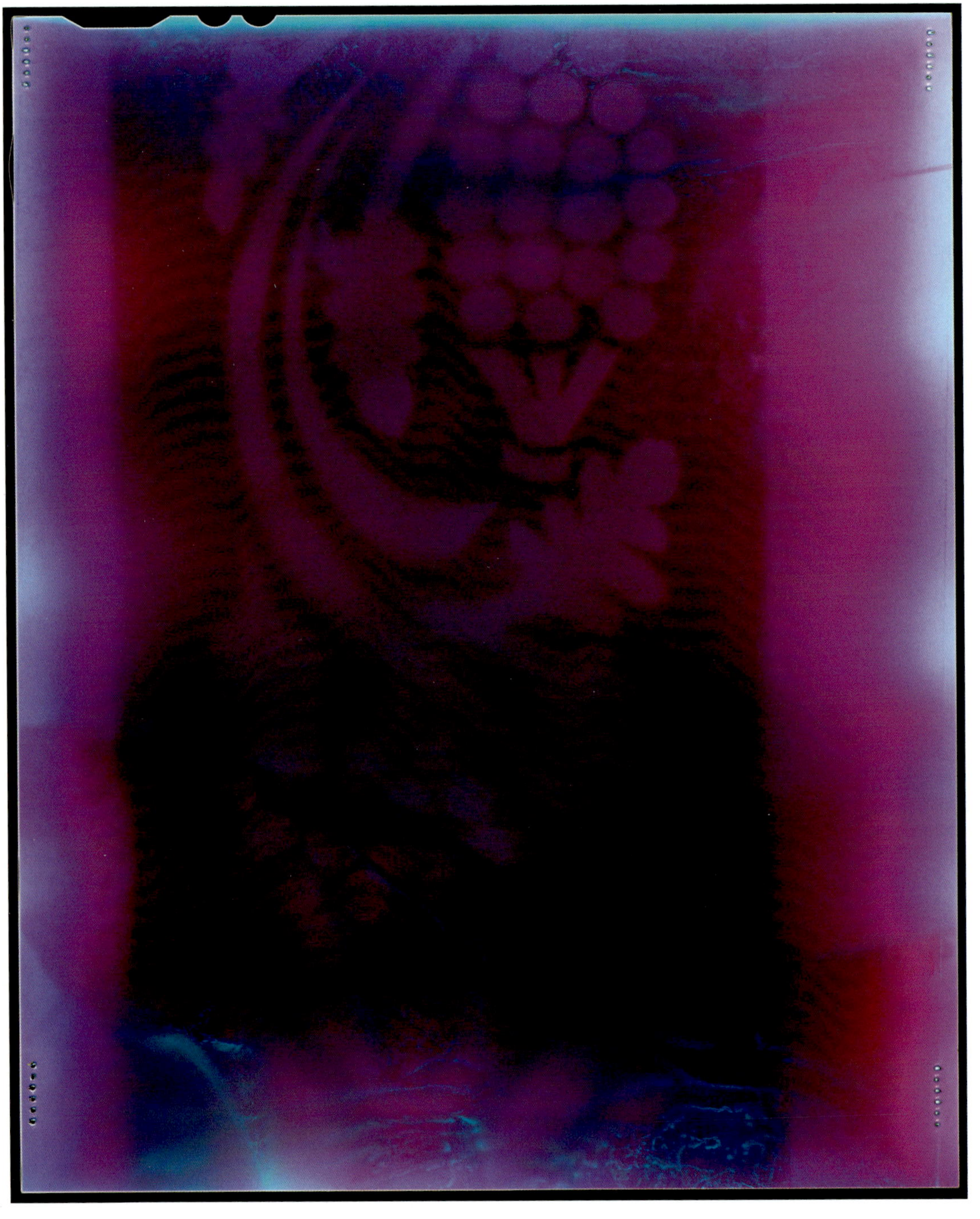

↑ *Vines*, 2020, archival pigment print
↗ *Vine*, 2021, archival pigment print

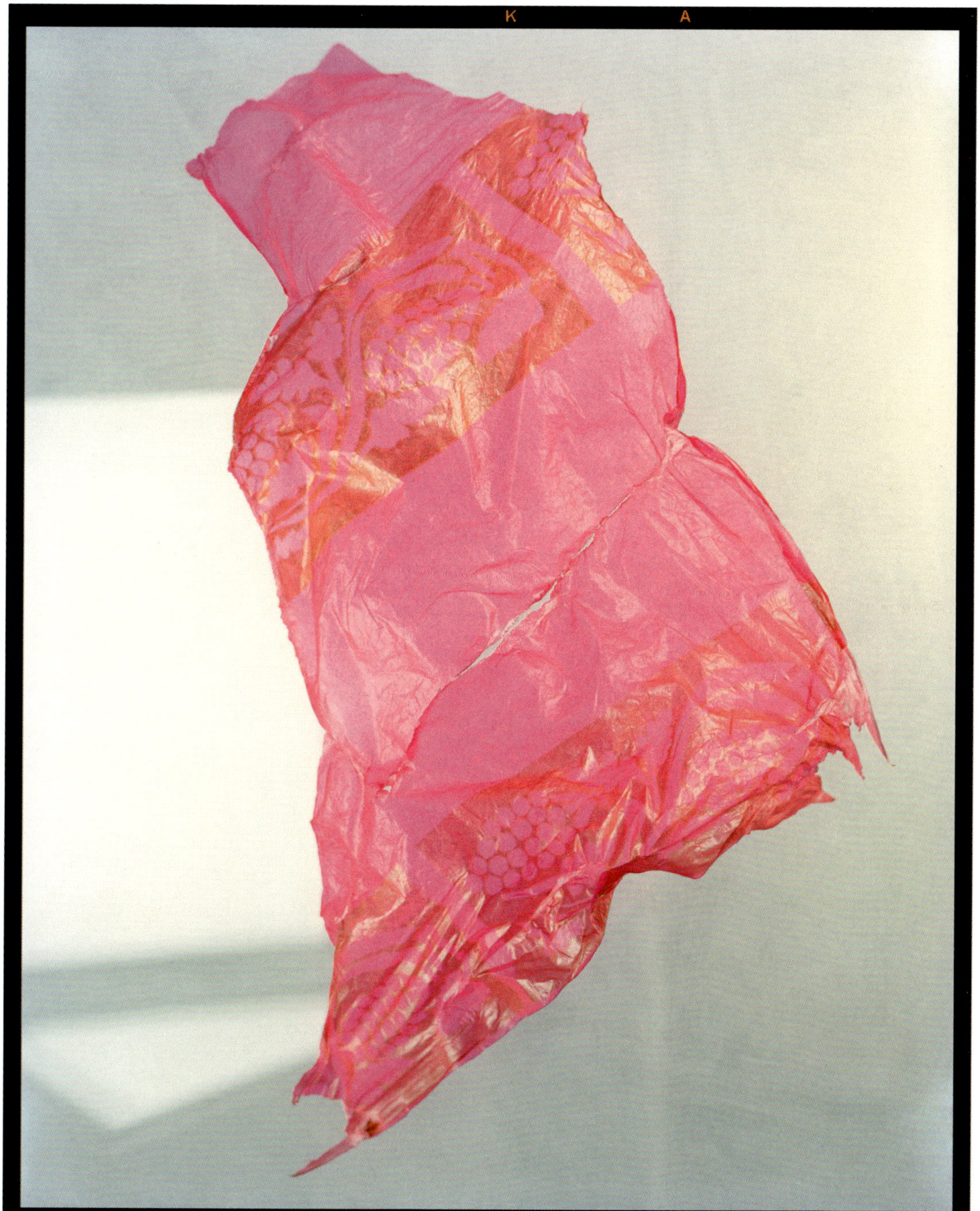

Ketuta Alexi-Meskhisvili

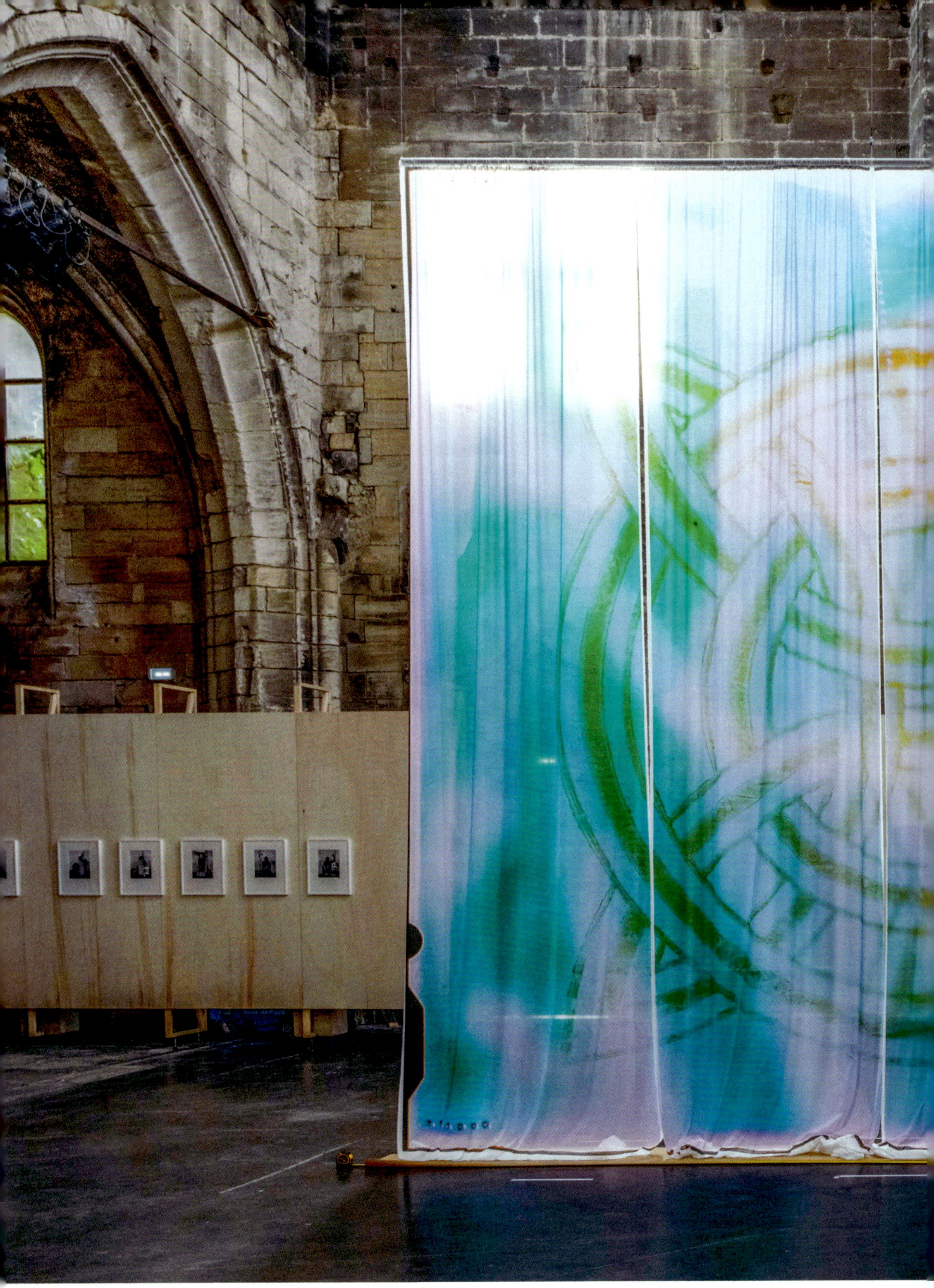

Installation view, *Georgian Ornament*, Les Rencontres de la photographie d'Arles, 2021

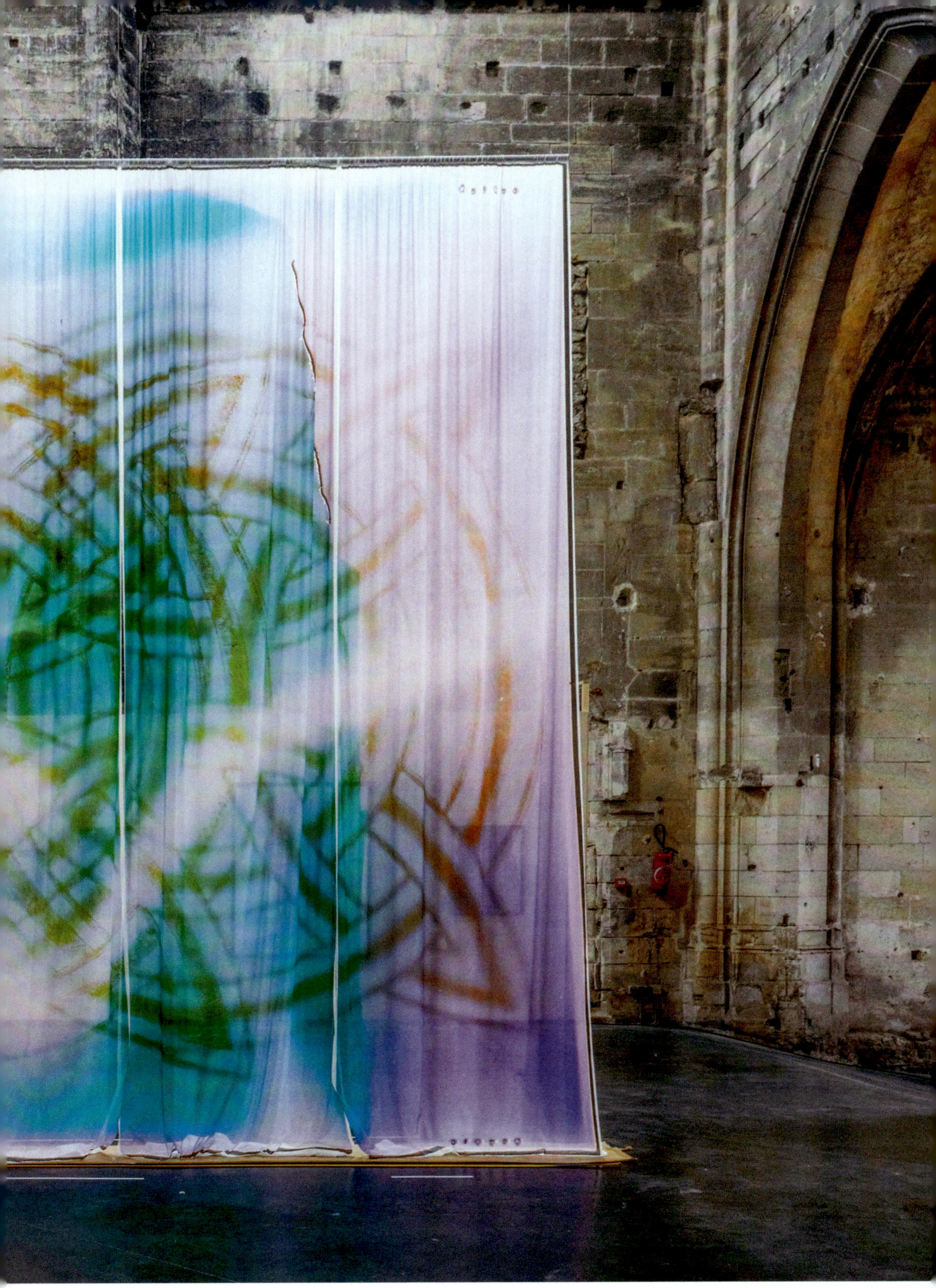

Ketuta Alexi-Meskhisvili

TEKLA ASLANISHVILI

&

GIORGI GAGO GAGOSHIDZE

Tekla Aslanishvili (b. 1988 in Tbilisi, Georgia) **is an artist, filmmaker, and essayist based in Berlin and Tbilisi**

Giorgi Gago Gagoshidze (b. 1983 in Kutaisi, Georgia) **is an artist and filmmaker based in Berlin**

The starting point of *Stone of Hell* (2021), an experimental documentary film by Tekla Aslanishvili and Giorgi Gago Gagoshidze, is Chiatura, a small town in the republic of Georgia whose economy has historically been dependent on mining. The area holds the largest manganese reserve in Georgia and one of the largest in the world. Charting the extraction of manganese, the filmmakers interweave archival video from Georgia's national broadcaster, new footage, historical photography, and animated reproductions of cave paintings.

The earliest-known human use of manganese compounds was in the Stone Age, when manganese dioxide was used as pigment in cave paintings. Today, manganese is predominantly used in metallurgical applications – almost all types of steel contain manganese. By tracing the processing and distribution of this metal, the film scrutinizes the geopolitical and economic interrelations that link this peripheral site of extraction to a vast network of places, subjects, and processes across the globe. It touches upon the material's use in construction as well as destruction (through images of tanks, weapons, and military aircraft). People living in the areas around Chiatura have called manganese the *stone of hell* for its toxic effects on the growth of specific domesticated plants like wheat. The film's experimental and layered form emphasizes how the effects of the material and its extraction ripple outward through the area's communities and environment.

● **Biographies** ASLANISHVILI'S works engage infrastructure design, history, and geopolitics. She graduated from the Tbilisi State Academy of Arts and holds an MFA from the Berlin University of the Arts. Her films have been screened and exhibited internationally at PACT Zollverein, Neue Berliner Kunstverein, Baltic Triennial, Short Film Festival Oberhausen, Kasseler Dokfest, Kunsthalle Münster, EMAF—European Media Art Festival, Videonale 18, and the Tbilisi Architecture Biennial. She was a 2018–19 Digital Earth fellow and was the recipient of the 2020 Han Nefkens Foundation—Fundació Antoni Tàpies Video Art Production Award.

GAGOSHIDZE works with film and video and explores the socio-political aspects of its contexts. He studied fine art at the State Academy of Arts in Tbilisi and at the Royal Academy of Fine Arts in The Hague, and experimental film and video with Hito Steyerl at the University of the Arts in Berlin. Gagoshidze has exhibited works at MUNCH, Oslo, Neuer Berliner Kunstverein, the 34th Biennial of Graphic Arts, Ljubljana, E.A. Shared Space, Tbilisi, Kunsthalle Wien, steirischer herbst, Graz, and Konsthall Minst ABF, Stockholm.

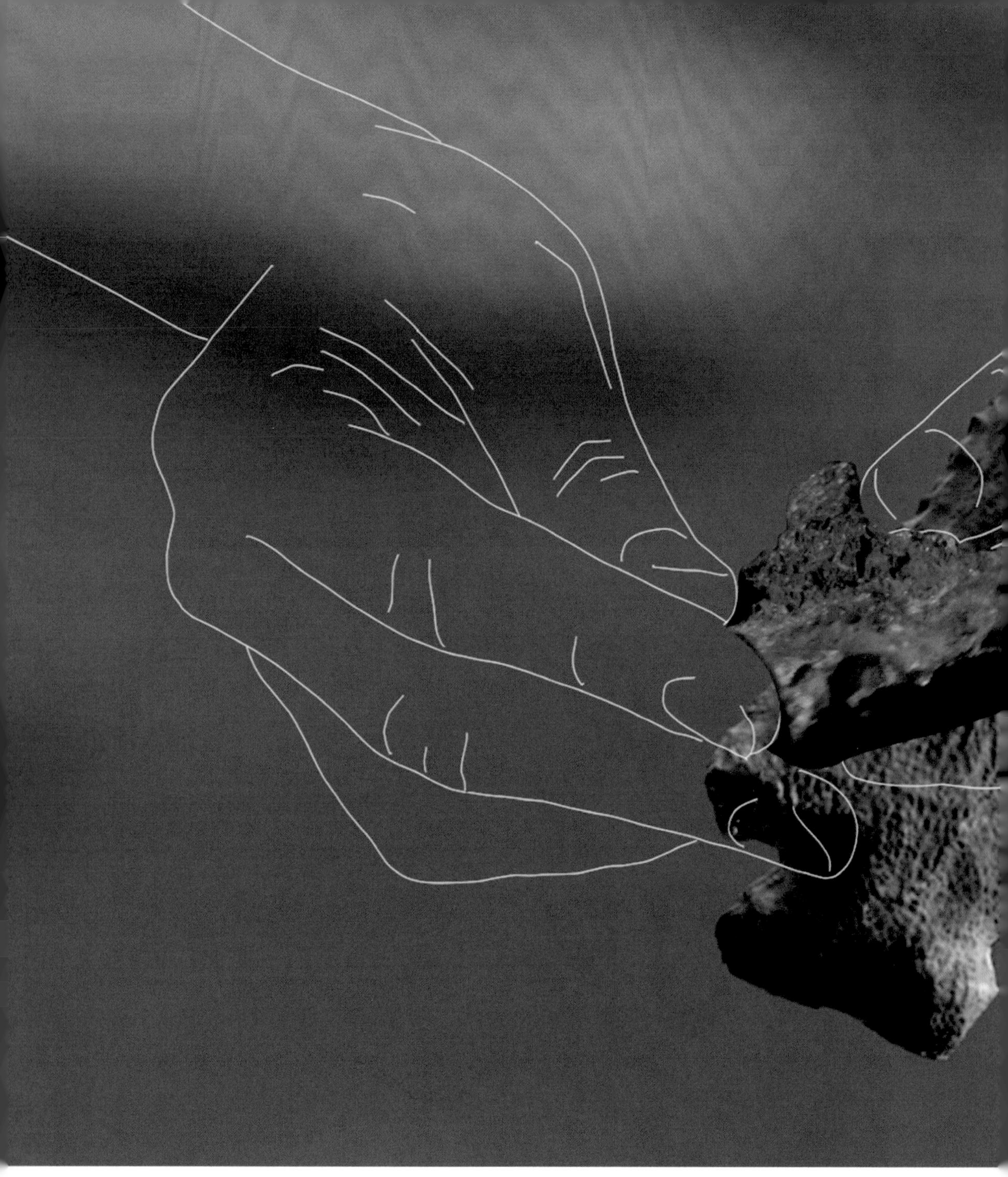

Still from *Stone of Hell*, 2021, single-channel color video with sound

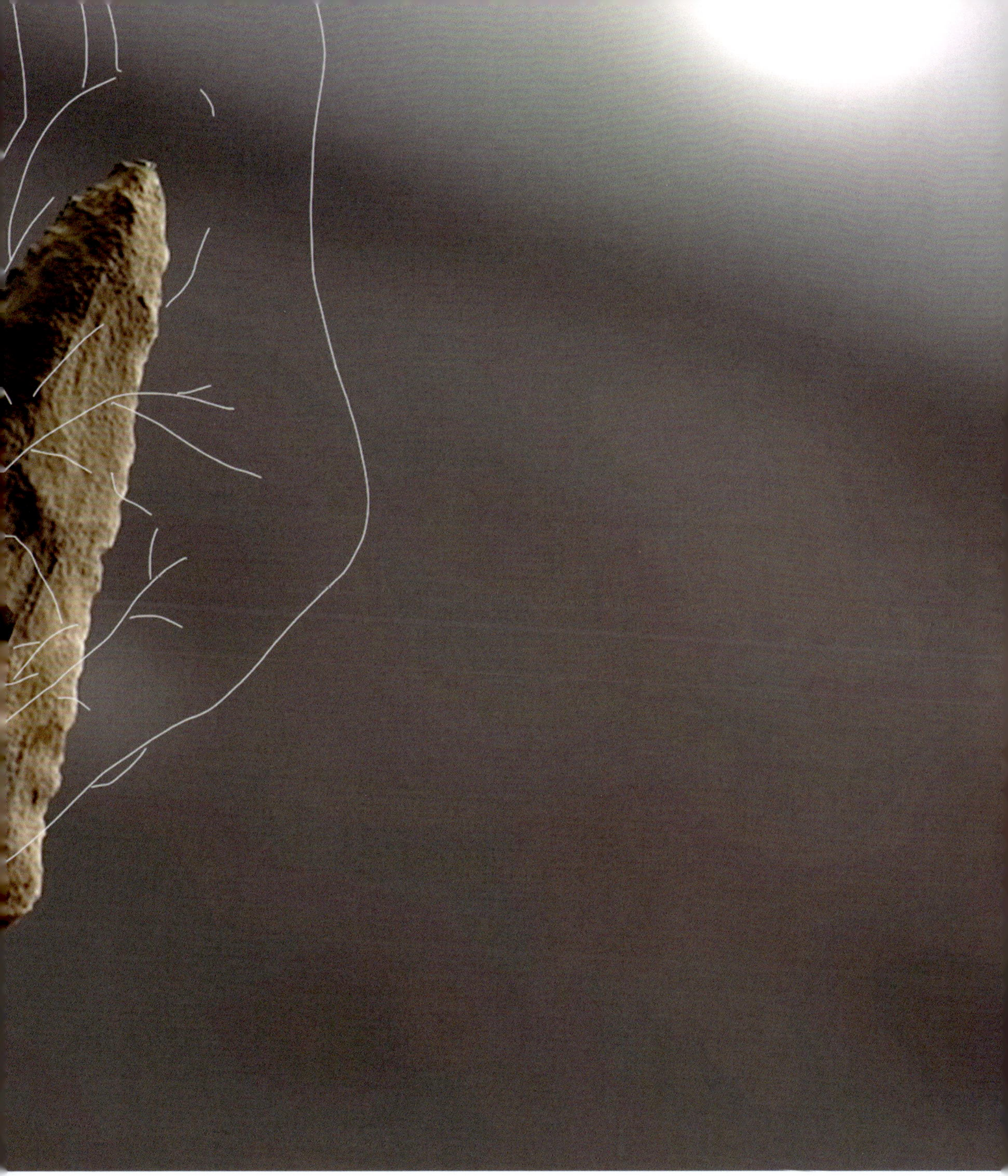

Tekla Aslanishvili & Giorgi Gago Gagoshidze

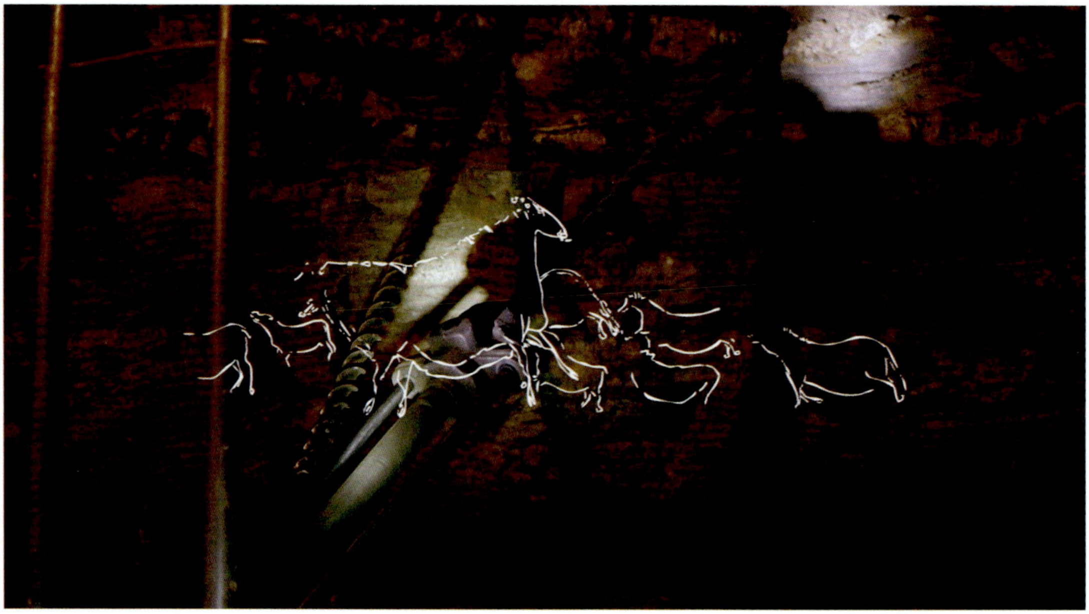

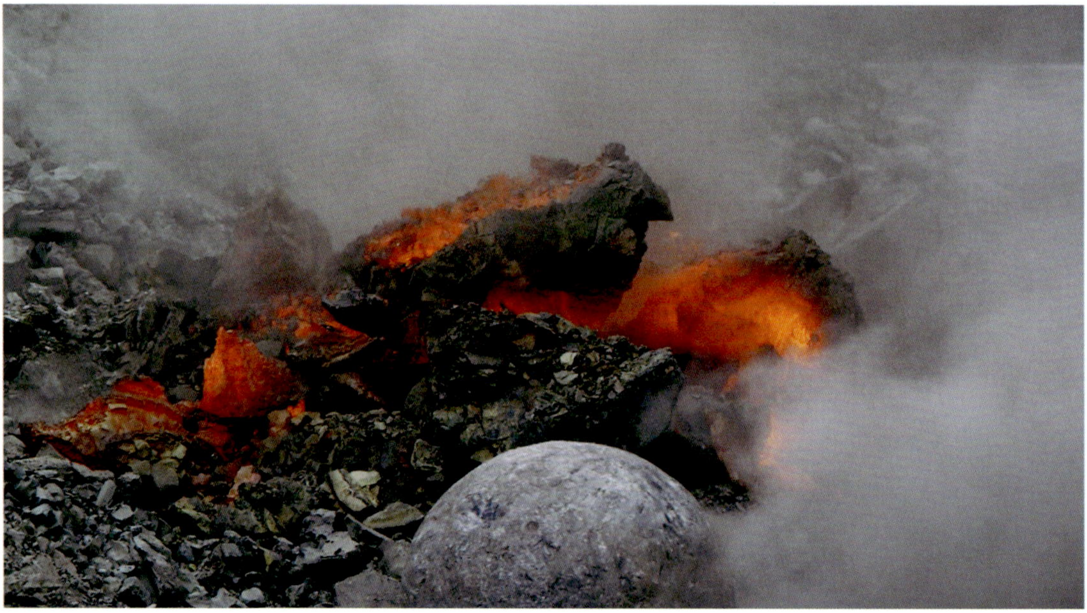

Stills from *Stone of Hell*, 2021, single-channel color video with sound

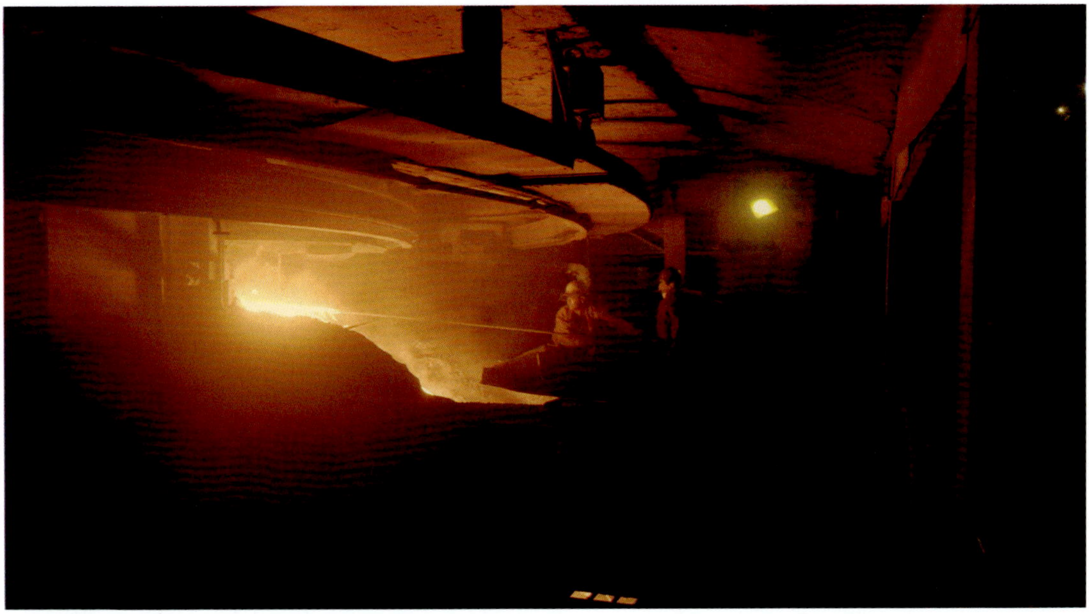

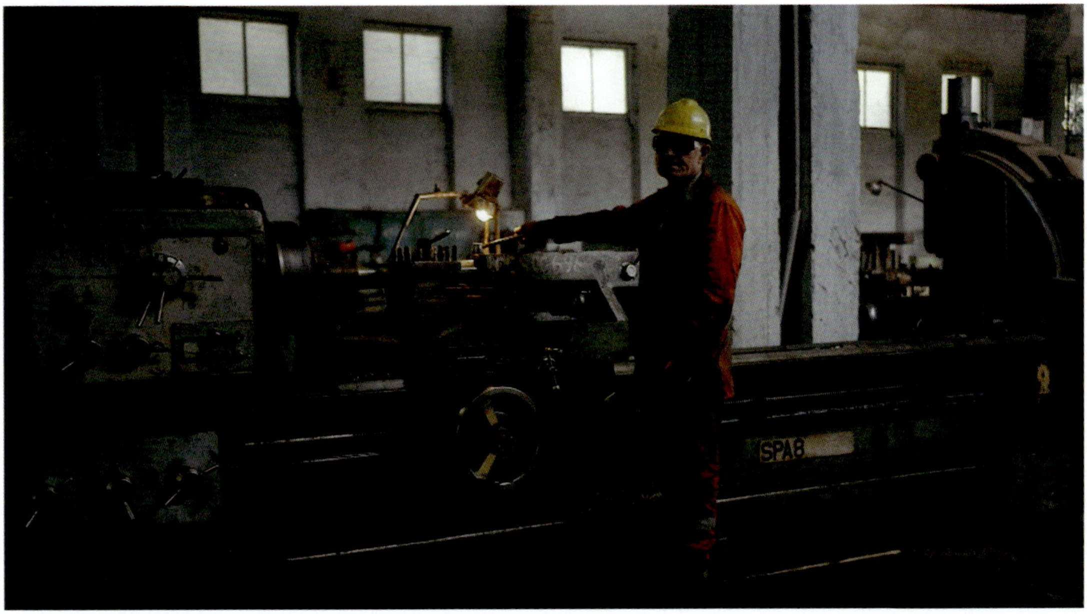

Tekla Aslanishvili & Giorgi Gago Gagoshidze

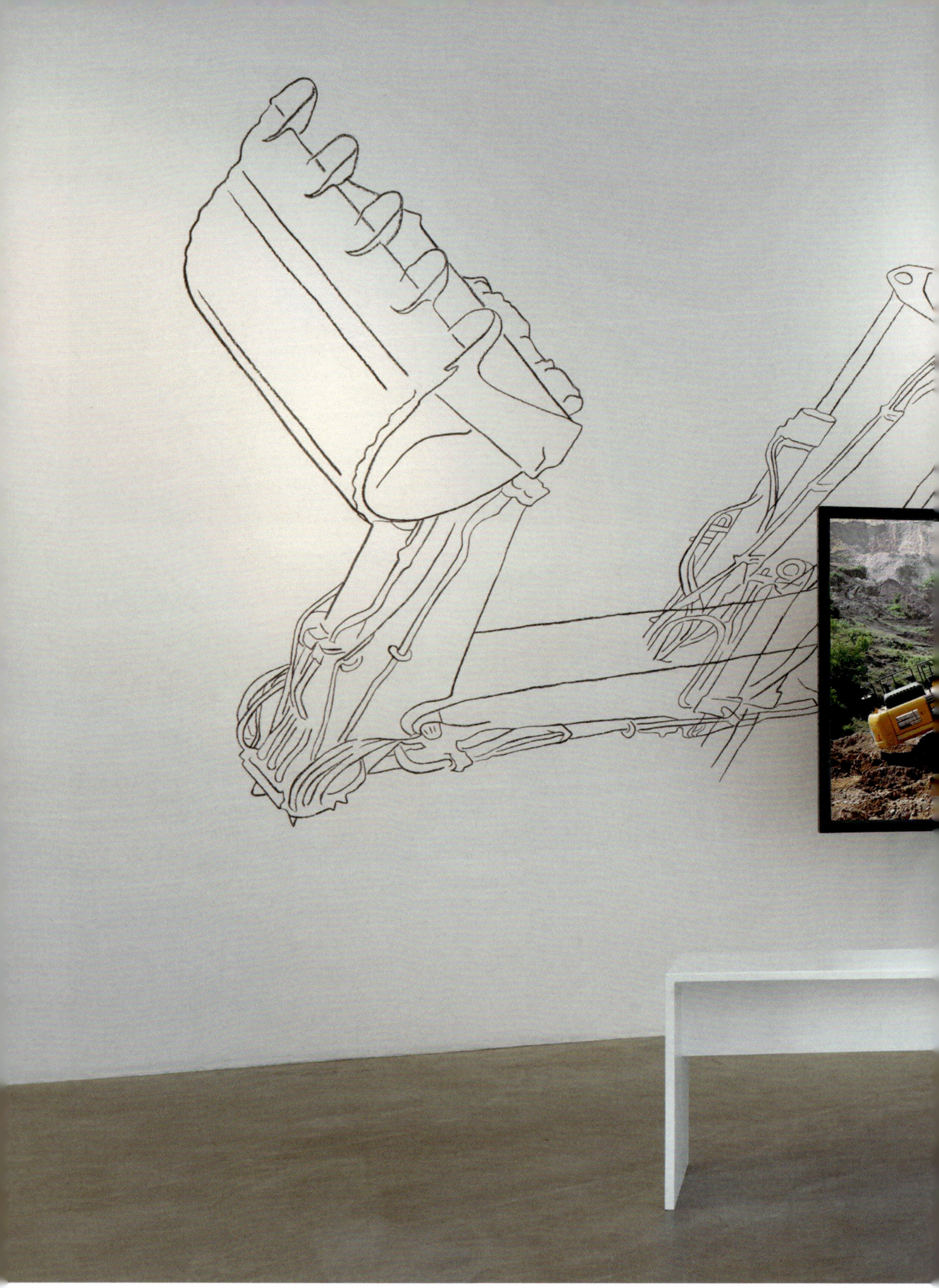

Installation view, *Thunder in Your Throat*, Neuer Berliner Kunstverein (n.b.k.), Berlin, 2022

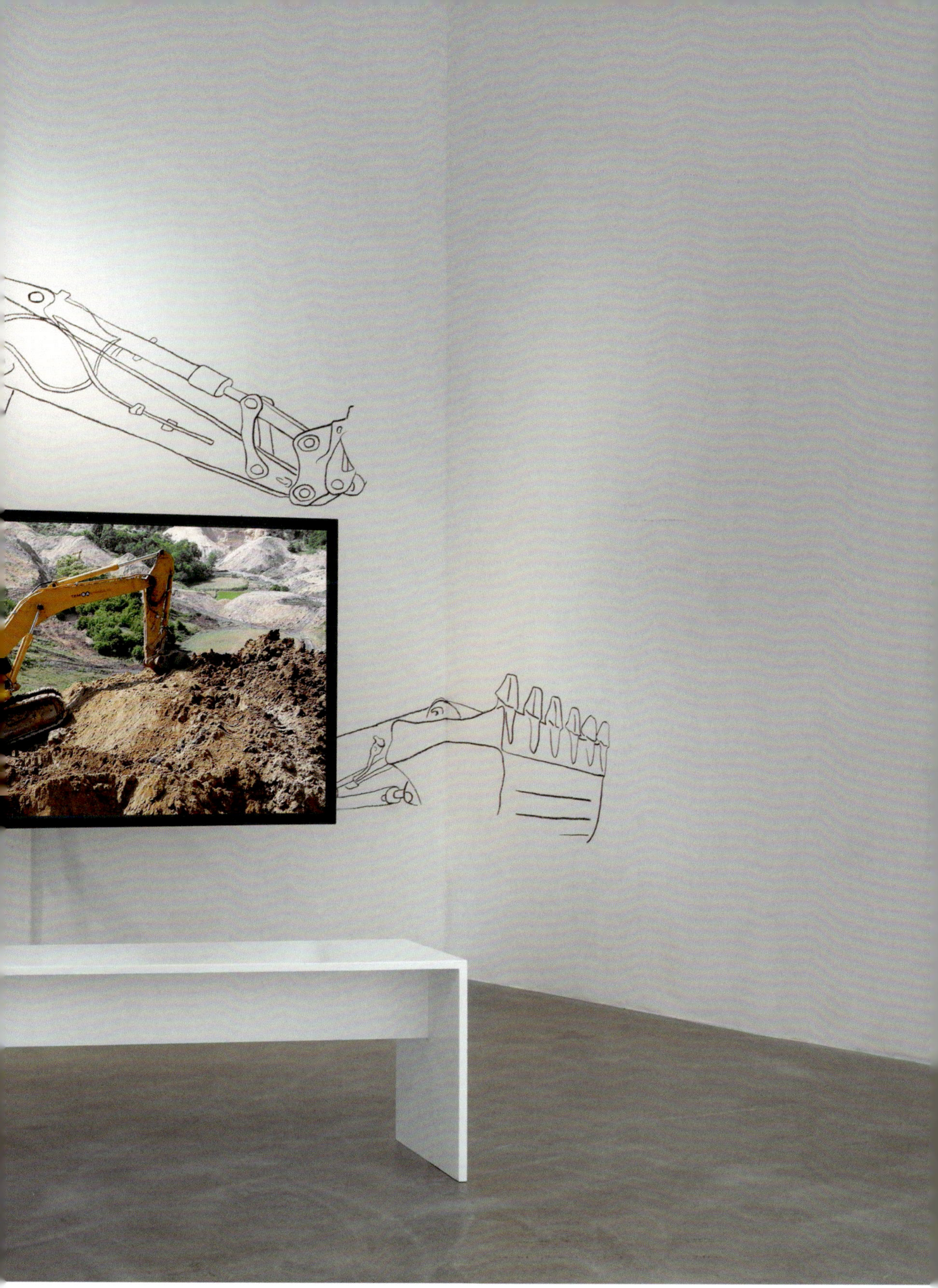

Tekla Aslanishvili & Giorgi Gago Gagoshidze

NEÏL BELOUPA

Neïl Beloufa (b. 1985 in Paris) **is based outside Paris and works across video, sculpture, and installation**

Neïl Beloufa's practice draws upon digital media culture, video games, reality television, and political propaganda. He uses these cultural and technological forms to interrogate the power relations and value systems of a society permeated by digital technology, where everything from food choices to human relationships are affected by algorithms that are in turn fed by data mined from our online activities.

Play and communication with diverse audiences are important to his work, which frequently involves interactive elements. In *New Visions 2023*, the video sculptures *Host B trying to reach out to its audience* (2021) and *Host C trying to reach out to its audience* (2021), actively approach the audience with sound, imagery, and interactive features on embedded screens. Visitors are invited to communicate with the "hosts," who, according to a script programmed for each exhibition, can perform various services, such as chat with an audience on Discord, give a speech, or take a selfie with visitors for uploading to a social media platform. By introducing elements of gamification, the hosts – which have been developed by Beloufa together with EBB – subject visitors to processes of data extraction. Founded by the artist in 2021, EBB is a decentralized experimental organization that creates tools and technologies for Web3 cultural production, linking IRL to URL. Beloufa's work with EBB furthers his interest in overturning the traditional roles and values assigned to art and in introducing modes of exchange that go beyond established forms of cultural distribution.

● **Biography** BELOUFA studied at Le Fresnoy, Studio National d'Art contemporain, Tourcoing, France; the Cooper Union, New York; and DNAP, École nationale supérieure des Beaux-Arts, Lyon. His work has been the subject of exhibitions at K11, Shanghai; Museum of Modern Art, New York; Schinkel Pavilion, Berlin; Institute of Contemporary Arts, London; Hammer Museum, Los Angeles; and Palais de Tokyo, Paris. His work is included in numerous museum collections, including the Centre Pompidou, Paris; the Museum of Modern Art, New York; Sammlung Goetz, Munich; and the Julia Stoschek Collection, Dusseldorf and Berlin.

Host B trying to reach out to its audience, 2021, TV screen, speakers, wood

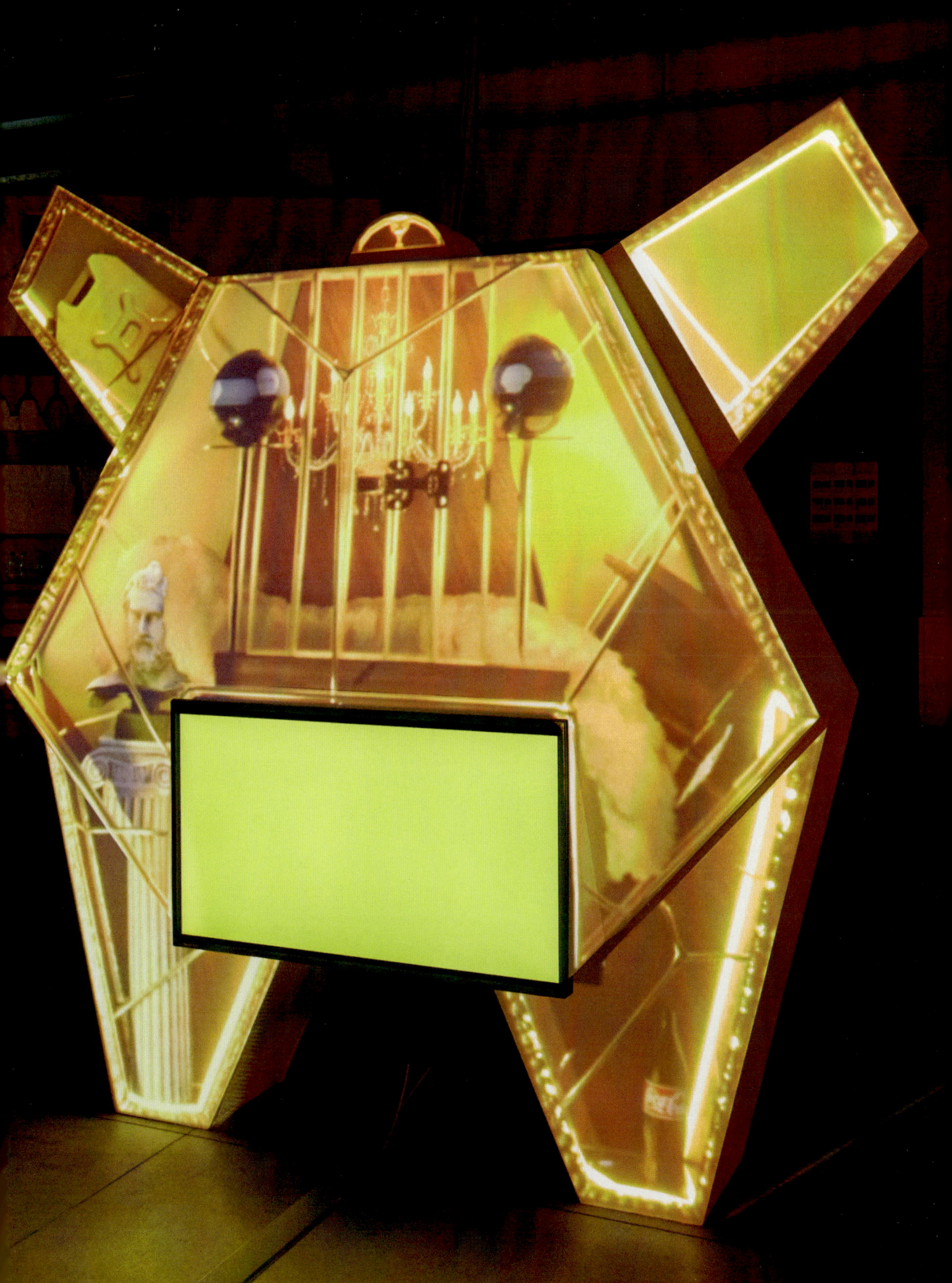

EBB & Neïl Beloufa

Host C trying to reach out to its audience, 2021, TV screen, speakers, wood

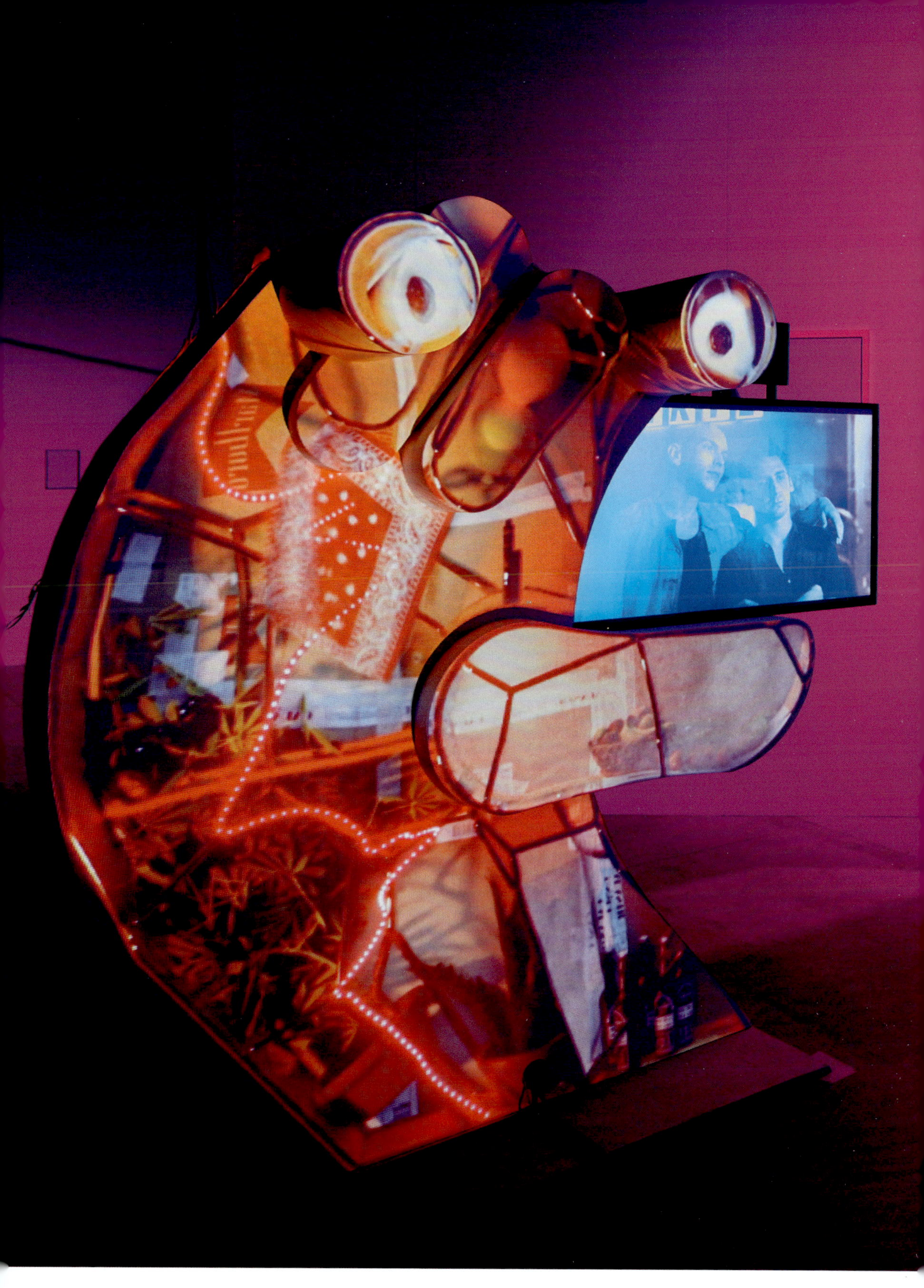

EBB & Neïl Beloufa

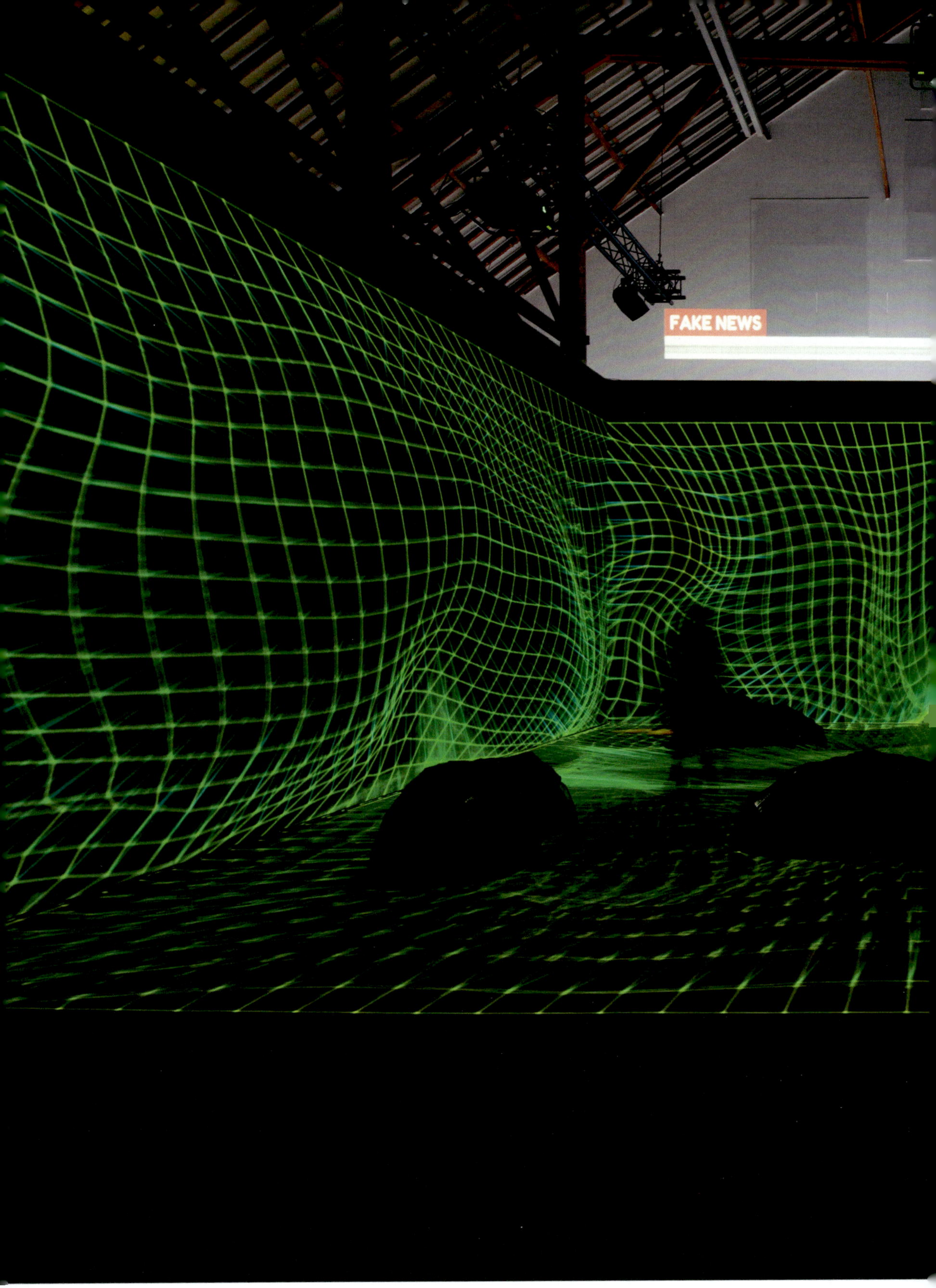

Installation view, *Pandemic Pandemonium*, CLEARING, Brussels, 2022

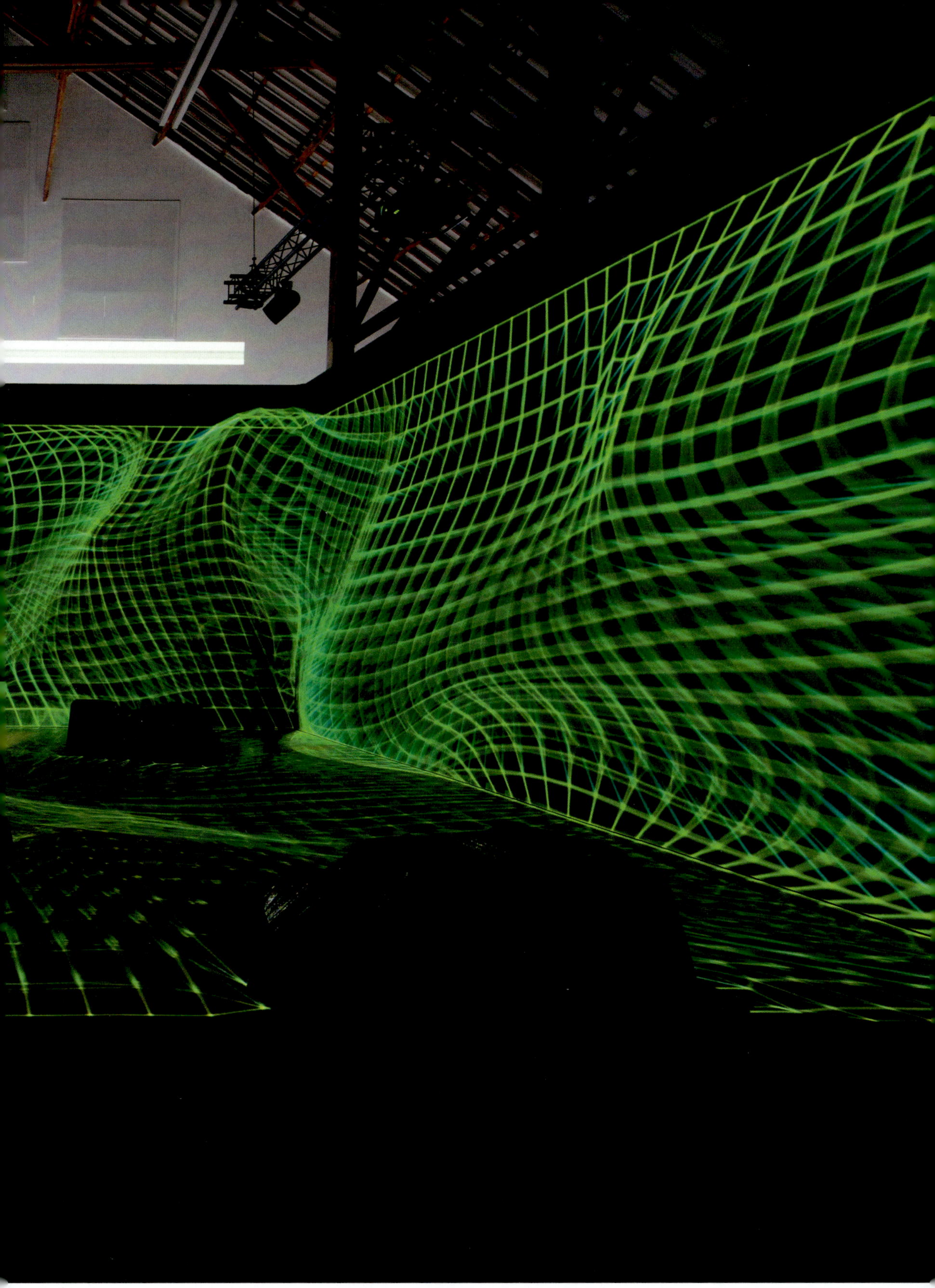

EBB & Neïl Beloufa

MYRIAM BOULOS

Myriam Boulos (b. 1992 in Beirut) **is a documentary photographer and artist based in Beirut**

What's Ours (2019–) is Myriam Boulos's ongoing photography series documenting the revolution in Lebanon that began on October 17, 2019. The photographs depict embodied struggle and resistance and the intimacies, pain, love, and frustration that accompany them. Fascinated by the proximity between bodies, moments when skin touches skin, Boulos's selection for *New Visions 2023* reclaims "what's supposed to be ours" through physical human contact. In the exhibition, the photographic prints are layered on the wall at different sizes and heights, assembling images of people together on the street, naked, intimate, or merely waiting in the months between October 2020 and January 2021.

This period saw the resumption of a revolution halted by COVID restrictions, by the August 4 explosion at the Port of Beirut and its aftermath, and by a deteriorating state. Here Boulos proposes desire for closeness and intimacy as emancipatory gestures, as a rejoinder to both virus and restriction, using the body and its changes to signify what is to come, whether through hope, sex, or death. Boulos conjures the social energy of this fraught moment with bodily tensions and attempts at disassociating from reality. According to the artist, the impulse animating this series is to unload data and emotions, to sweep away psychological baggage, so that she and her viewers can "start feeling subtle things again, [like] delicacy and magic."

● **Biography** BOULOS graduated in 2015 with a master's degree in photography from the Academie Libanaise des Beaux-Arts, Beirut. She has captured a tumultuous period in Lebanese history for *Time*, *Vogue*, and *Vanity Fair* and has taken part in numerous international exhibitions such as *Close Enough* at the International Center of Photography, New York; *Infinite Identities* at Huis Marseille, Amsterdam; and the Third Biennial of Photographs of the Arab World at the Institut du Monde Arabe, Paris. In 2020, she co-founded and became the photo editor of *Al Hayya*, a bilingual magazine that publishes literary and visual content on the work, interests, and struggles of women in her region. In 2021, she was awarded the Grand prix ISEM and the second prize of the PhMuseum women's grant. She was also named as a Foam talent and joined Magnum the same year.

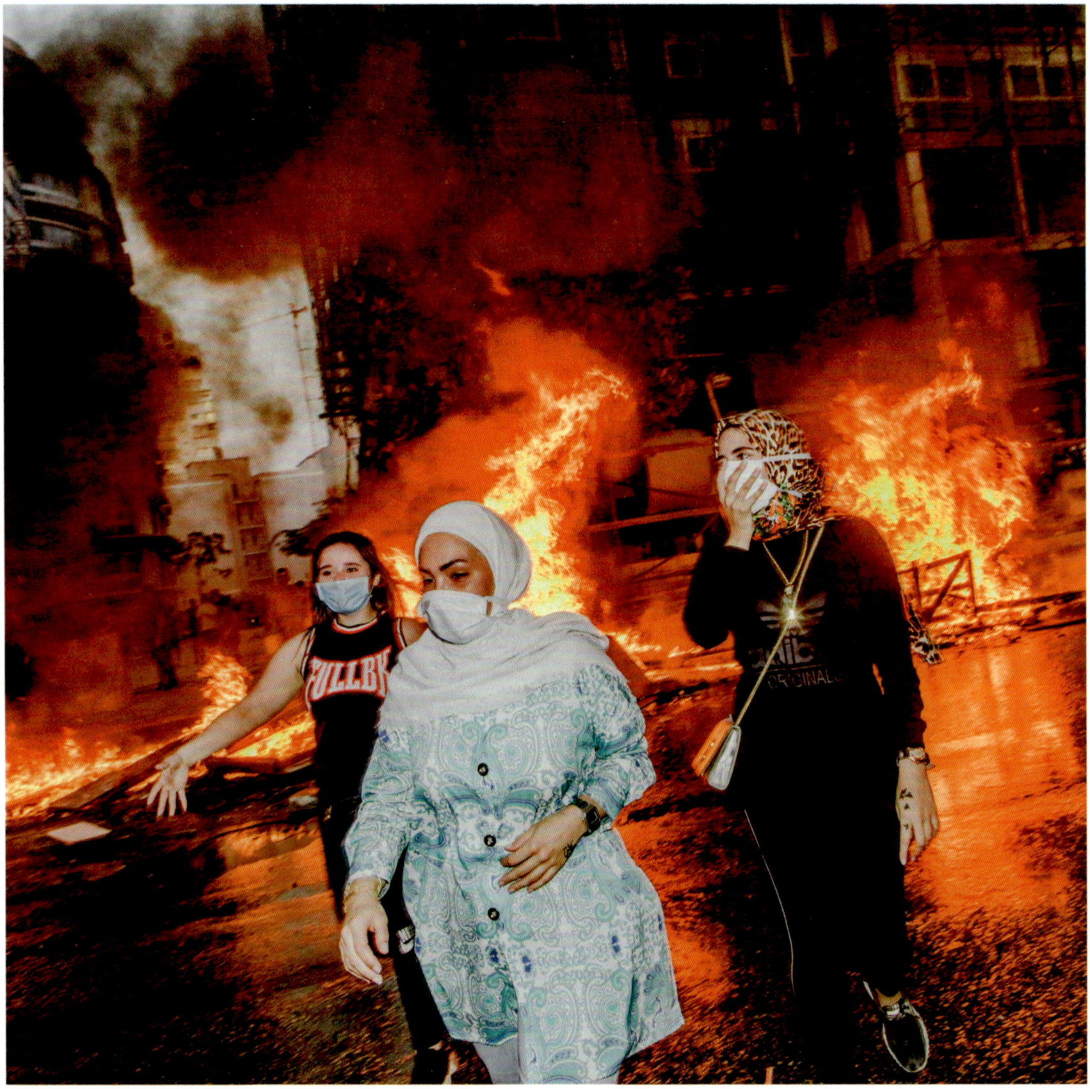

↑ *What's ours*, Beirut, Lebanon, 2019, inkjet print
↗ *Tell the trees to smile*, Sour, Lebanon, 2021, inkjet print

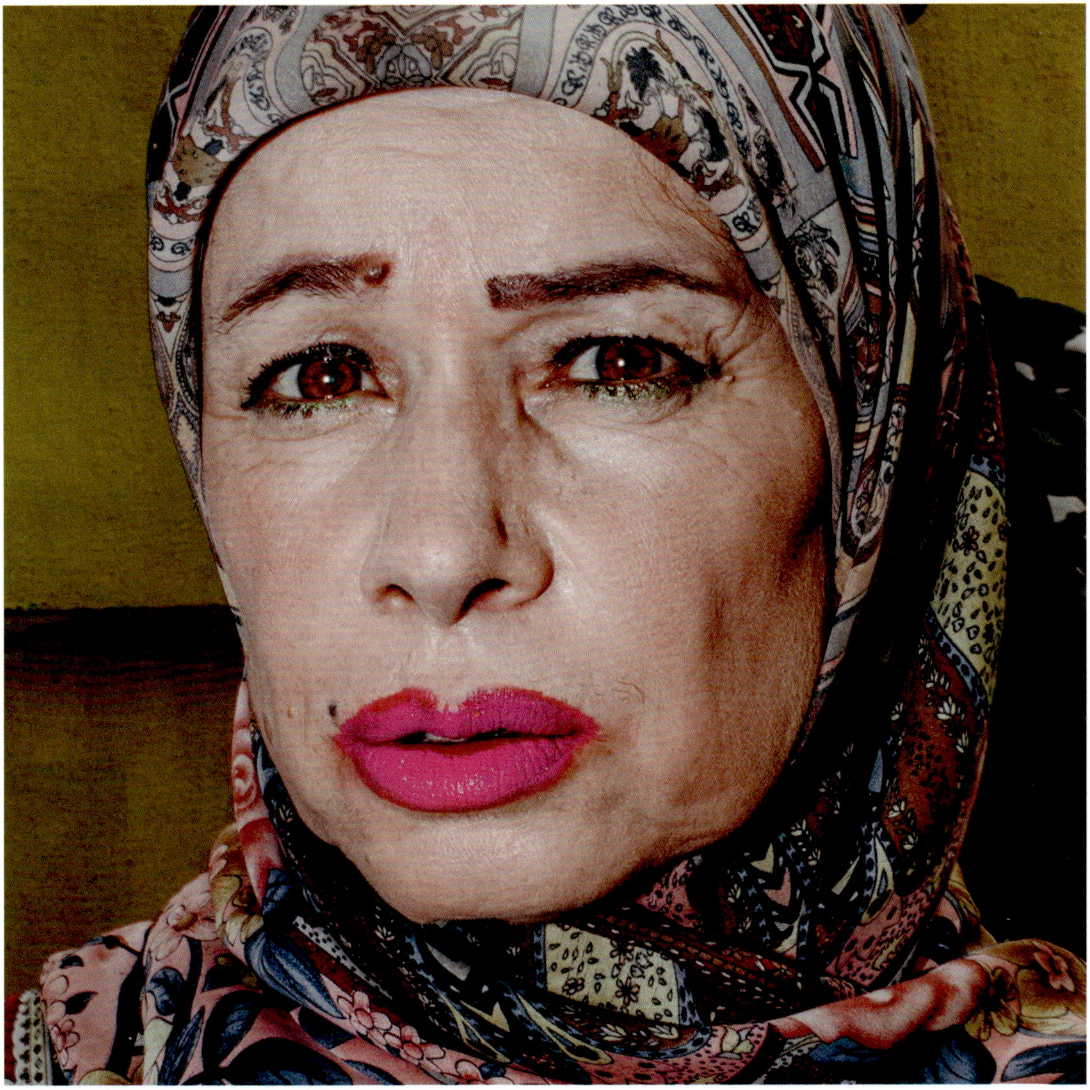

Myriam Boulos

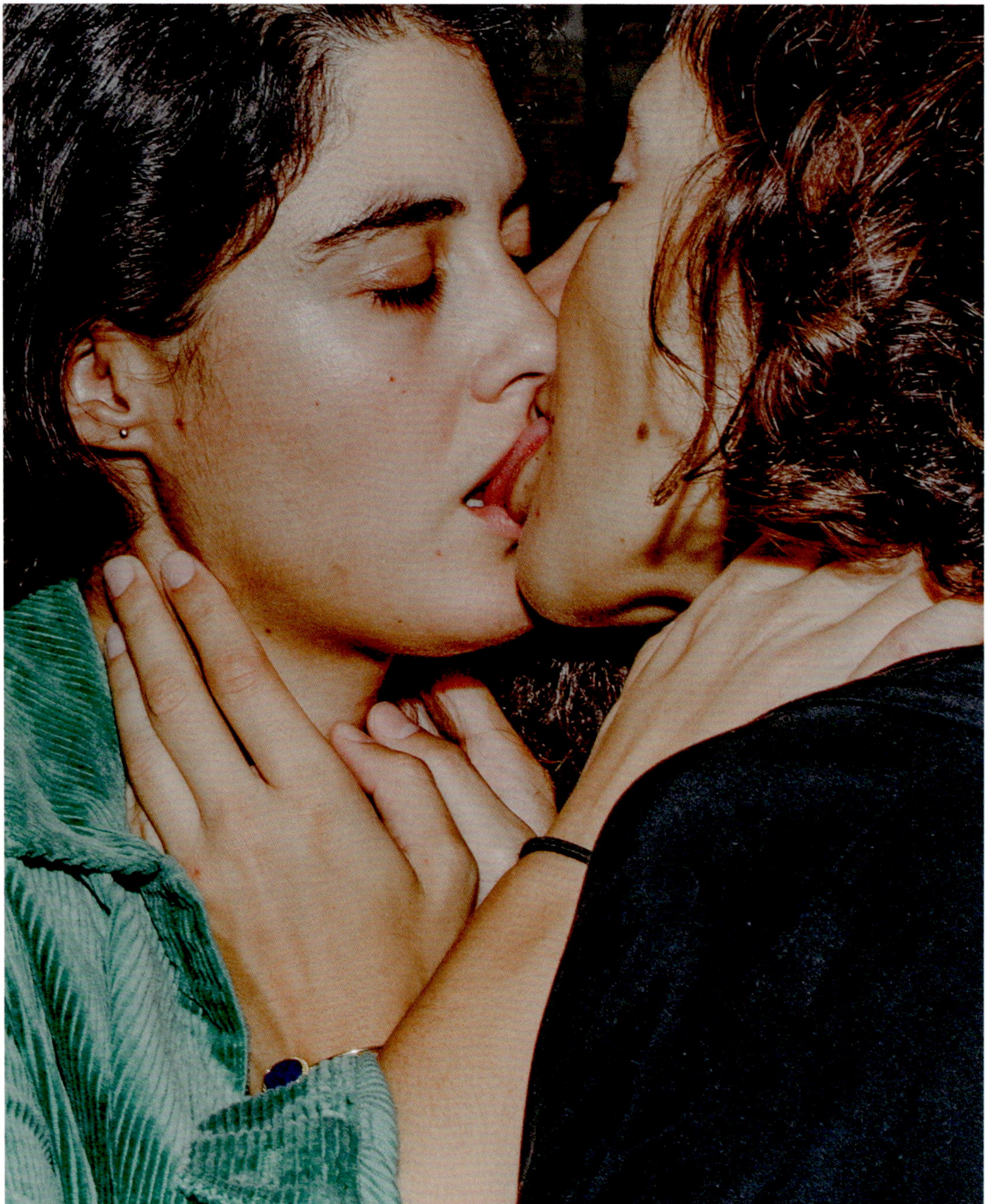

↑ *What's ours*, Beirut, Lebanon, 2019, inkjet print
↗ *Tenderness*, Beirut, Lebanon, 2018, inkjet print

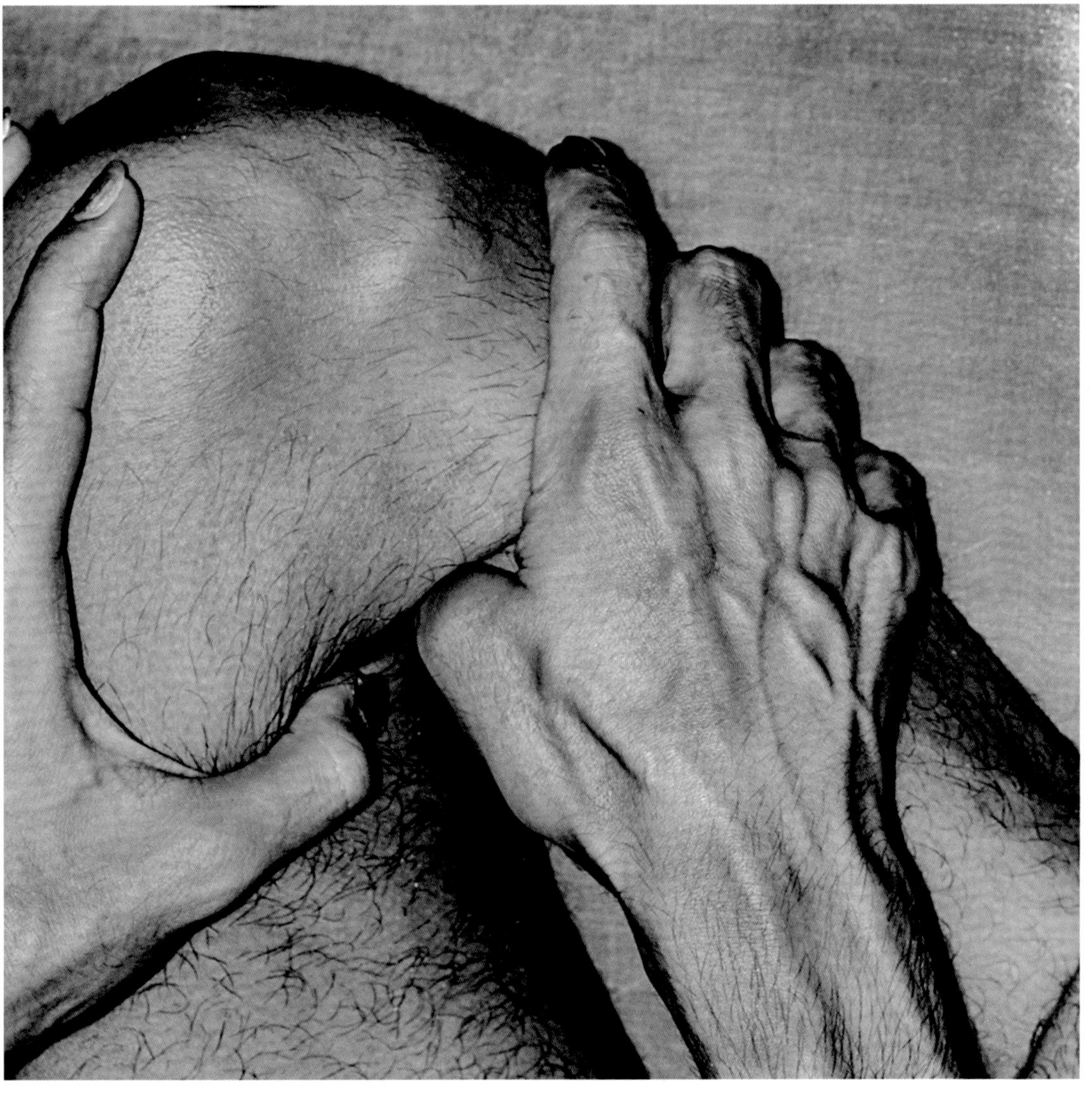

Myriam Boulos

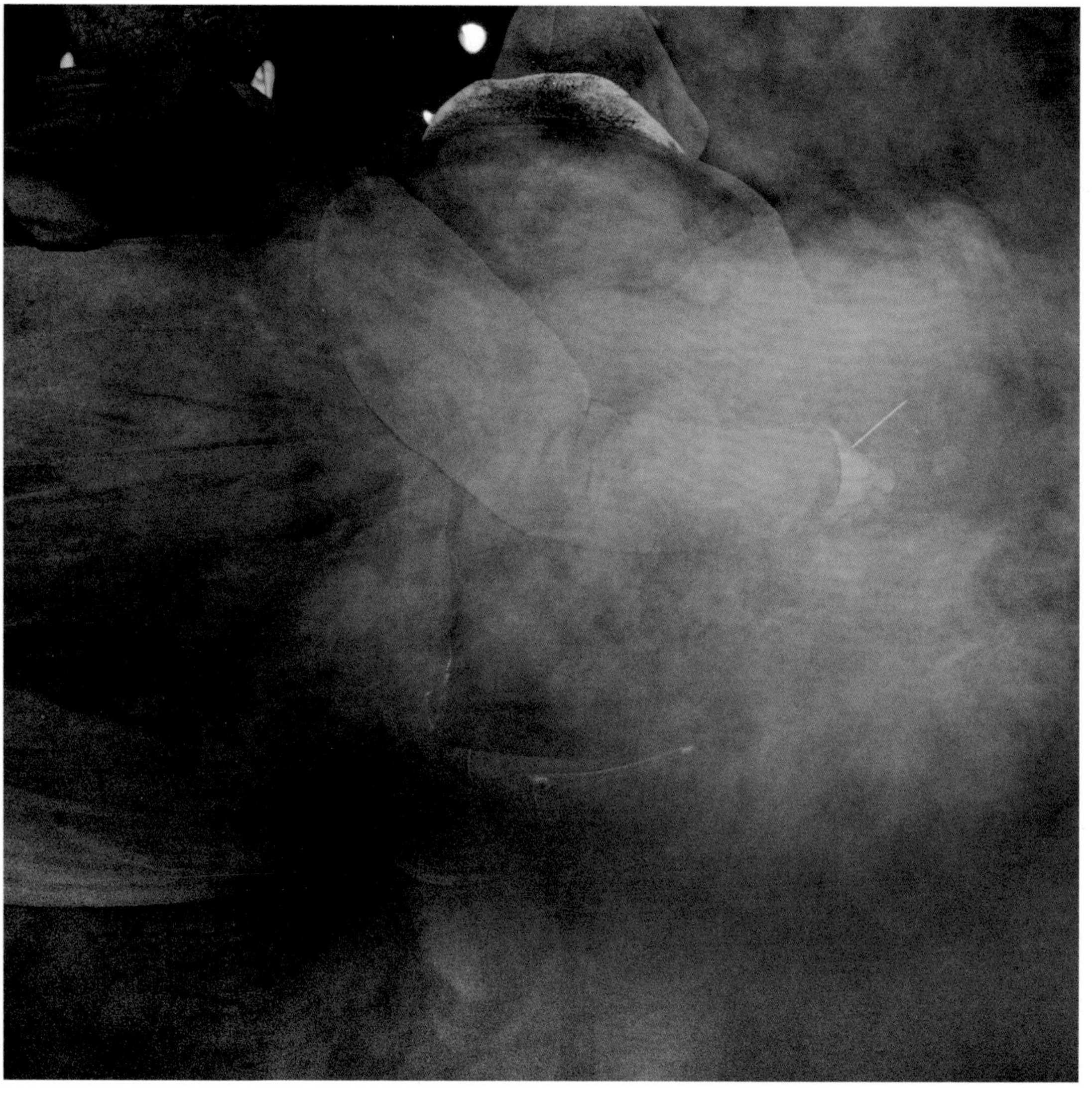

↑ *What's ours,* Beirut, Lebanon, 2020, inkjet print
↗ *What's ours,* Lebanon, 2019, inkjet print

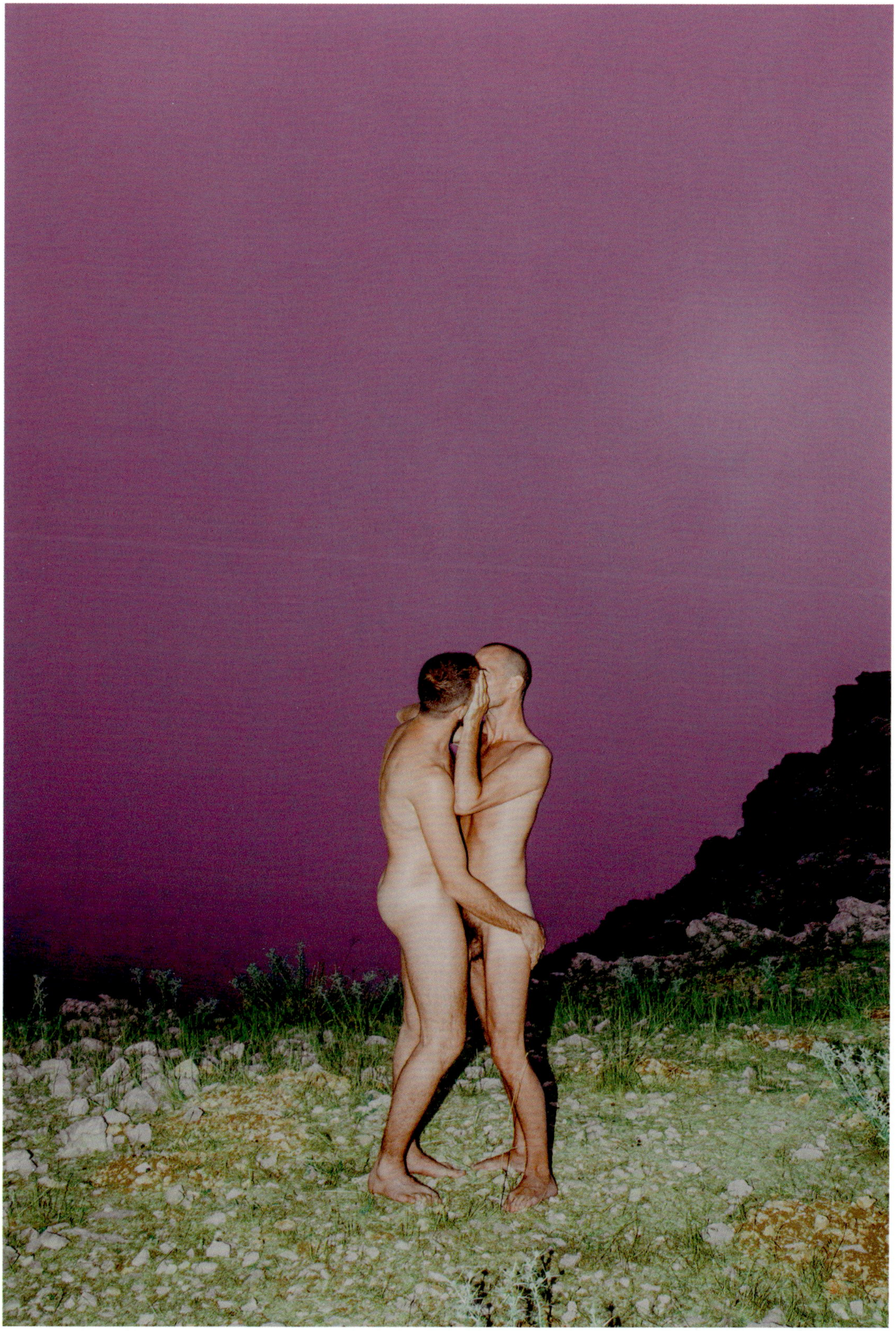

Myriam Boulos

MARAT DILMAN

Marat Dilman (b. 1990 in Almaty, Kazakhstan) **is a documentary photographer based in Almaty**

Marat Dilman's photographs blend interfaces, robots, and other markers of technological progress with traditional elements of Kazakh culture to construct a distinct mythological and symbolic iconography. His vividly colored blend of futurism and folklore is inspired by his country's fast-changing, visually hybrid landscape.

The photographs presented in *New Visions 2023* show motifs from small- and large-scale national celebrations across Kazakhstan. To capture the Nauryz holiday, the public celebration of the spring equinox, the artist has photographed the installation of a stage in a public square. A robot featuring a traditional Kazakh hat is the outcome of a school competition in robotics, for which the jury asked participants to make the robots human-like. In a shopping mall, Dilman has captured a security camera and an amulet side by side, two objects that are believed to offer protection. Another image shows a yurt as a decorative element next to an artificial ceiling, a sign of a repair strategy using cheap materials to modernize interior spaces. Dilman's works reflect how processes of transformation and nation-building in the young post-Soviet state entwine new technologies and traditions.

● **Biography** DILMAN is a photographer who travels around Kazakhstan shooting uncanny, unpredictable vistas. His recent exhibitions include *The Eurasian Utopia: Post Scriptum* at Suwon IPark Museum of Art, Suwon, South Korea; the Astana Art Show in Astana, Kazakhstan; and *Act of Creation*, part of the ARTBAT FEST in Almaty. Dilman was a winner of the 2019 Halyk Art Prize.

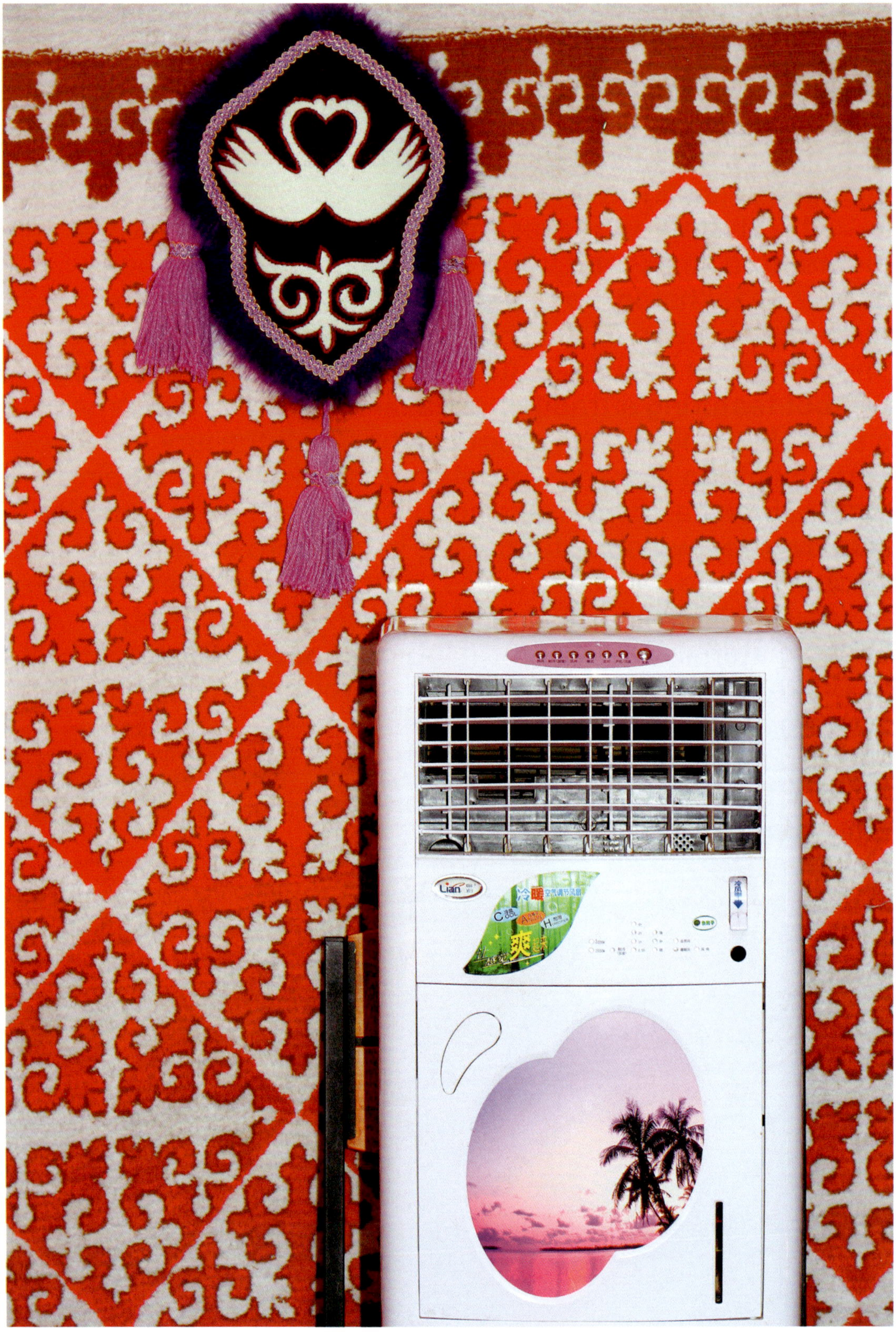

↑ *Untitled*, 2017, inkjet print
↗ *Untitled*, 2017, inkjet print

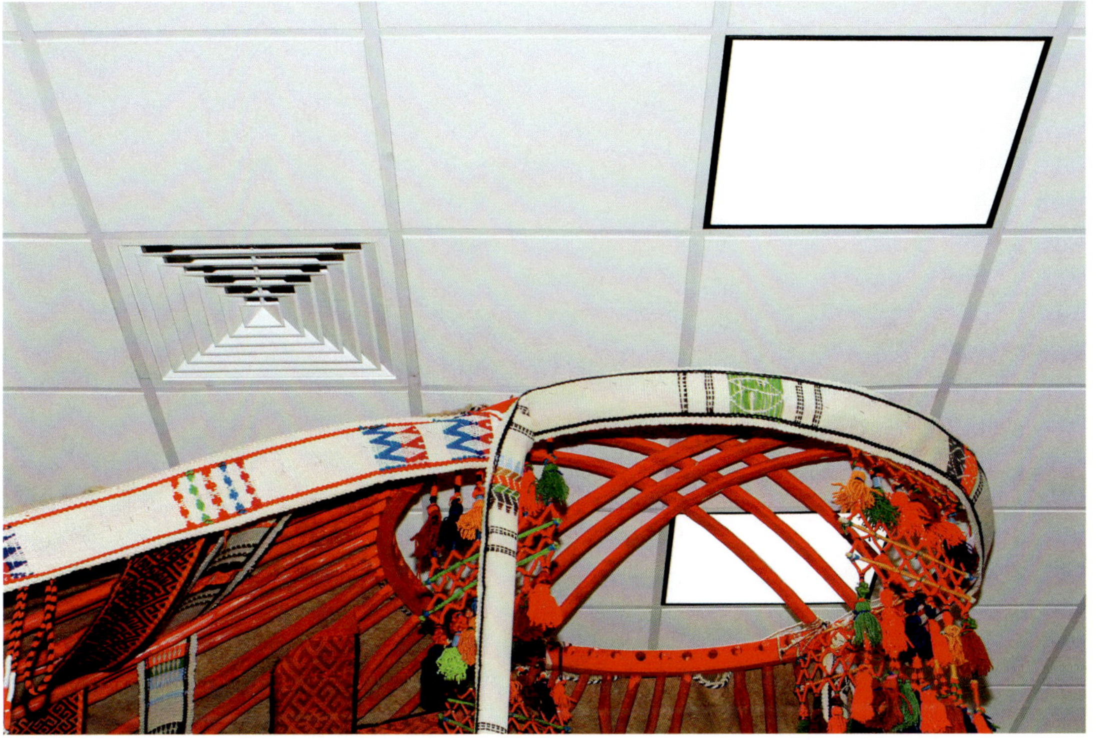

Marat Dilman

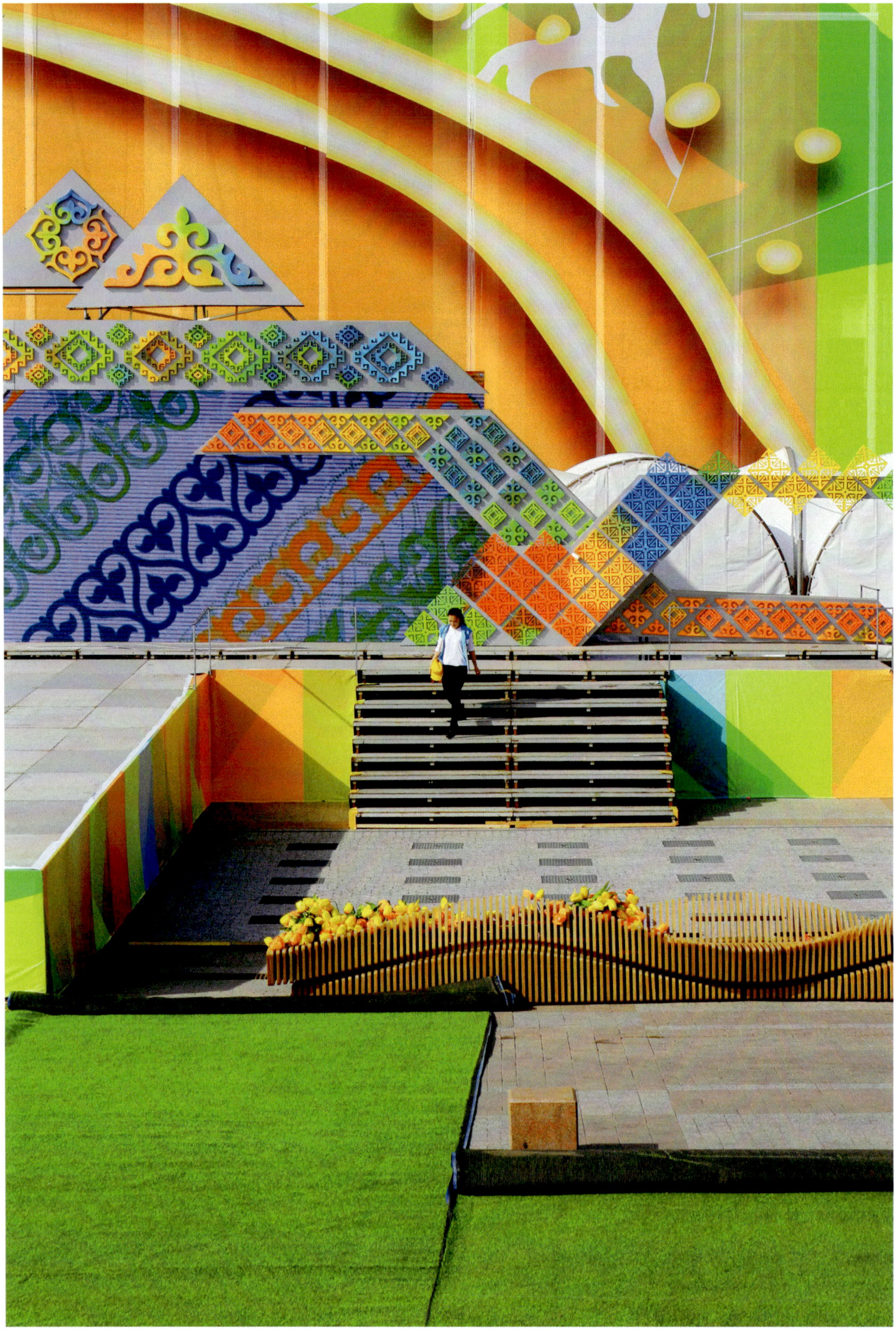

↑ *Untitled*, 2018, inkjet print
↗ *Untitled*, 2019, inkjet print

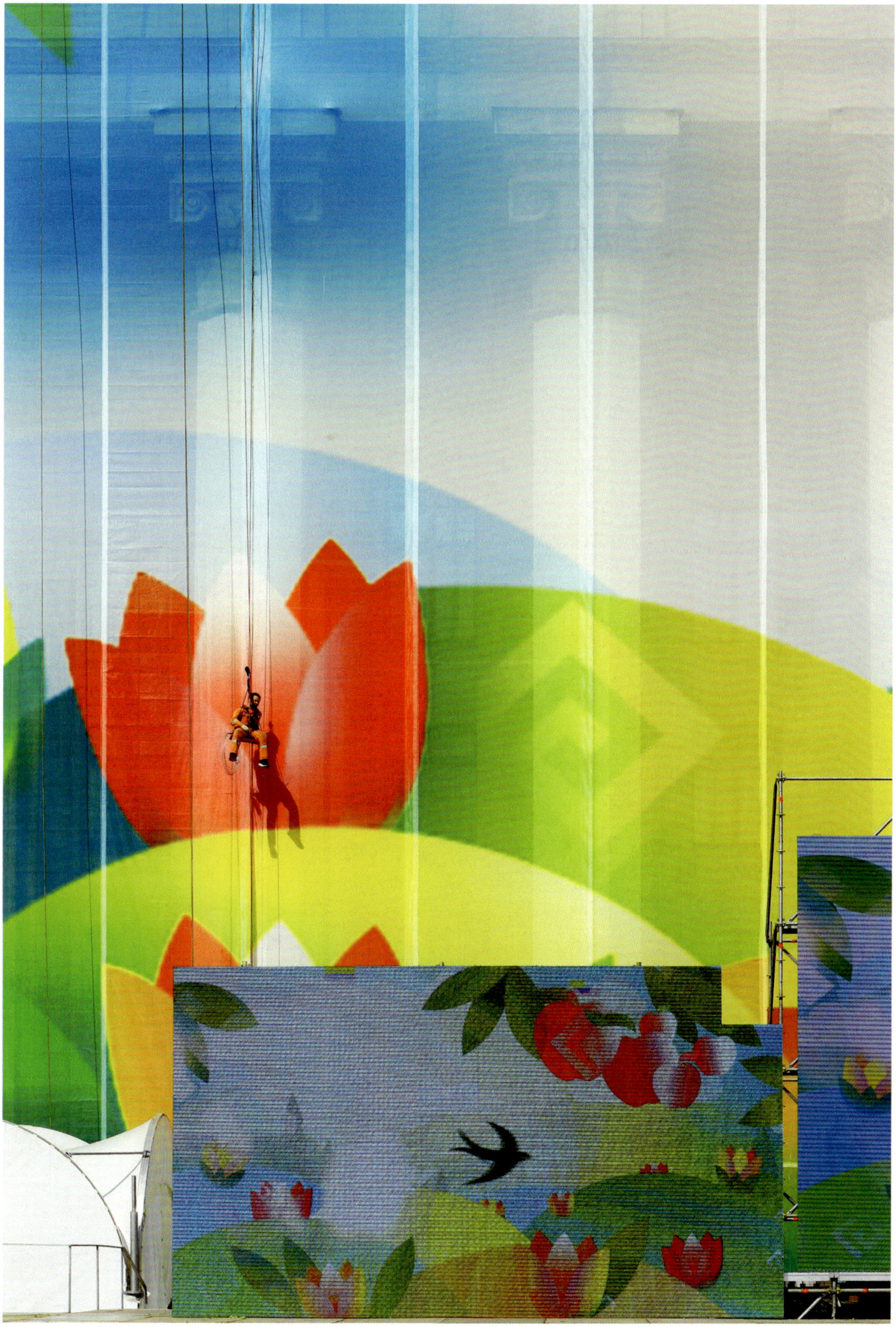

Marat Dilman

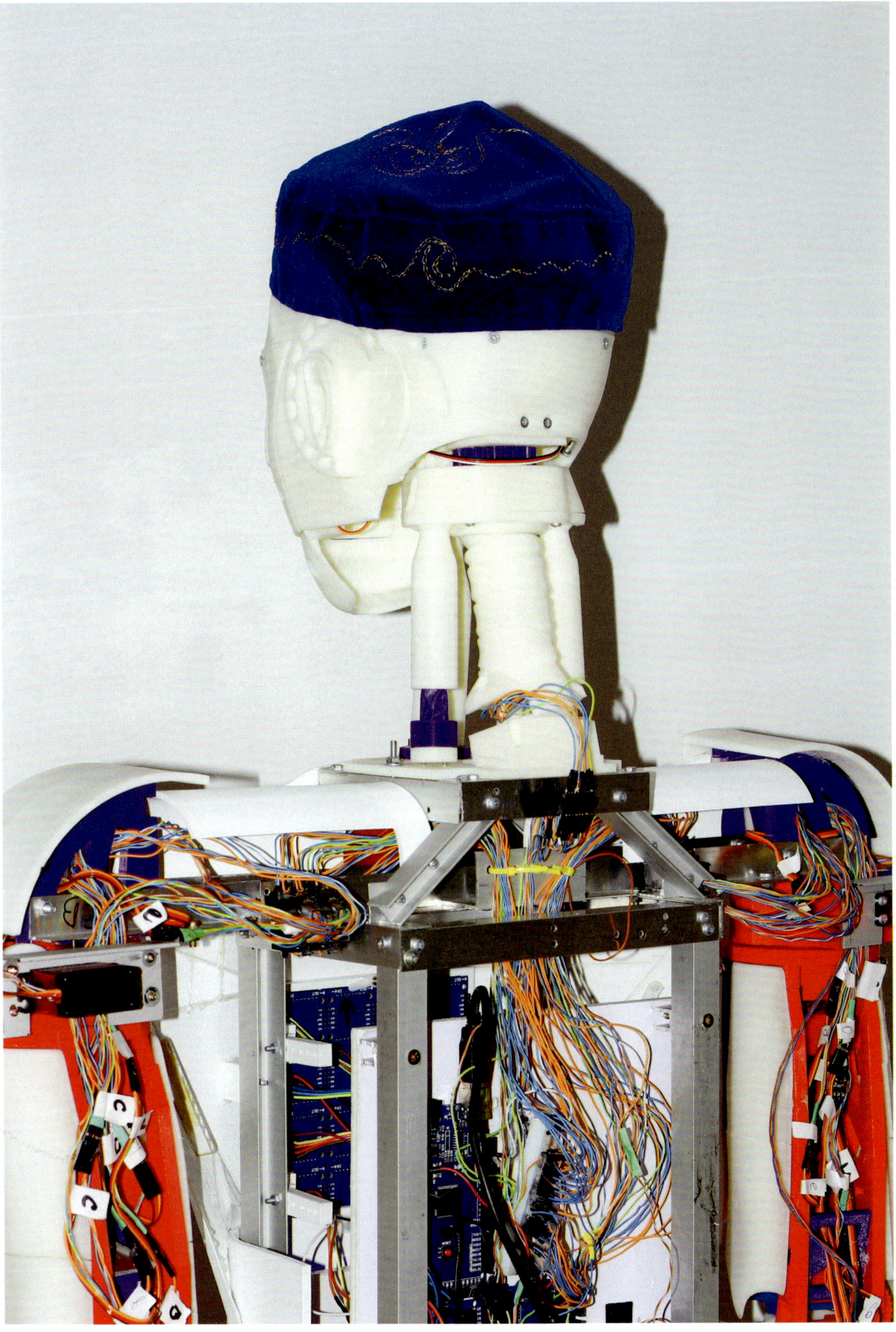

↑ *Untitled*, 2019, inkjet print
↗ *Untitled*, 2020, inkjet print

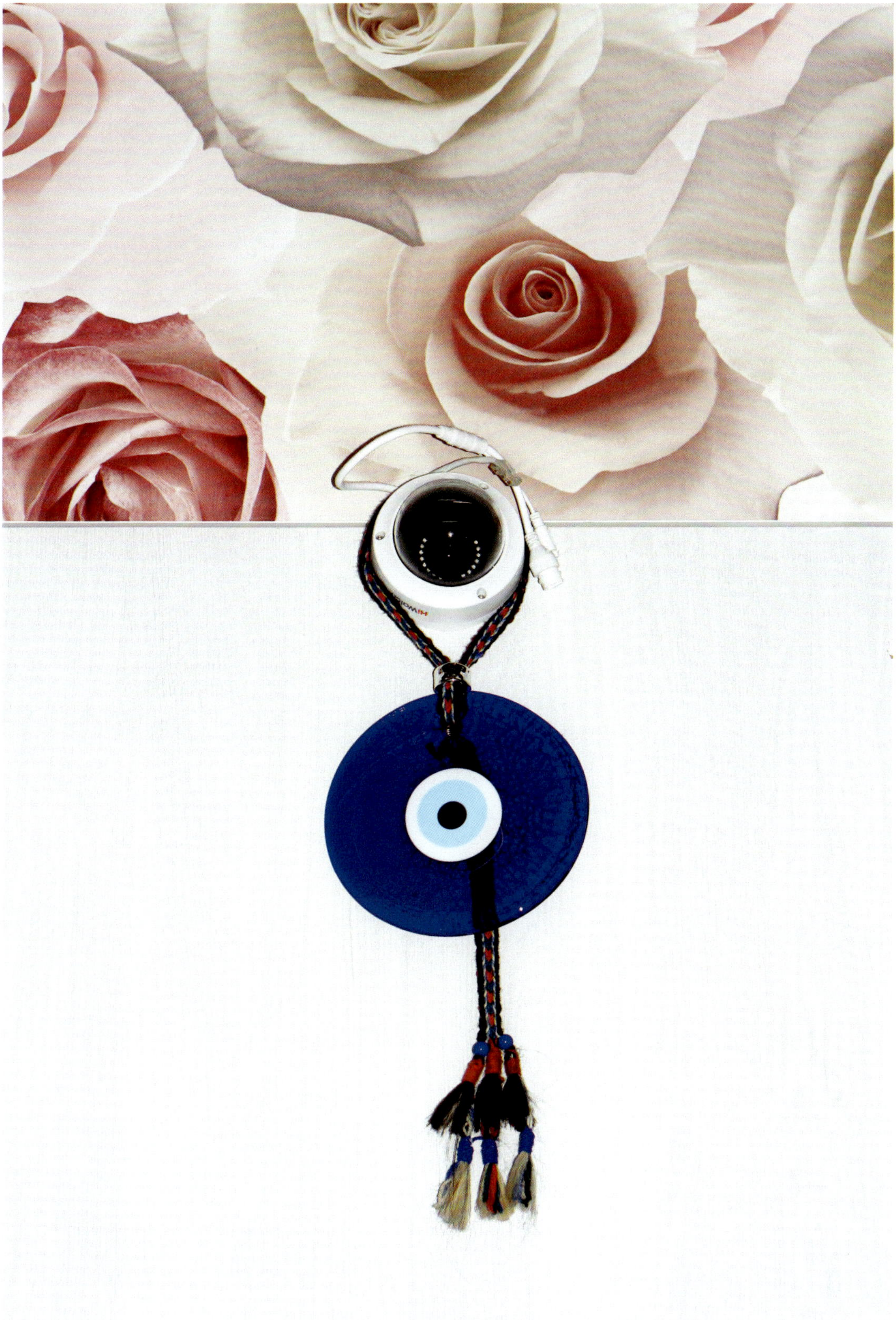

Marat Dilman

ANNA EHRENSTEIN

Anna Ehrenstein (b. 1993 in Germany) **is a diaspora Albanian transdisciplinary artist based in Berlin**

"For a person who has never seen the Orient, a lotus is still a lotus; for me, it is only a kind of onion." These lines, attributed by Edward Said to French Romantic author Gérard de Nerval, point to the shifting perspectives on what Westerners have called "the Orient" and inspired the title of Anna Ehrenstein's ongoing project *A Lotus Is a Lotus* (2017–).

The work explores the Western consumption of cultural differences through fake and folkloric objects across the digital and physical realms. Through lenticular photographic prints, which appear to change as they are viewed from different angles, and a video work, Ehrenstein conjures a dreamscape of historic and contemporary Orientalist artifacts. Two image planes appear in the prints. One shows lotus flowers from textiles produced on the west coast of India that Ehrenstein has processed into new objects using origami techniques and photographed. The other plane consists of documentary photos of objects typically found in tourist markets in countries of the former "Orient": Egypt, Morocco, Albania, China. As the viewer moves, the image shifts: is it an onion, or is it a lotus?

In the video, a guide to the illegal backdoor spaces of the Pearl Market in Beijing muses on her experiences of the tastes and preferences of different tourist groups. *A Lotus Is a Lotus* continues Ehrenstein's longstanding exploration of how and by whom cultural, economic, and aesthetic value is produced and judged, and how these values are upheld and upended in today's neocolonial conditions.

● **Biography** EHRENSTEIN studied photography at the University of Applied Arts and Sciences in Dortmund, media arts at the Academy of Media Arts in Cologne, and curatorial practice at the University of Malta and through the Lagos Biennale. She often works with groups on joint artistic projects and has exhibited, individually and collectively, at the Screen City Biennale in Berlin, the Ural Biennale in Yekaterinburg, the Biennale für aktuelle Fotografie in Mannheim, Germany, and Amanet, at the Triennale of Photography in Hamburg, where she was an artist, initiator, and co-curator. Her solo shows include *Tools for Conviviality* at Landesmuseum in Linz, Austria, and *The Albanian Conference: Home Is Where the Hatred Is* at KOW in Berlin.

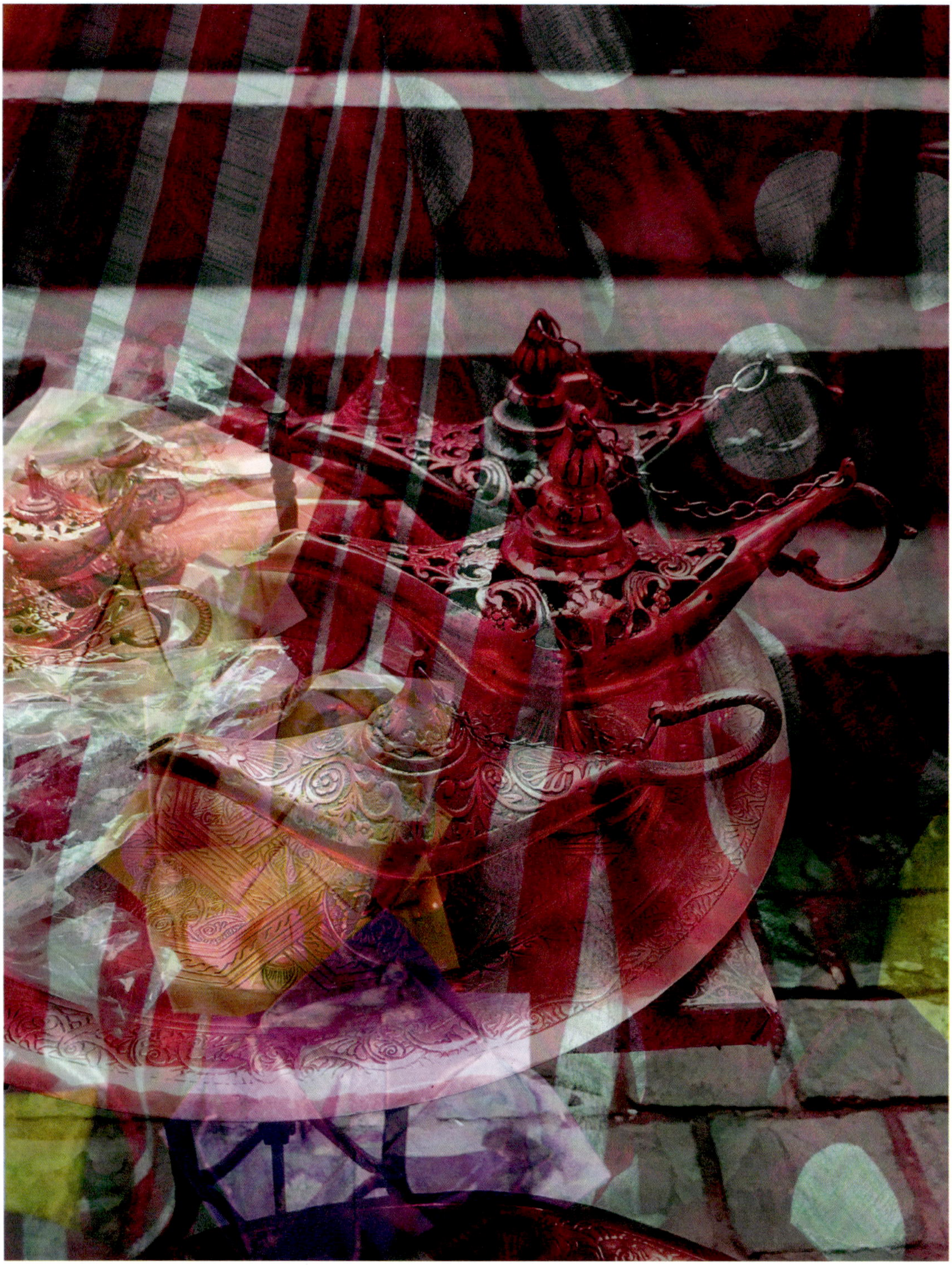

A Lotus Is a Lotus, 2017–, lenticular prints

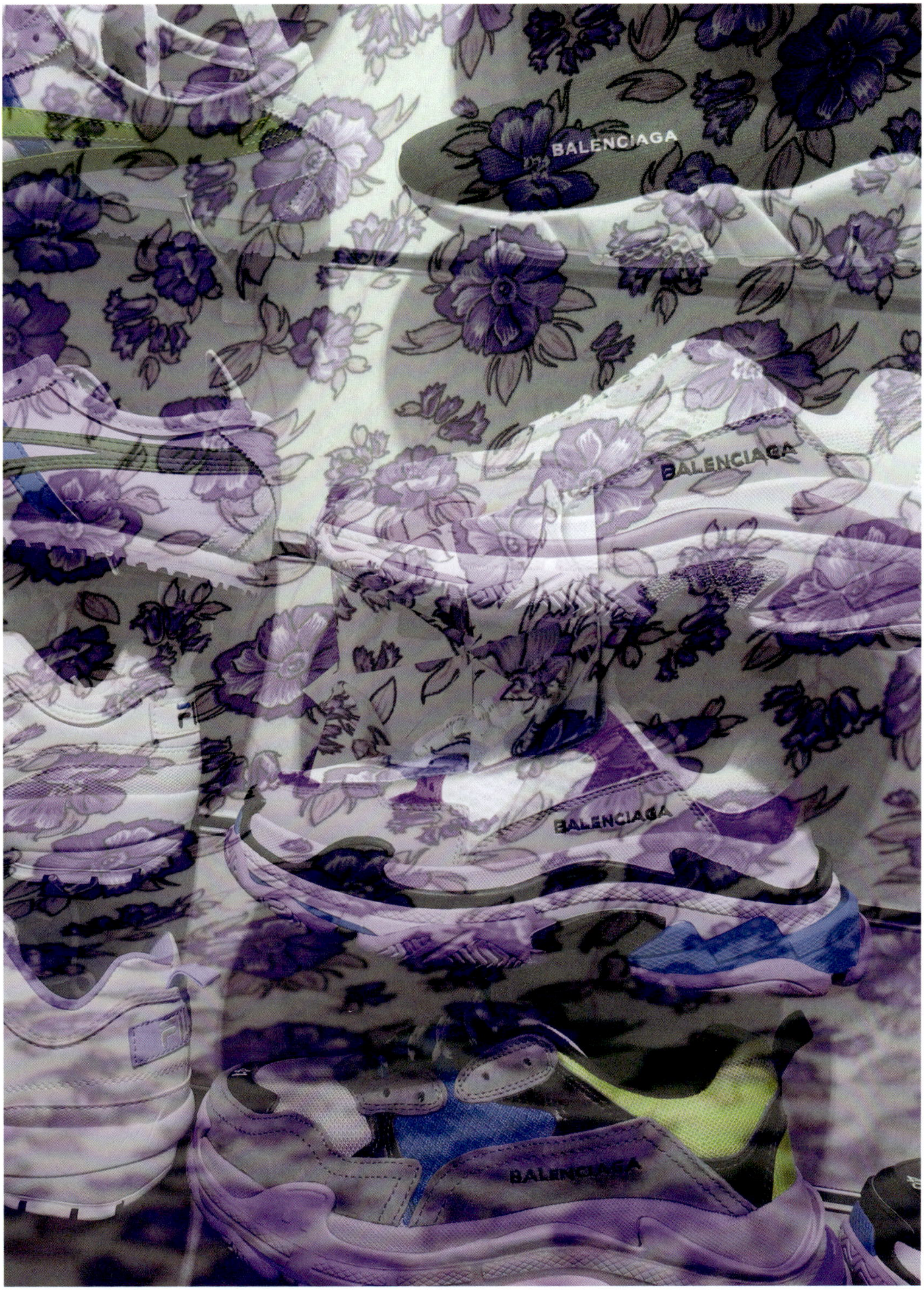

Anna Ehrenstein

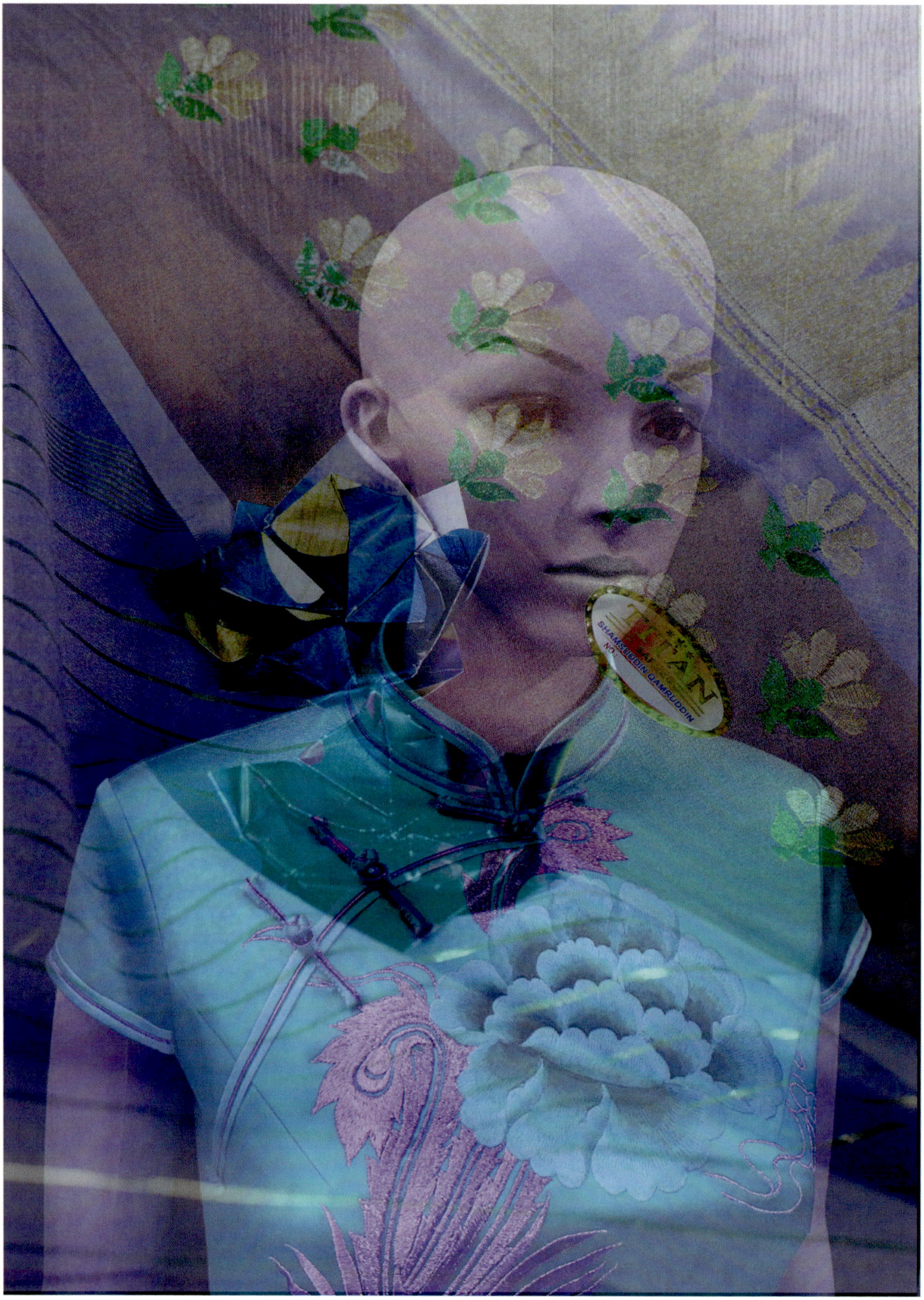

A Lotus Is a Lotus, 2017–, lenticular prints

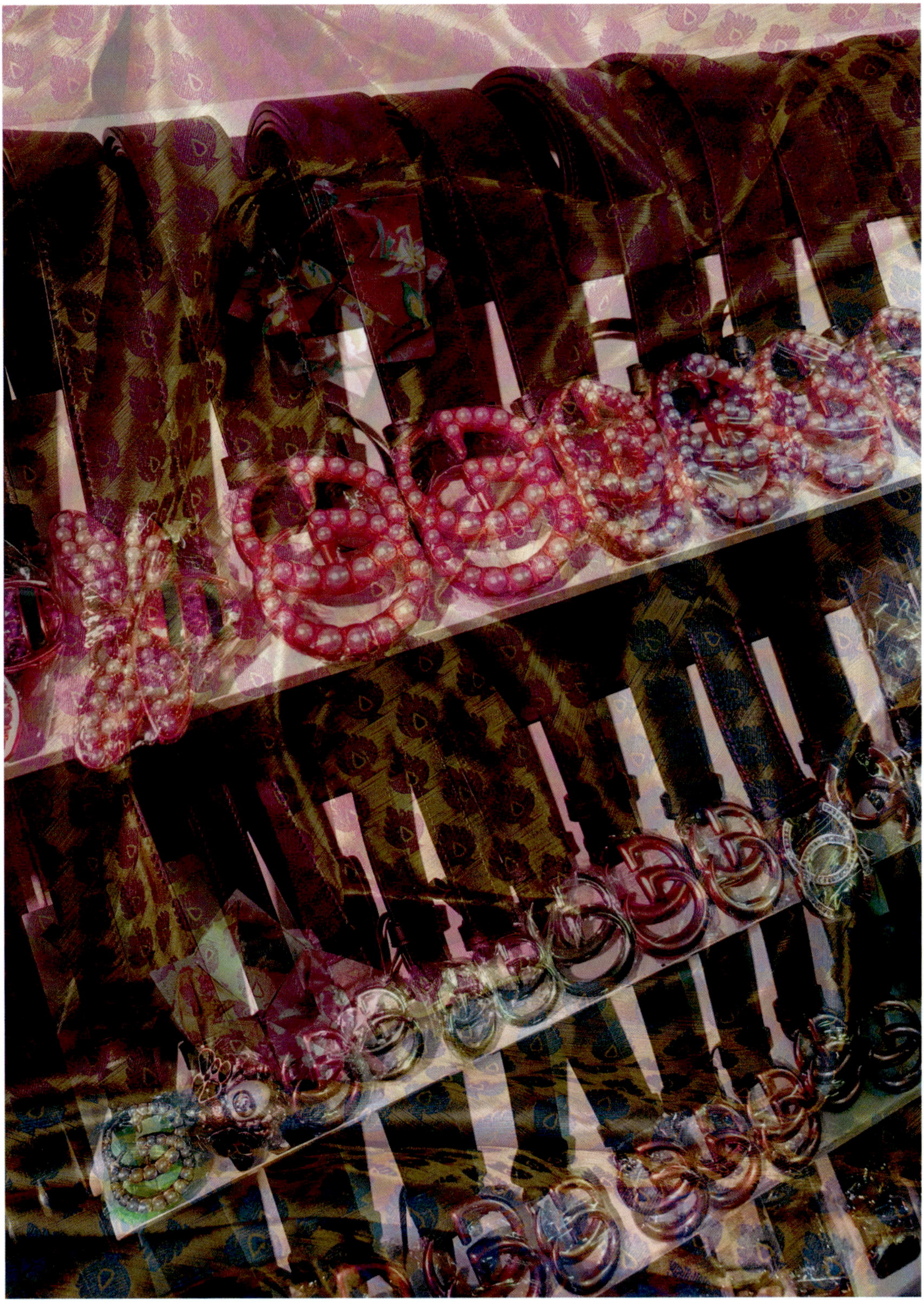

Anna Ehrenstein

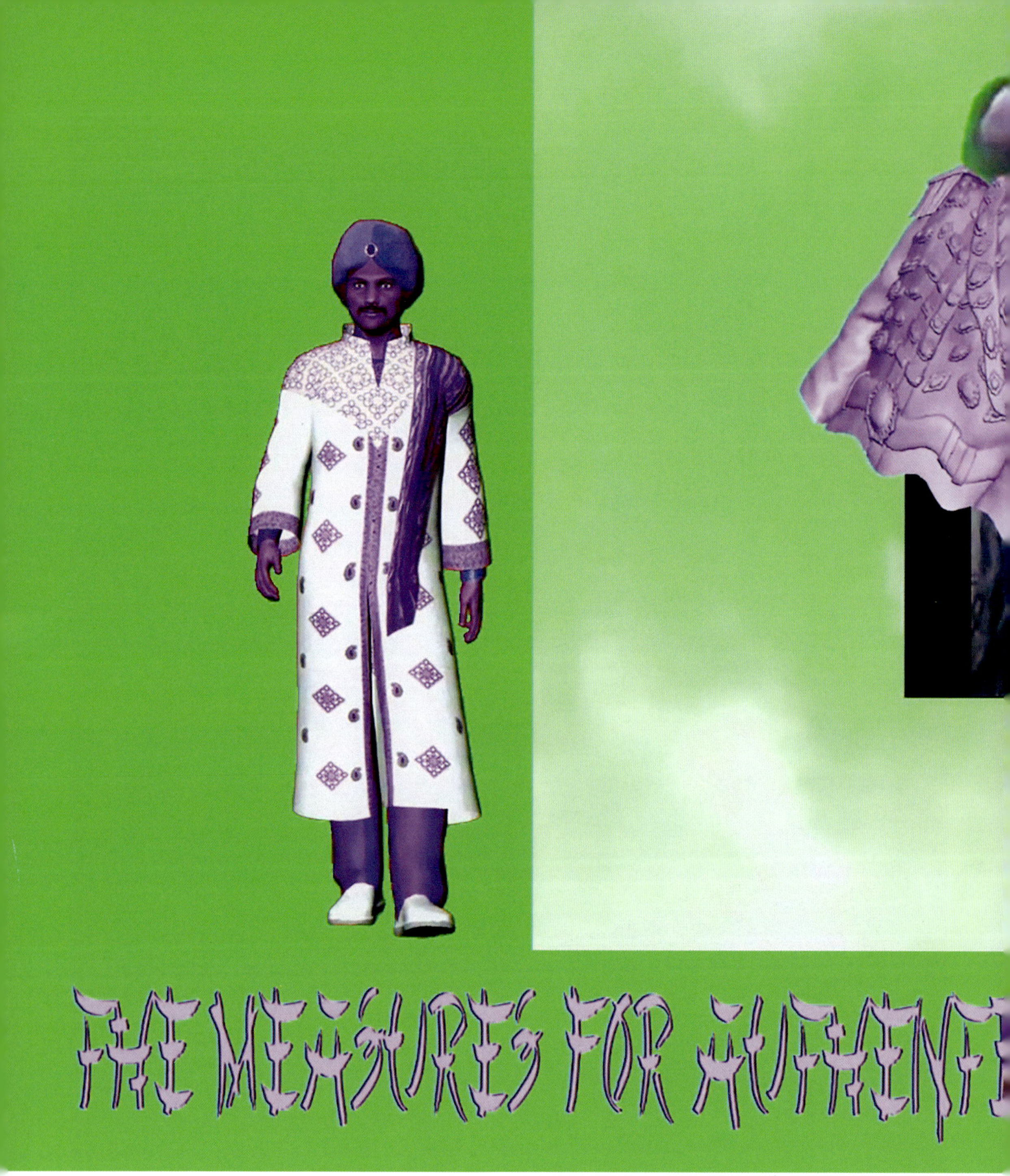

Still from *Capitalocene Safari Collage*, 2019, single-channel color video with sound

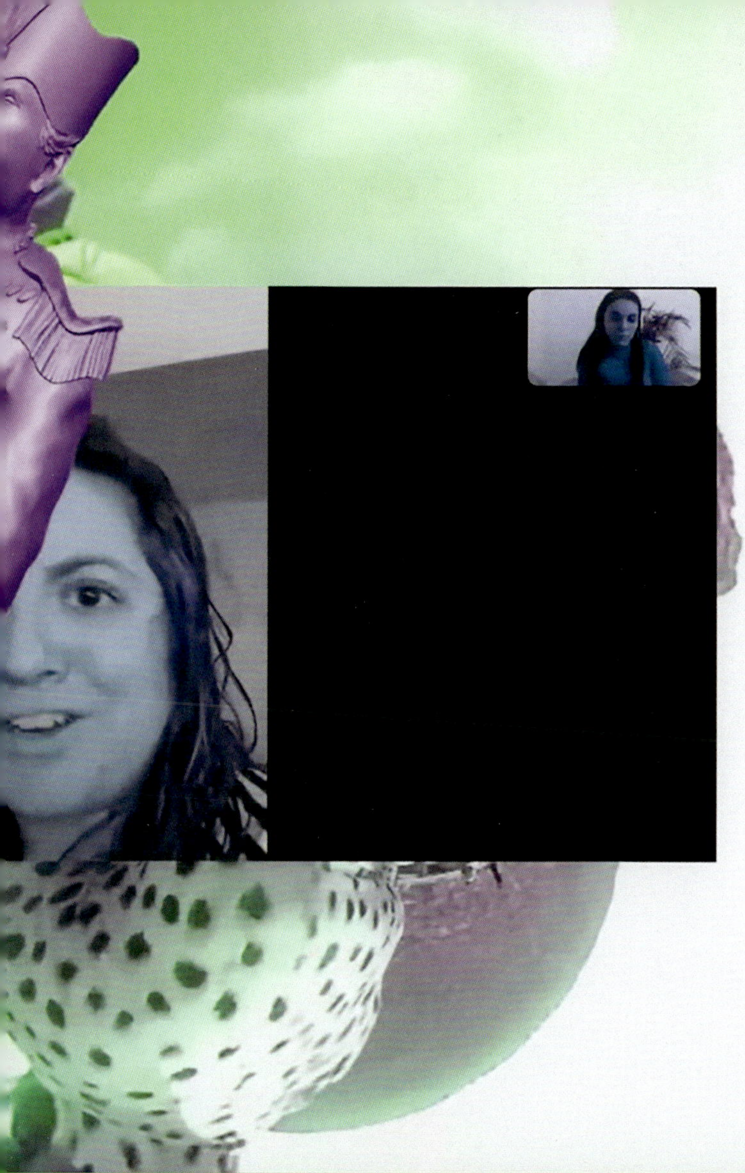

FX ARE OUR CULTURAL CHOICE

Anna Ehrenstein

ANNA ENGELHARDT & MARK CINKEVICH

Anna Engelhardt (b. 1996 in Rostov-on-Don, Russia) **is the alias of a research-based media artist and writer**

Mark Cinkevich (b. 1994 in Lahoysk, Belarus) **is an interdisciplinary researcher and artist based in Warsaw**

In their new video installation *Onset* (2023), Anna Engelhardt and Mark Cinkevich explore Russian colonialism through conventions from horror films. A demon roams through an ominous synthetic environment constructed from satellite images of the Russian air bases Khmeimim, in Syria, Baranovichi, in Belarus, and Belbek, in Ukraine. This parasitic force pervades the air bases, passing through their deserted corridors, interrogation rooms, and electricity substations. Devastation follows in its wake. In this single-channel video installation, Engelhardt and Cinkevich use a combination of medieval demonology, open-source intelligence, and CGI animation to uncover the hidden life of these military outposts. Over the course of the film, the horror of Russian colonialism becomes manifest in the process of possession – the imposition of external control that gradually destroys an organism from within.

● **Biographies** ENGELHARDT investigates topics from military cybernetics to cyber warfare across multiple media, including videos, software, and hardware interfaces. She also writes, lectures, and publishes to promote decolonial approaches to cyberspace and to situate digital conflicts within a broader colonial matrix. Her works and activities have been featured at Transmediale in Berlin, Venice Architecture Biennale, Ars Electronica, and the Kyiv Biennial and in *Digital War* and *Funambulist*.

CINKEVICH holds a master's degree in cultural studies from the University of Helsinki and is currently pursuing a PhD in anthropology at the University of Warsaw. He is interested in critical, speculative, and experimental aspects of art that operate at the intersection of fact and fiction. His work focuses on the post-Soviet infrastructural and social landscape, including nuclear and infrastructural colonialisms, extractivism, and monstrosity. Cinkevich has exhibited his work across Europe. With Engelhardt, he was a 2022 artist-in-residence at Transmediale in Berlin.

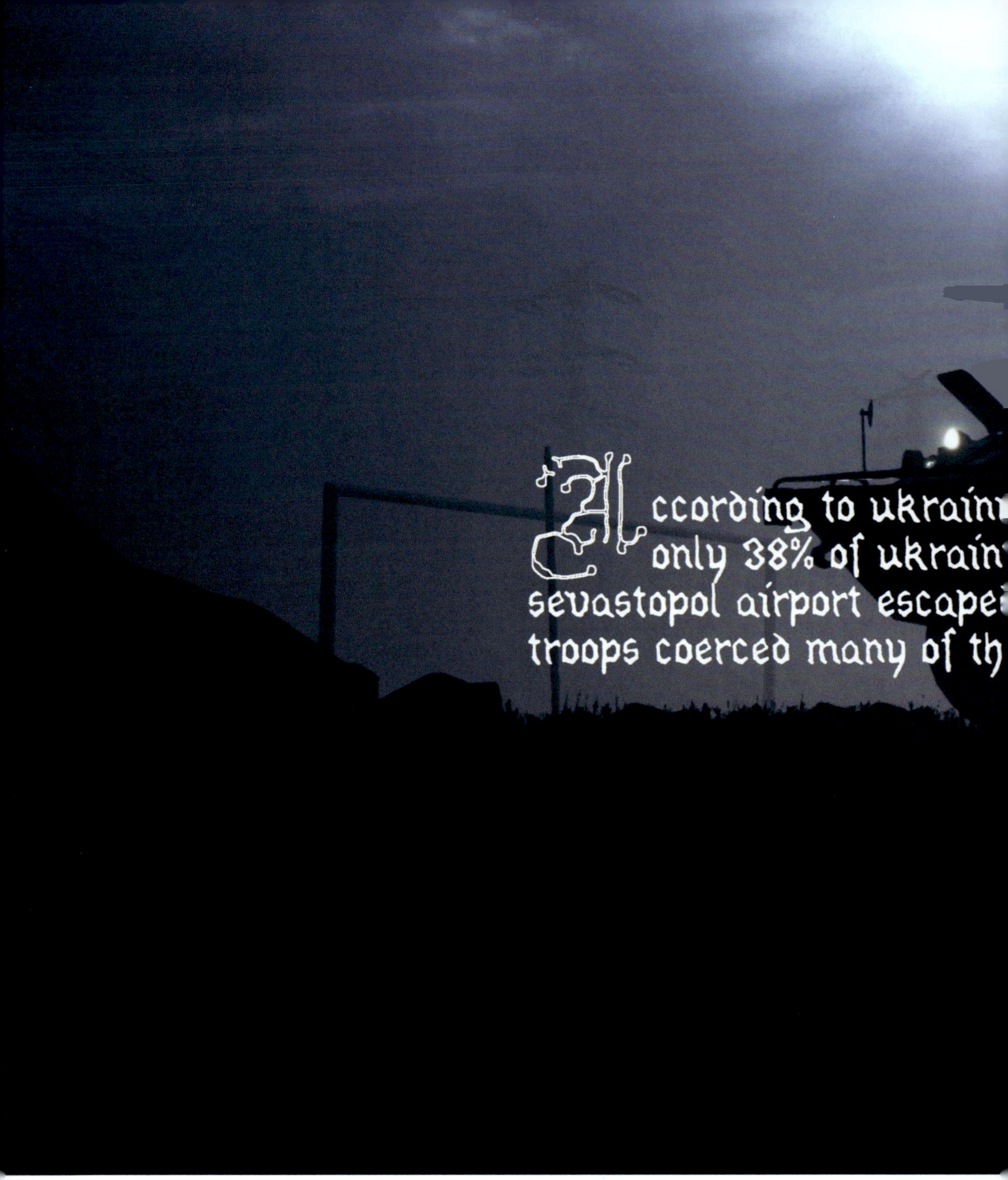

Still from *Onset*, 2023, single-channel video installation

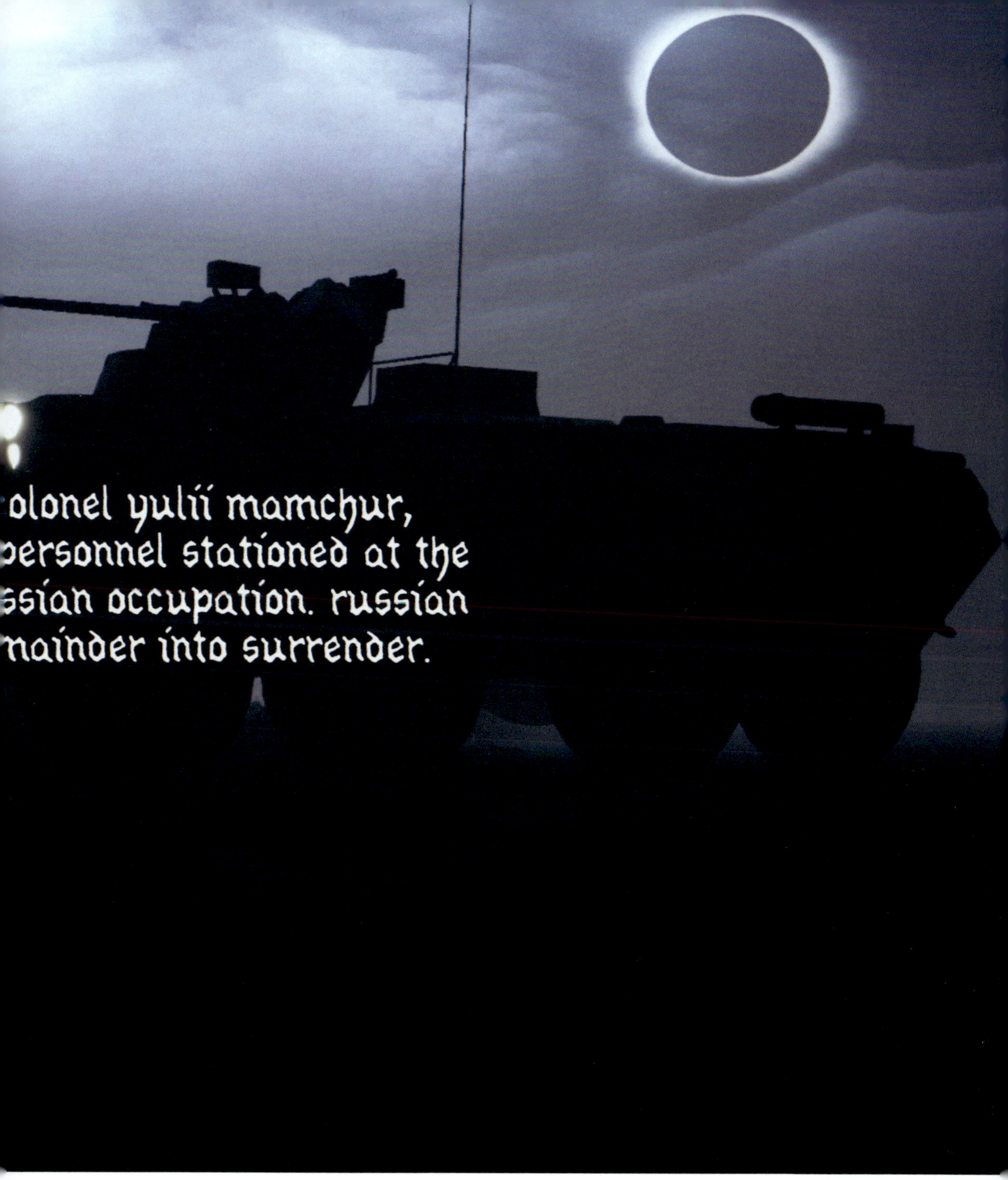

Anna Engelhardt & Mark Cinkevich

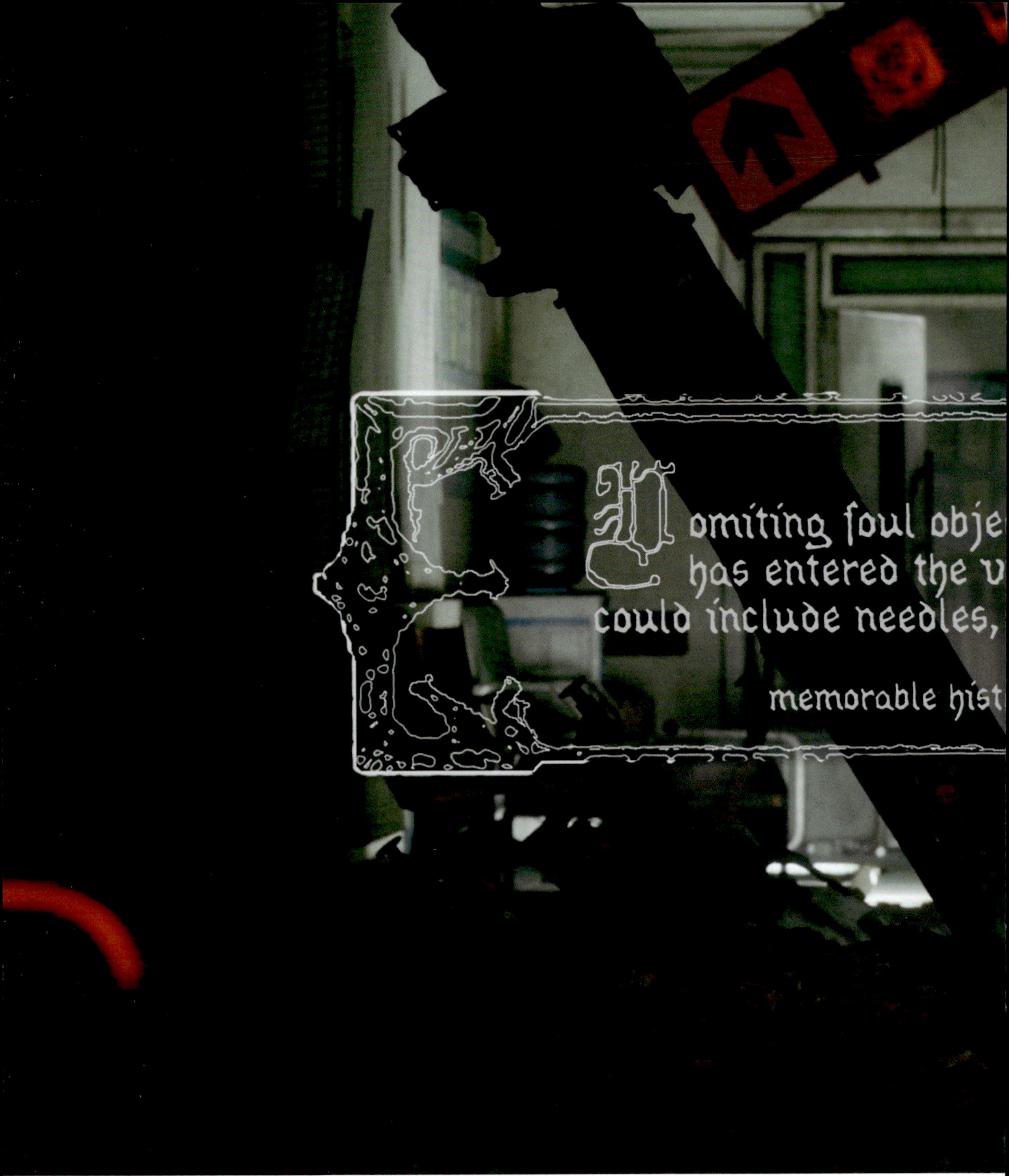

Still from *Onset*, 2023, single-channel video installation

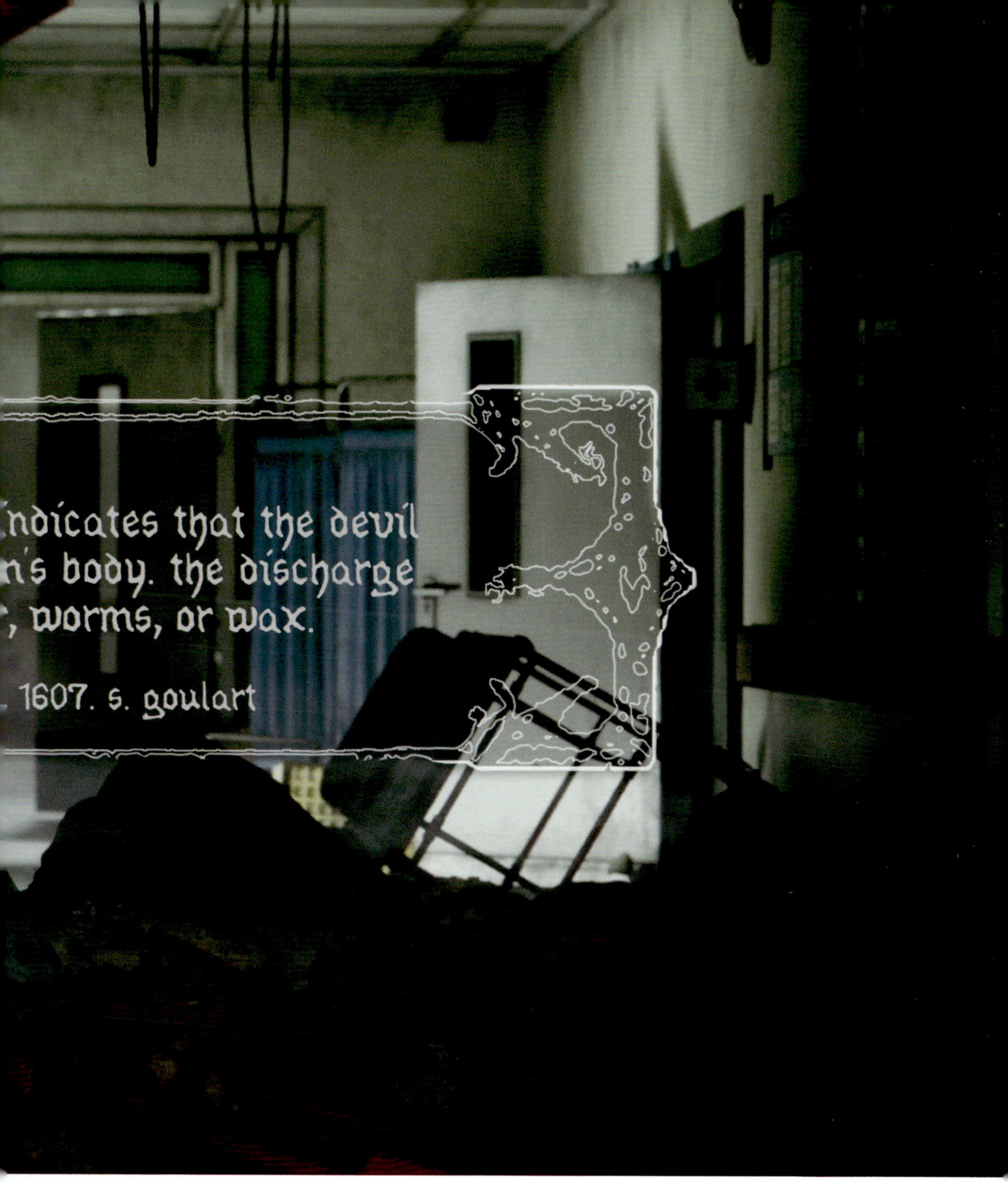

Anna Engelhardt & Mark Cinkevich

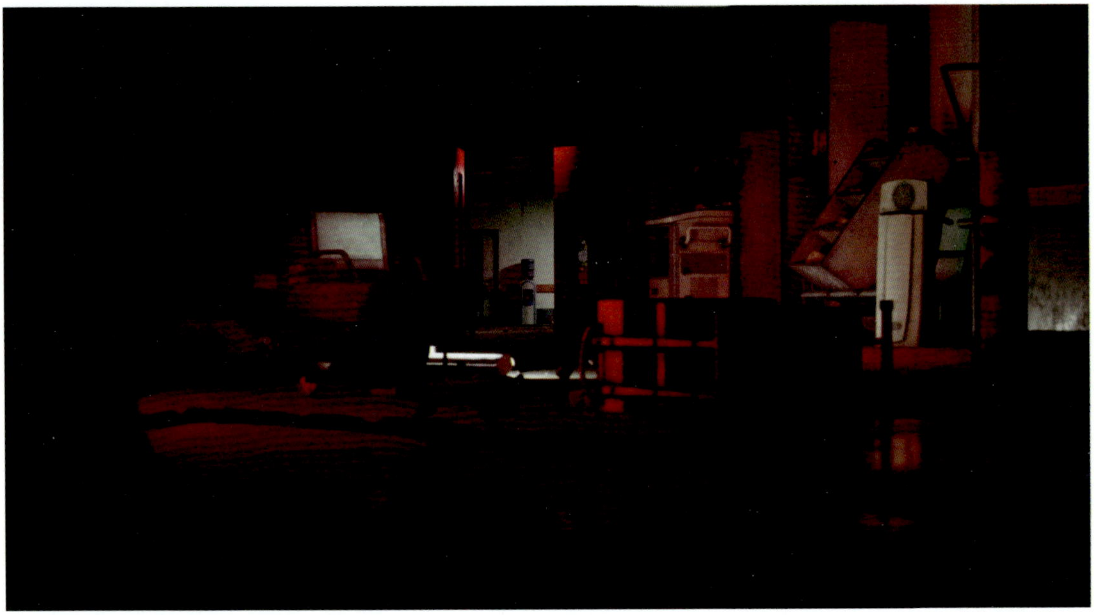

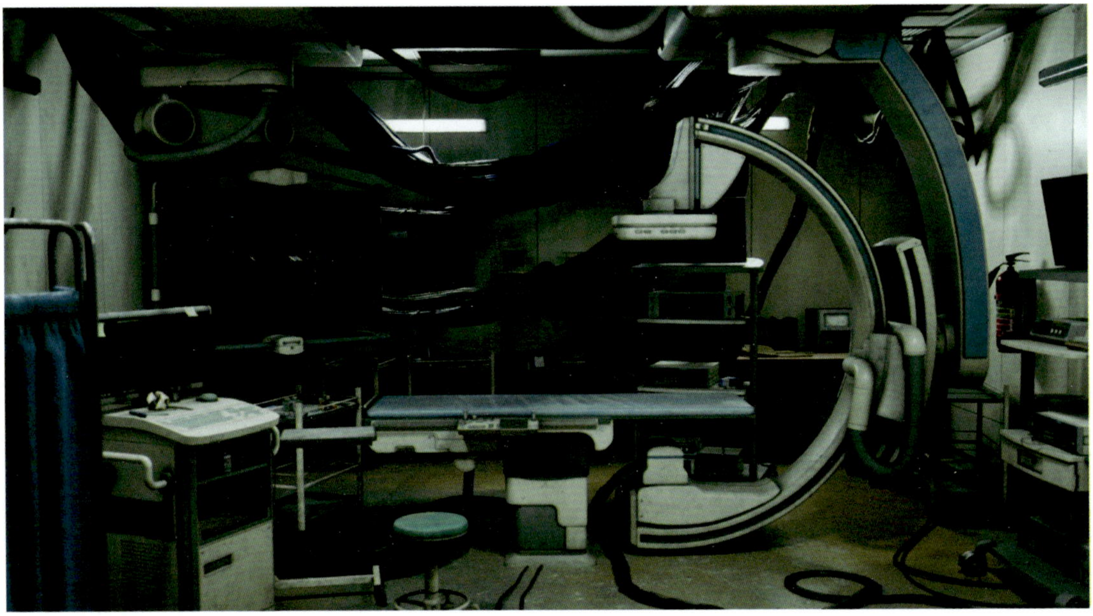

Stills from *Onset*, 2023, single-channel video installation

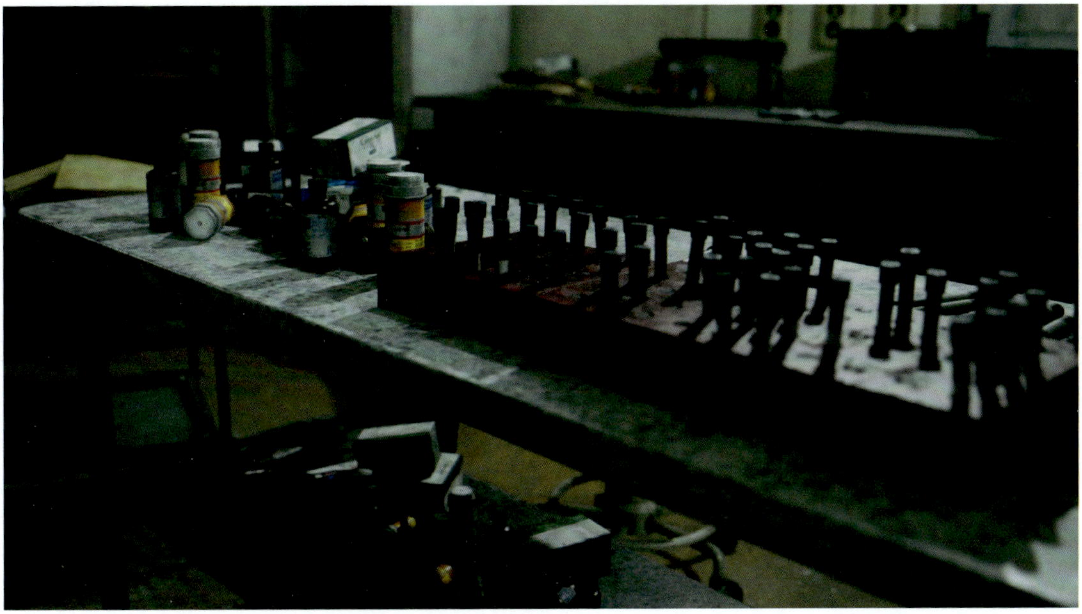

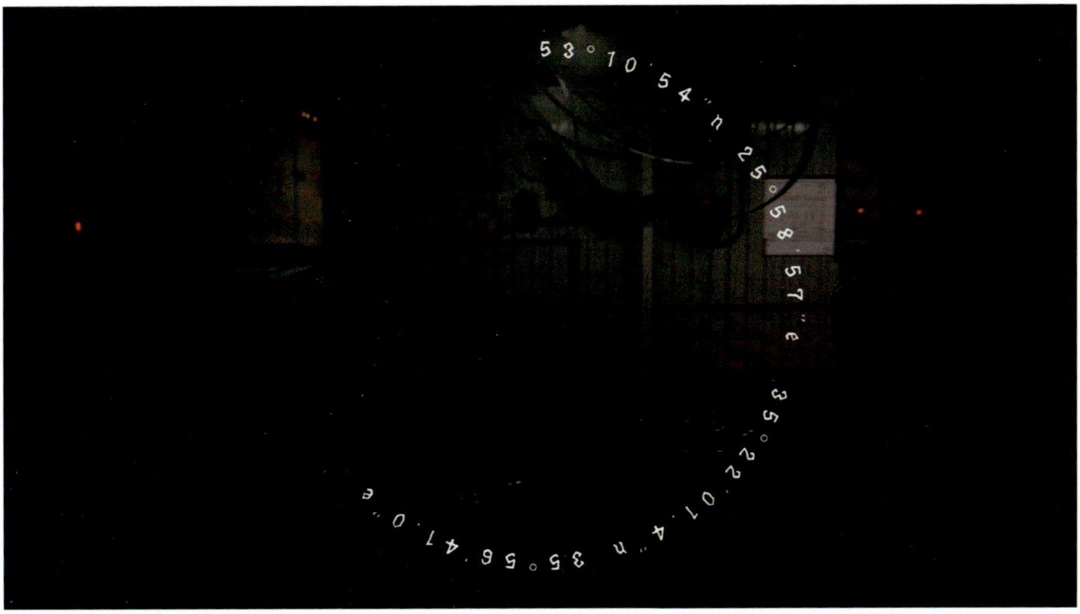

Anna Engelhardt & Mark Cinkevich

KÖKEN ERGUN & SASHA AZANOVA

Köken Ergun (b. 1976 in Istanbul) **is a Berlin-based artist working in film and installation**

Sasha Azanova (b. 1985 in Yekaterinburg, Russia) **is based in Bergen and works with photography, video, and text**

For *New Visions 2023*, Köken Ergun and Sasha Azanova present a newly commissioned collaborative work centered on the Polar Silk Road, its relation to Norway, and the melting of Arctic ice. The Polar Silk Road is a new maritime route conceived by China with Russian collaboration that passes through the Russian waters of the slowly melting Arctic and terminates at newly built ports on Norway's Arctic shores. This work continues Ergun's ongoing research into China's global expansion and features two maps and a video made in collaboration with ethnographers, historians, sociologists, artists, and infrastructural specialists. Ergun and Azanova lay out the Polar Silk Road on Chinese cartographer Hao Xiaoguang's vertical world maps that center the northern and southern hemispheres. Poetry, songs, and stock imagery in the video further contextualize Xiaoguang's novel cartography. The deliberate upending of perceptual norms underscores the geopolitical struggle over energy resources in the Arctic. Further, the work questions the roles of infrastructure and representation as agents of soft power, expansionism, and extractivism.

● **Biographies** ERGUN studied acting at Istanbul University, completed his postgraduate degree in ancient Greek literature at King's College London, and earned an MA in art history at the Bilgi University, Istanbul. After working with American theater director Robert Wilson, Ergun became involved with video and film. His video installations have been exhibited at Documenta 14; Palais de Tokyo, Paris; SALT, Istanbul; Stedelijk Museum Bureau Amsterdam; and Casino Luxembourg. Ergun's films have received the Tiger Award for Short Film at the 2007 Rotterdam Film Festival and the Special Mention Prize at the 2013 Berlinale.

AZANOVA holds a master's degree in fine arts from The Art Academy's department of contemporary art at the University of Bergen, Norway. She has previously exhibited at Bokboden, Rom8 (part of the Borealis festival of experimental music), Prøverommet, Bergen Kjøtt, and Bergen Kunsthall, all in Bergen, and at CLB, Berlin.

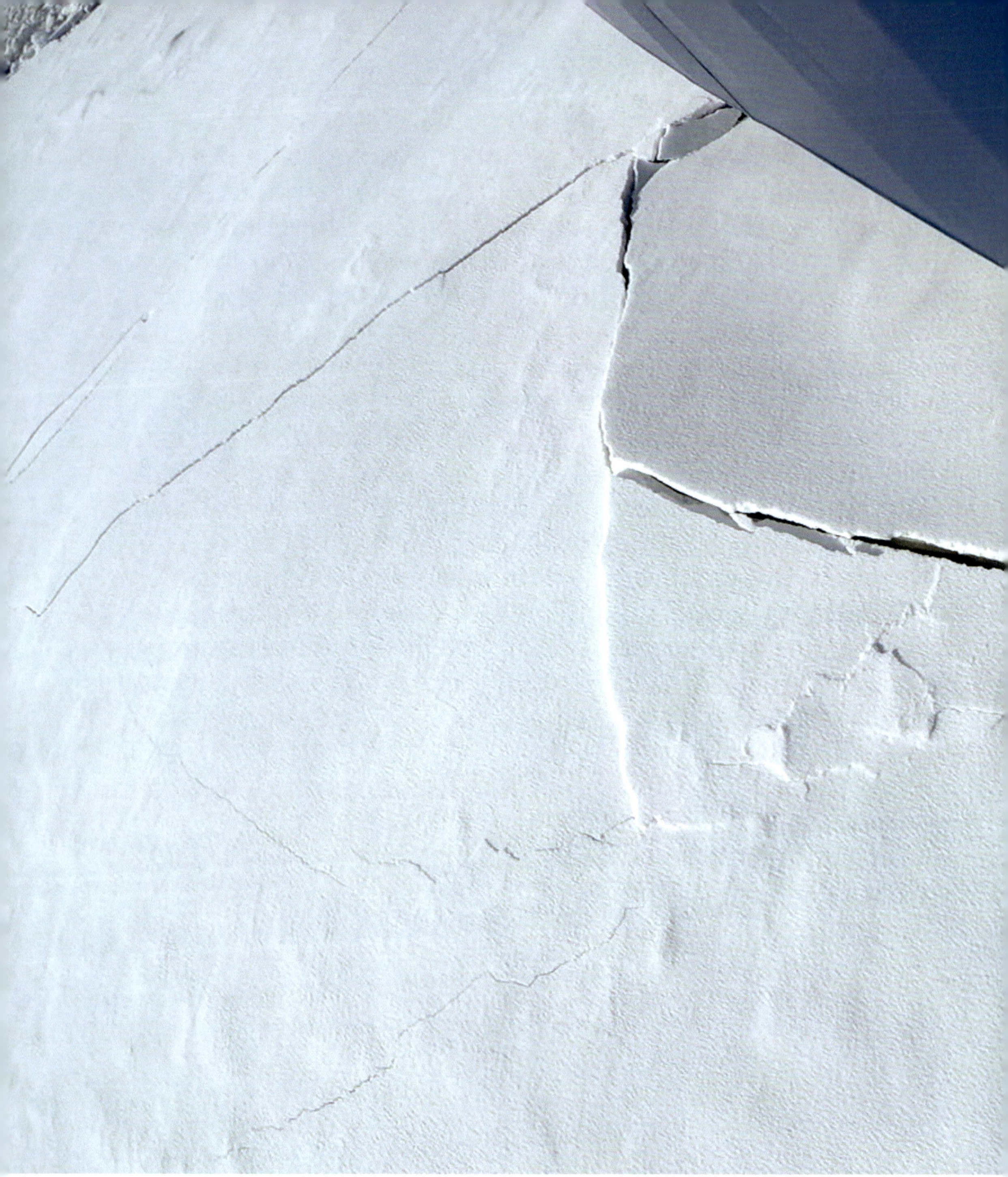

Still from *Polar Silk Road*, 2023, single-channel color video with sound
Image is used with permission of Aker Arctic

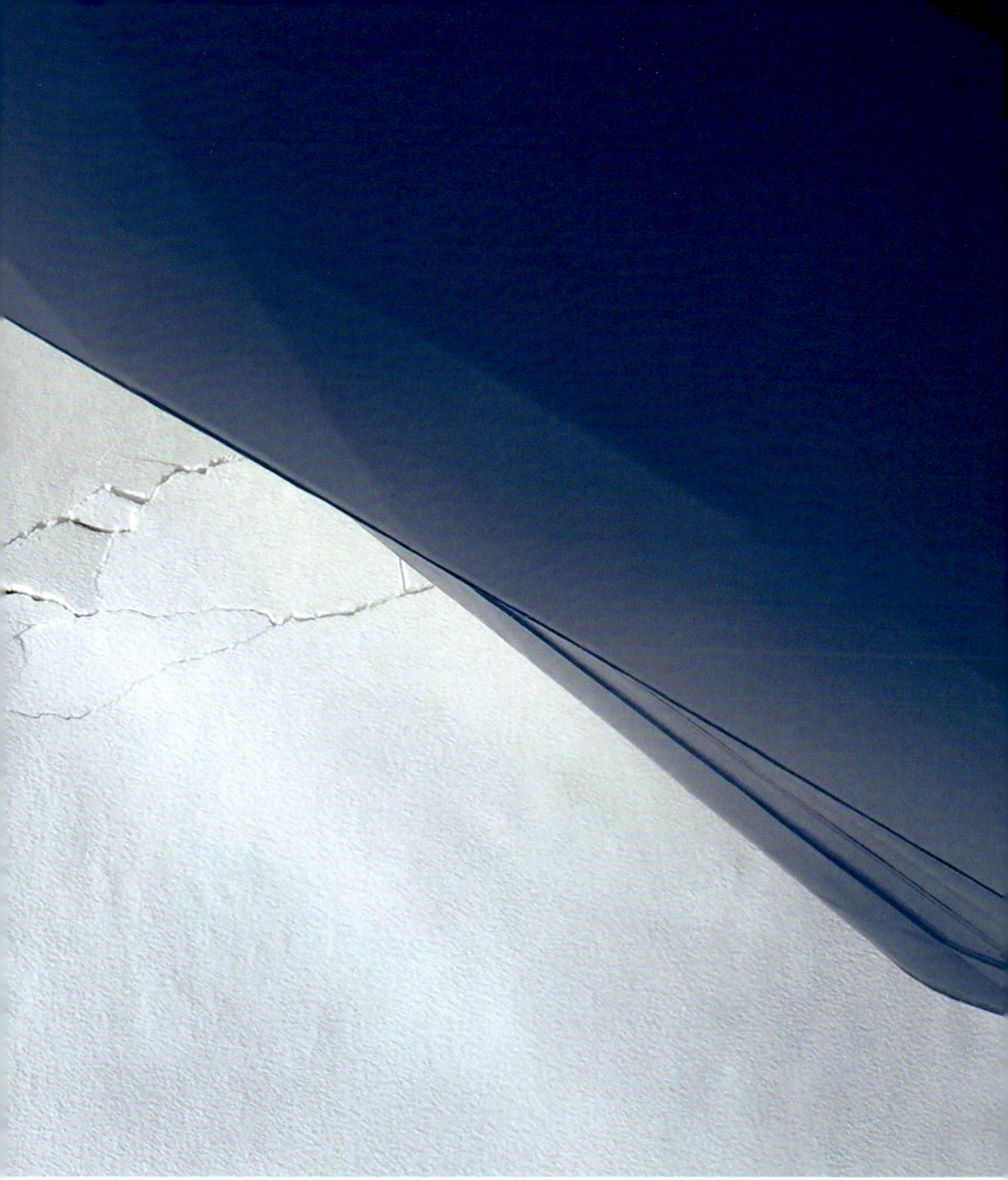

Köken Ergun & Sasha Azanova

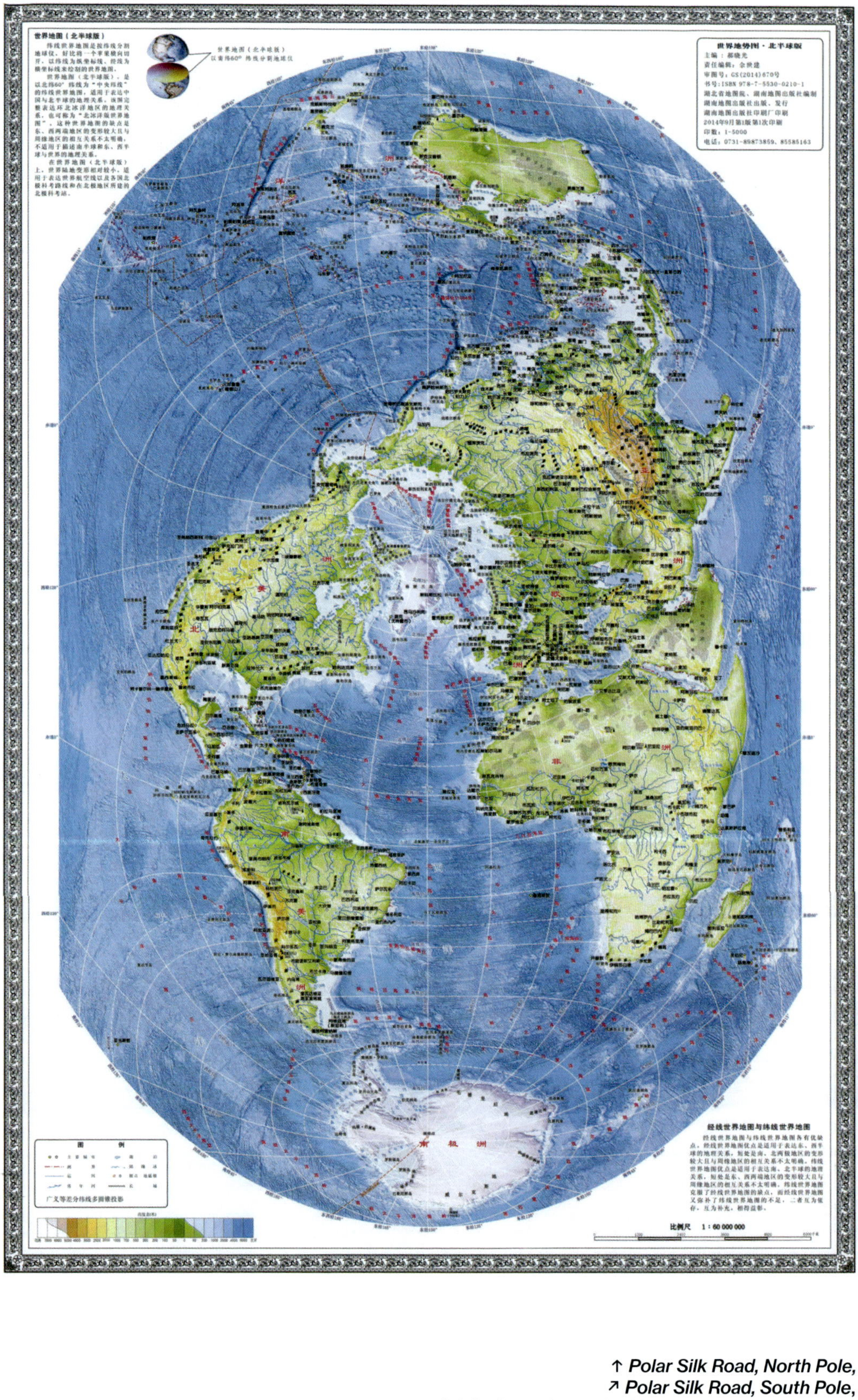

世界地势图

北半球版

↑ *Polar Silk Road, North Pole, 2023*

↗ *Polar Silk Road, South Pole*, 2023

Original map is used with permission of Hao Xiaoguang

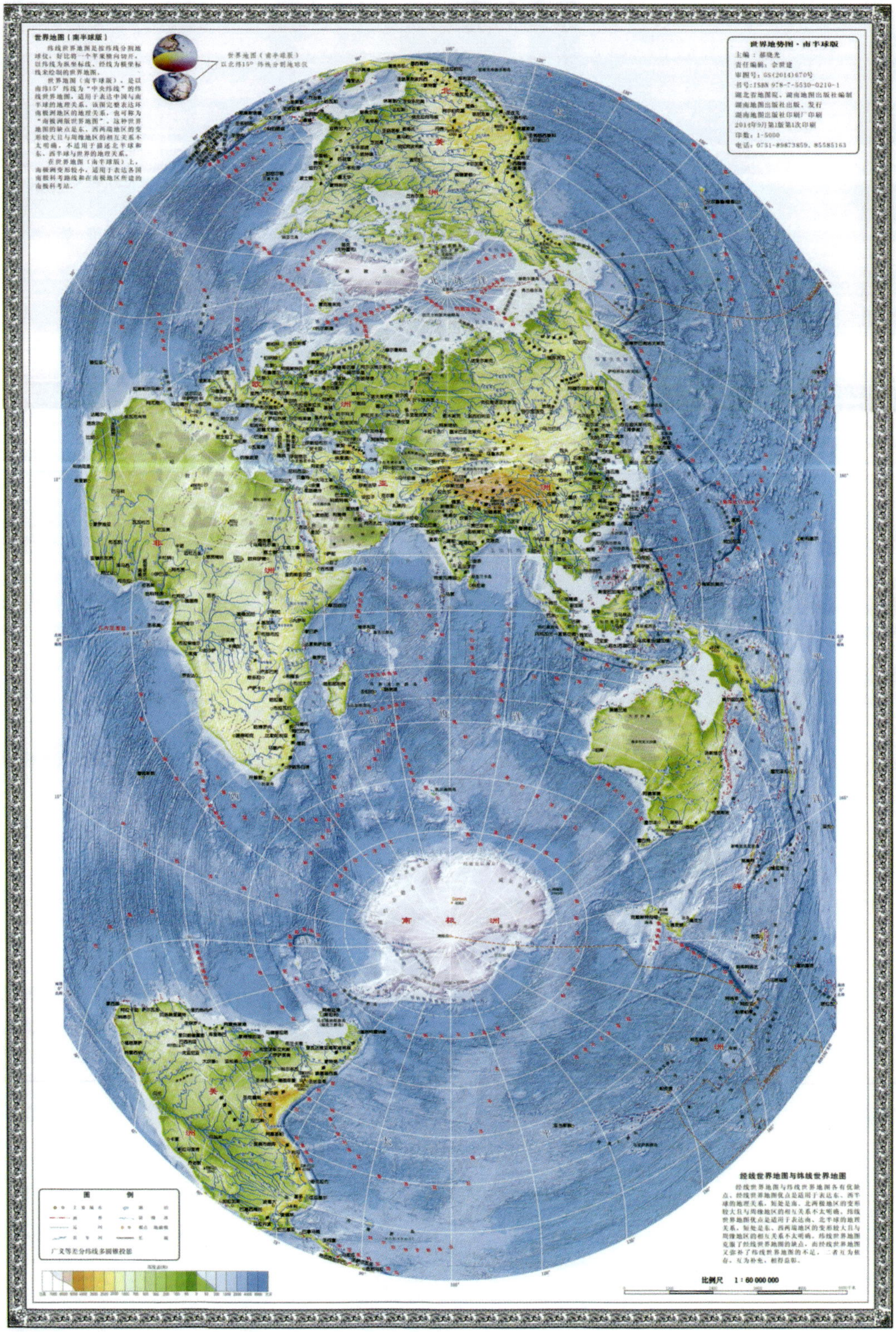

世界地势图

南半球版

Köken Ergun & Sasha Azanova

DILYARA KAIPOVA

Dilyara Kaipova (b. 1967 in Tashkent, Uzbekistan) **is an artist based in Tashkent who works with textiles**

Dilyara Kaipova mixes traditional Uzbek silk and cotton textiles and motifs with characters and symbols from modern Western pop culture to comment on the processes of globalization and question the possibility of preserving traditions. In her new series, she prints photographs of symbols for cotton flowers found in public spaces across Uzbekistan onto cotton garments produced in the country.

Cotton – also known as "white gold" – was grown in the region long before the Russian and Soviet occupation and was crucial to the development of Uzbekistan's economy. During the 1960s, when the Soviet administration launched a major water-diversion project on the arid plains of Kazakhstan, Uzbekistan, and Turkmenistan, cotton production was dramatically altered, leading to forced-labor systems and environmental destruction. The Soviet era also saw a proliferation of cotton symbols in public spaces and on everyday objects; the stylized flower of cotton was applied everywhere, from tableware and clothing to physical infrastructure.

For *Curse of Cotton* (2022), Kaipova traveled across the country taking photos of those cotton flowers. Working with the shape of the *chapan*, a traditional cotton robe, she inscribes a critical tension onto it through adding these images, asking: Can we look at the material without seeing the violence of its making?

● **Biography** KAIPOVA has recently presented solo exhibitions at the State Silk Museum in Tbilisi, Georgia and the Asanbay Center in Bishkek, Kyrgyzstan. She has participated in the Astana Art Show, *Black Animals* at the National Gallery of Uzbekistan, Tashkent, and *Women in Art* in Dubai. Kaipova's works are in the collections of the State Silk Museum in Tbilisi, the National Gallery of Uzbekistan, Tashkent, the MARKK Museum, Hamburg, the Stedelijk Museum, Amsterdam, the Royal Ontario Museum, Toronto, and the Victoria & Albert Museum, London, among other institutions.

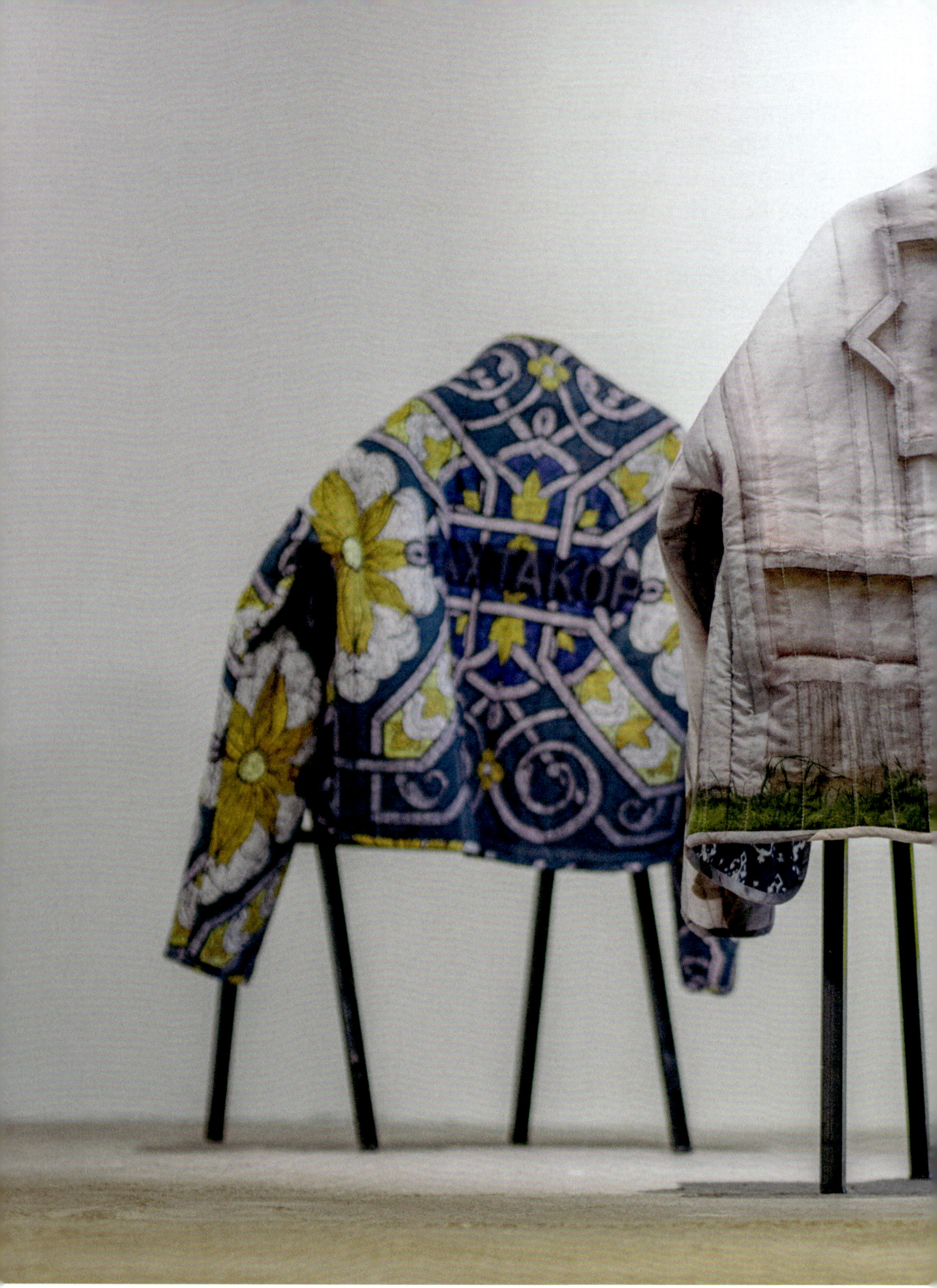

Curse of Cotton, 2022, photographic print on cotton

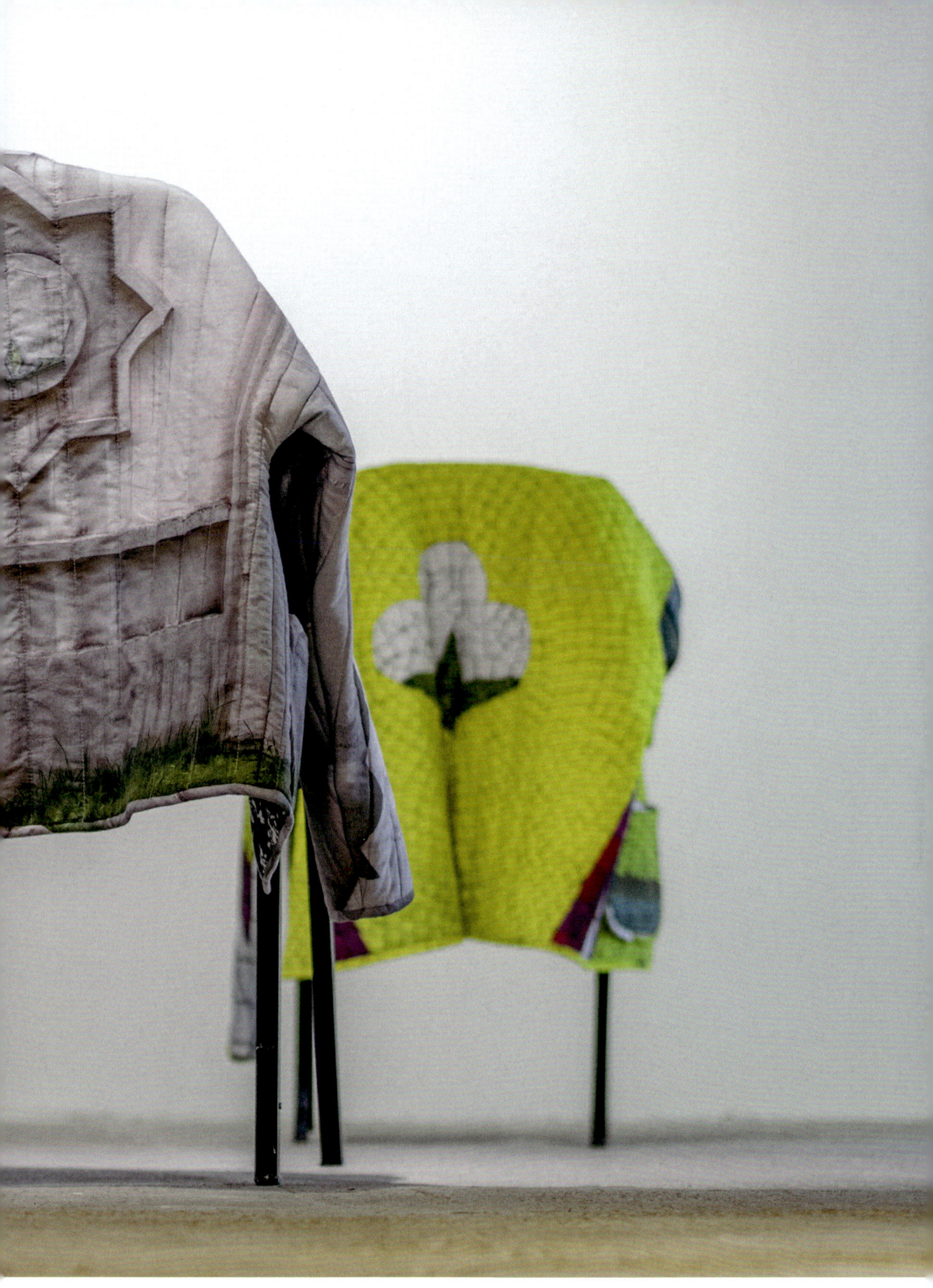

Dilyara Kaipova

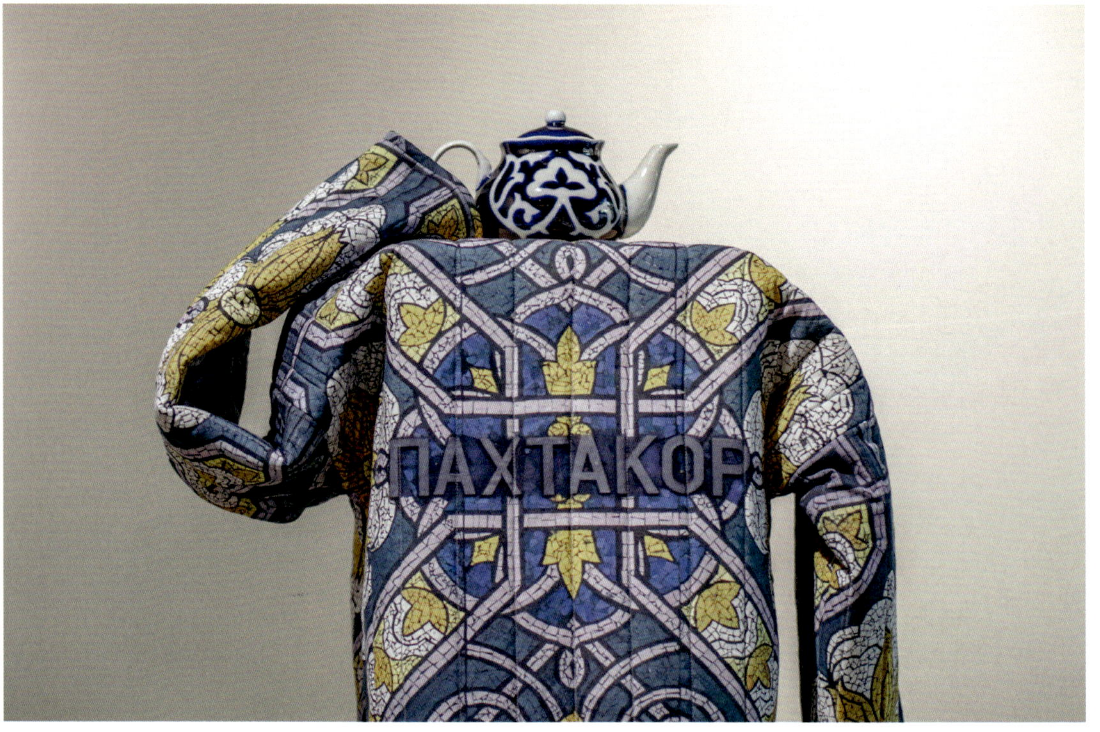

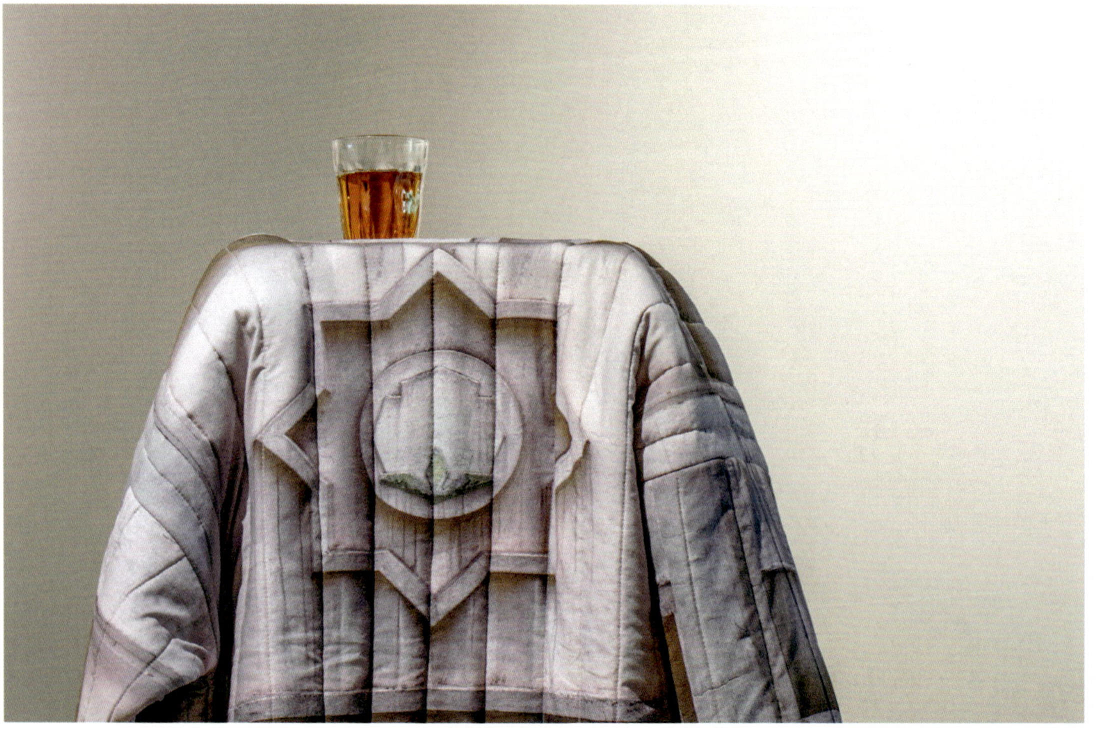

Curse of Cotton, 2022, photographic print on cotton

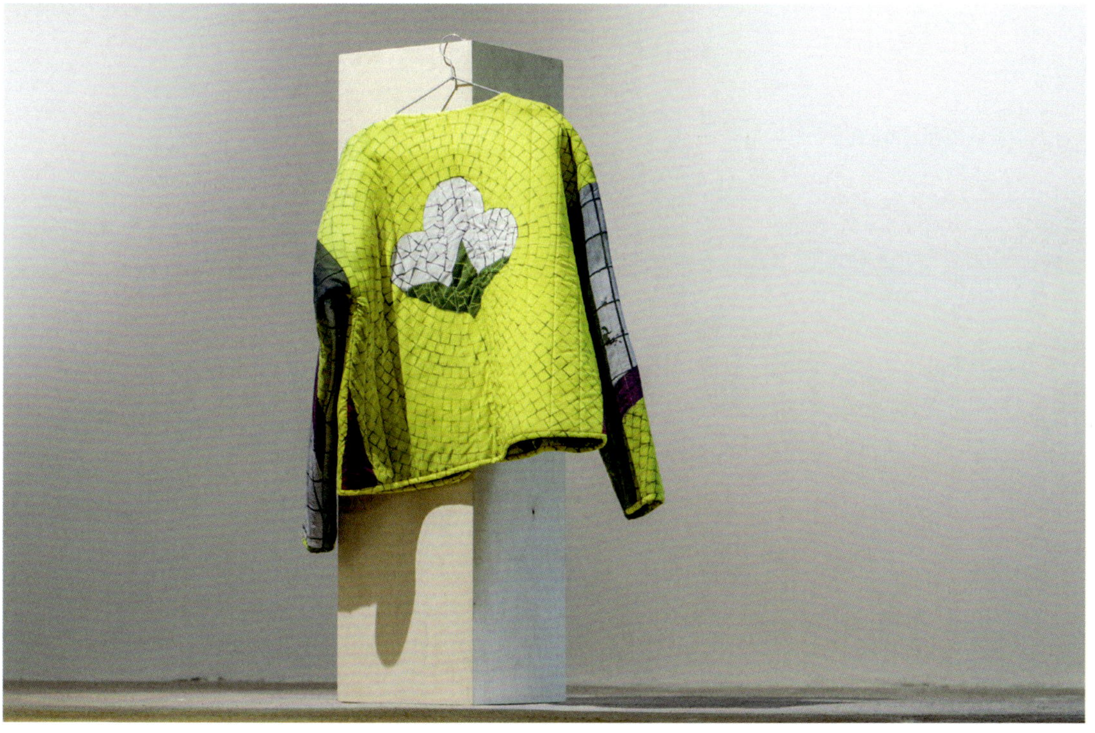

Dilyara Kaipova

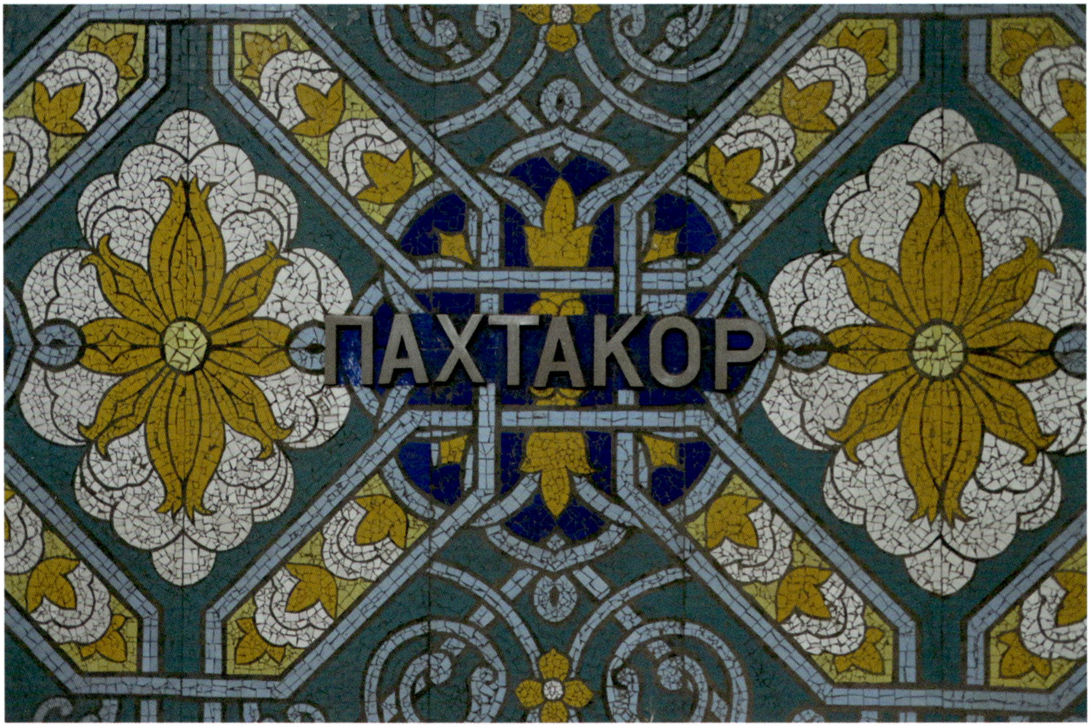

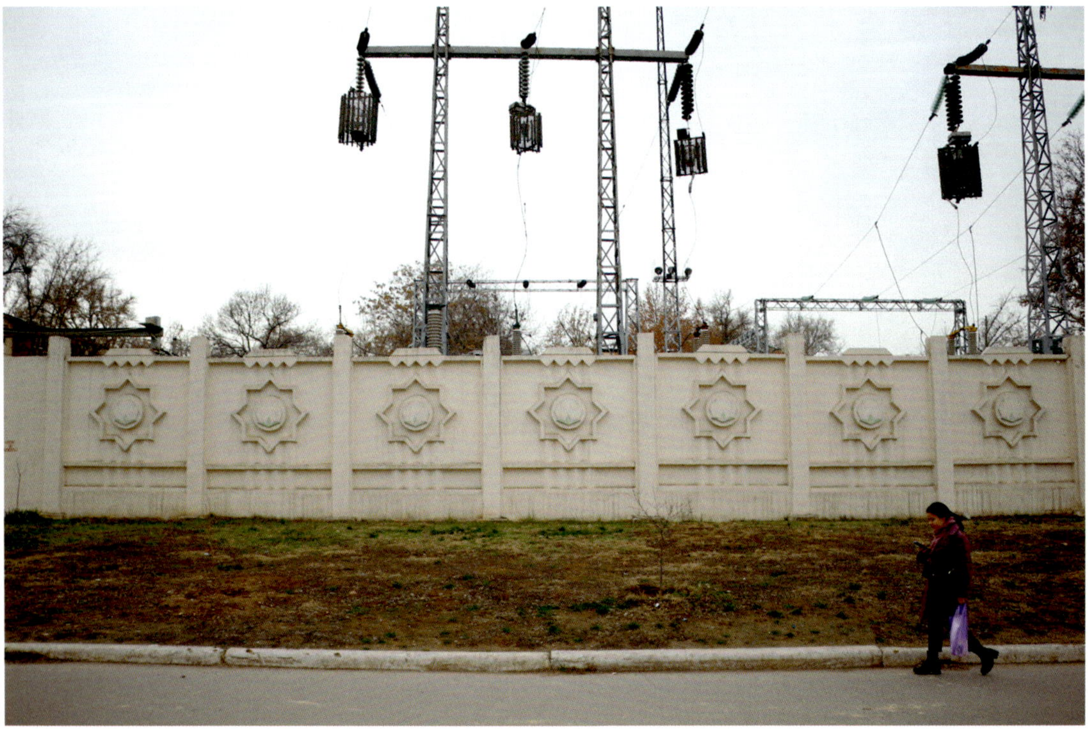

Symbols for cotton flowers in public spaces
Images: Juriy Vedenin

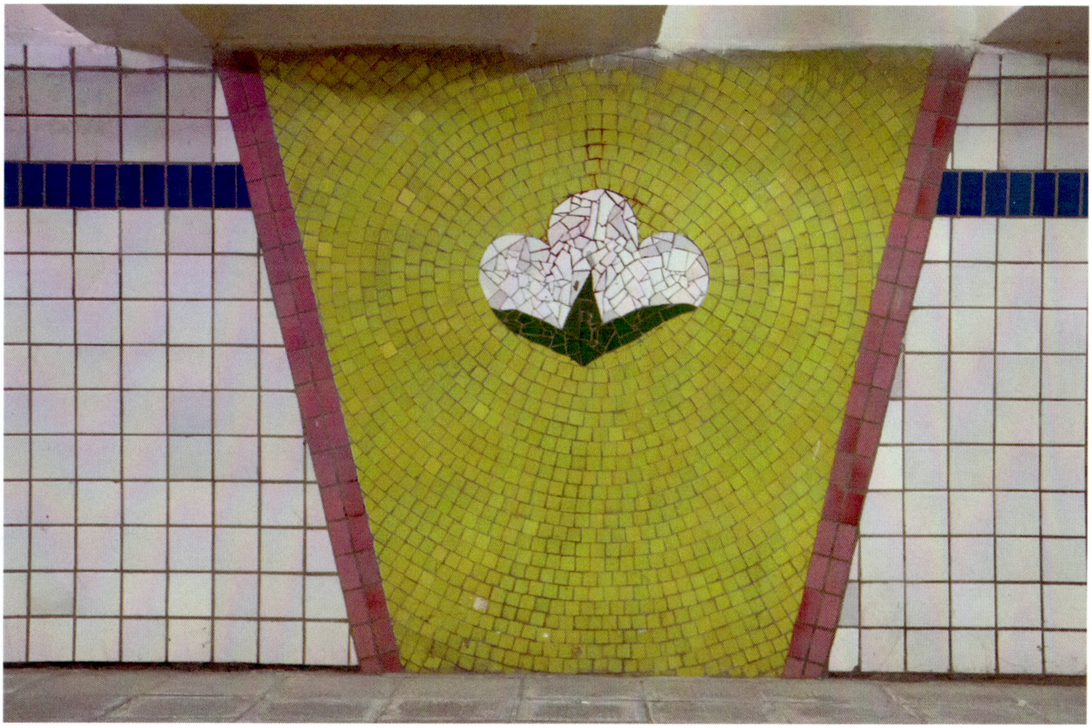

Dilyara Kaipova

SEIF KOUSMATE

Seif Kousmate (b. 1988 in Essaouira, Morocco) **is a self-taught photographer based in Morocco**

For the project *Waha* (2020–; "oasis" in Arabic), Seif Kousmate has photographed deserted and deteriorating oases in his native Morocco. Once agricultural centers, trade hubs, sites of architectural and cultural heritage, and biosphere reserves, oases suffer from overexploitation of their raw materials and are devastated by cycles of drought. Their surface area is decreasing; according to official figures, Morocco has lost two-thirds of its palm trees over the last decade and an equivalent percentage of the country's oasis habitats has vanished.

For *Waha*, Kousmate has expanded his documentary practice to include experiments with distortions and the degradation of prints. He has described his need for a different photographic vocabulary to capture the situation and to avoid reproducing Orientalist, "Edenic" representations of the oases. The images depict towering palm trees, dried-out irrigation ditches, and close-ups of henna-adorned hands, among other subjects. By staining his images with acid and fire and corrupting them using remnants of local flora, Kousmate materially and conceptually conveys the degradation of these once-fertile areas.

● **Biography** KOUSMATE specializes in social issues and is the co-founder of KOZ collective. After working in the civil engineering sector, he dedicated himself to photography in 2016. A National Geographic Explorer since 2018, he was selected as a 6×6 Global Talent Program candidate by World Press Photo in 2020 and is a Magnum Foundation, Prince Claus, and Arab Documentary Photography Program grantee. In 2022, his work was presented in the Foam *Talent* exhibition at Fotografiemuseum, Amsterdam and in the Louis Roederer Discovery Award exhibition at Les Rencontres de la photographie d'Arles. His work has been published in international magazines and newspapers such as the *New York Times*, *Newsweek*, *The Guardian*, and *El Pais*, among others.

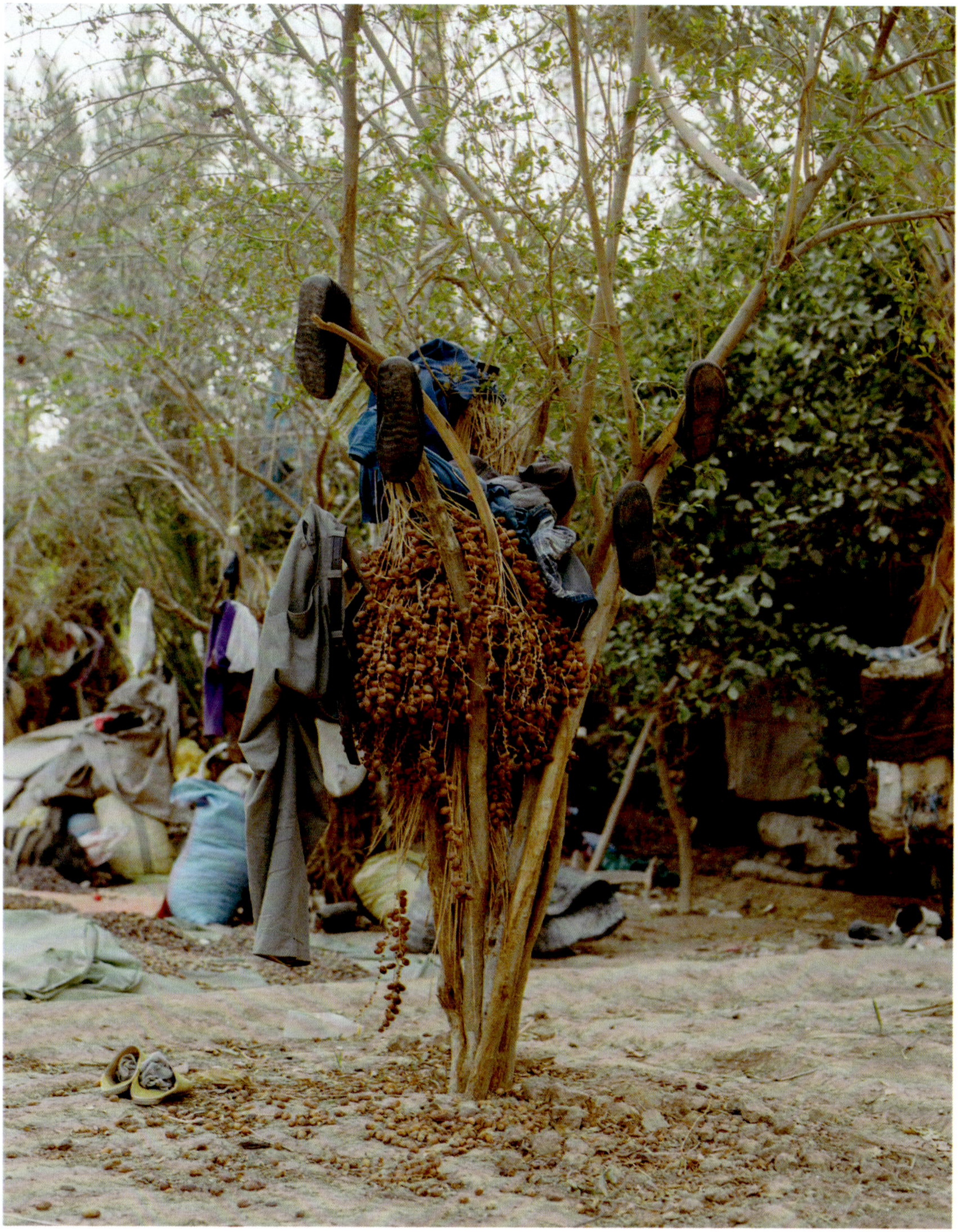

↑ *Waha*, 2020–, giclée print
↗ *Waha*, 2020–, acid on giclée print

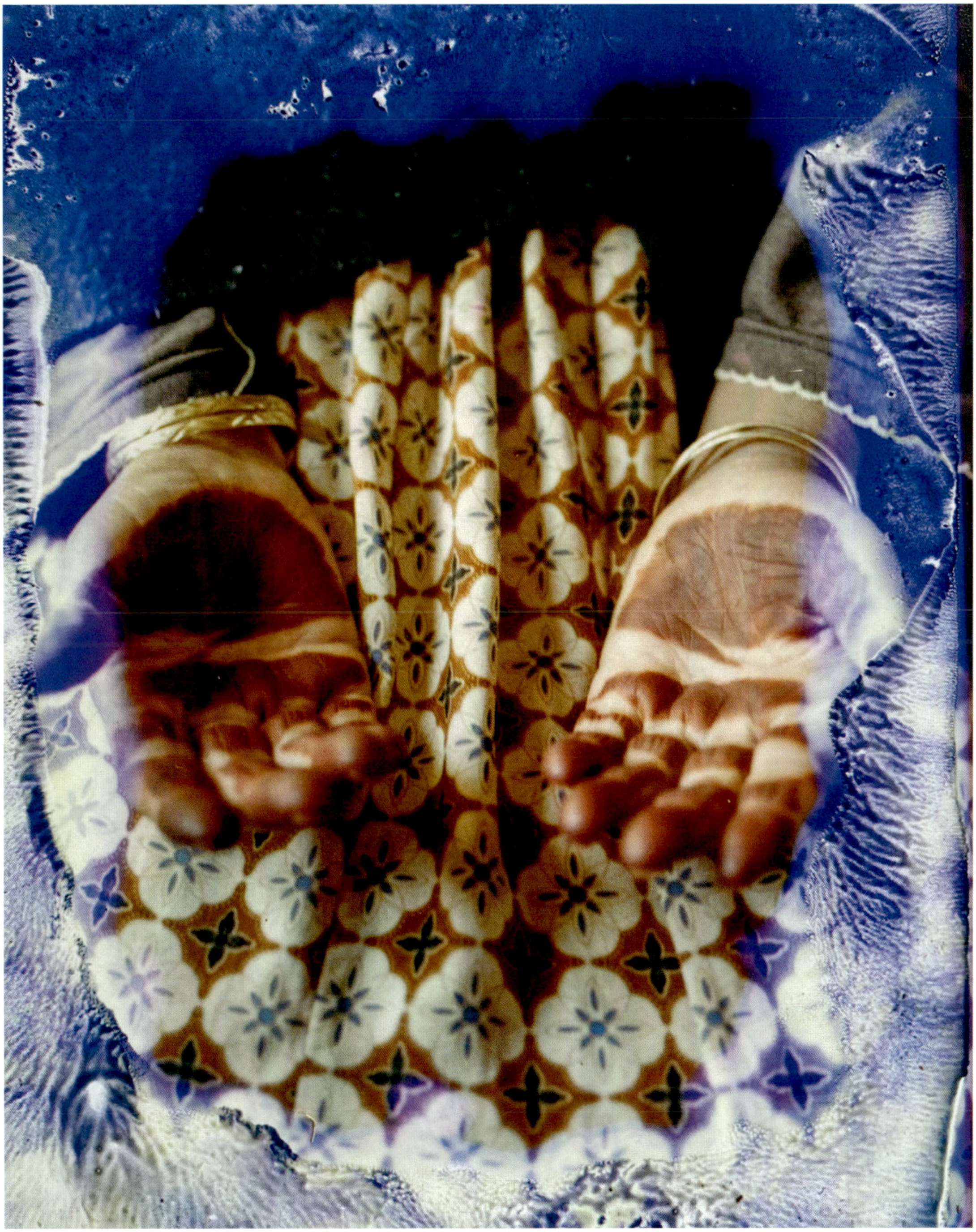

Seif Kousmate

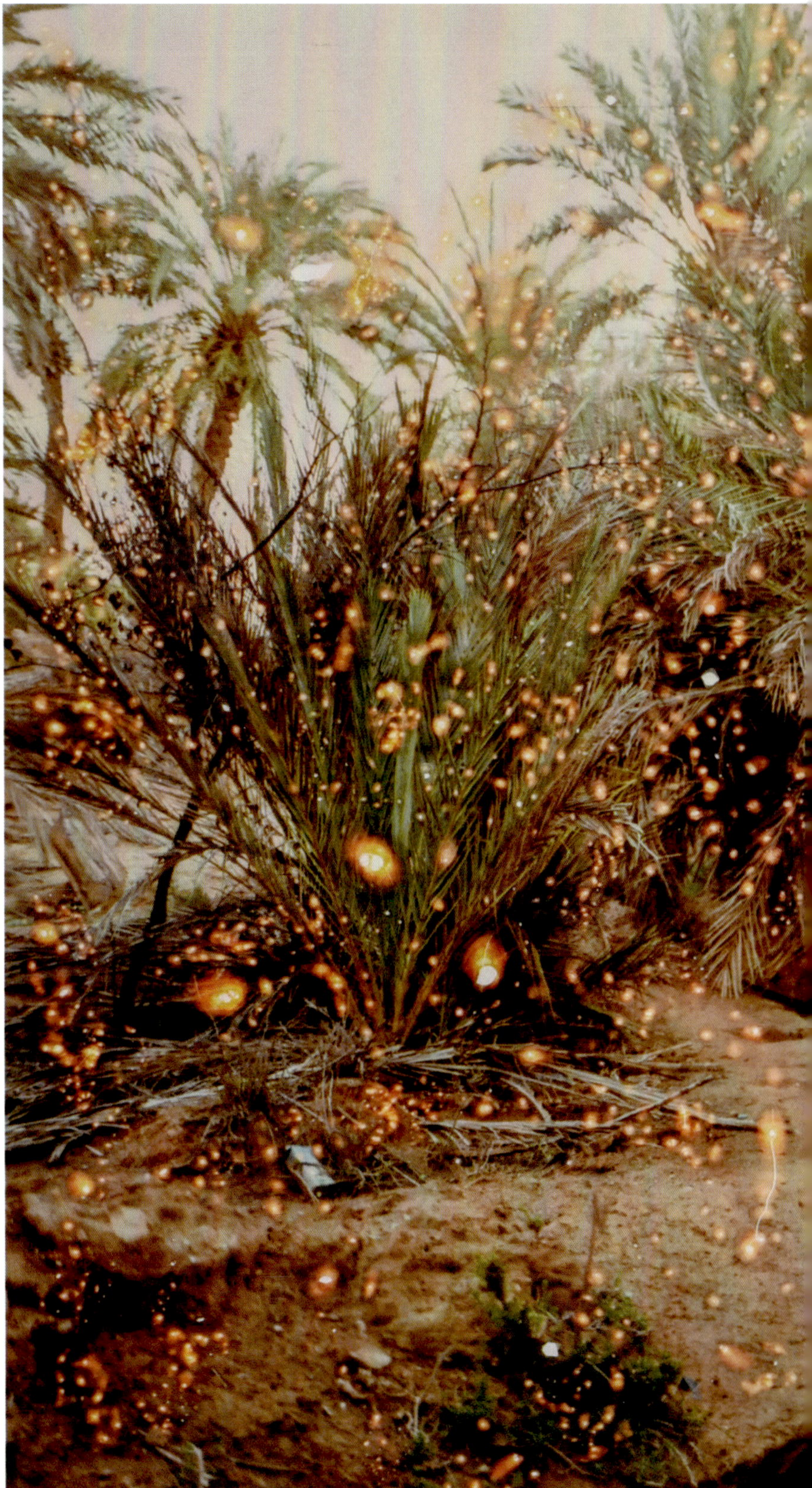

From the series *Waha*, 2020–, fire on giclée print

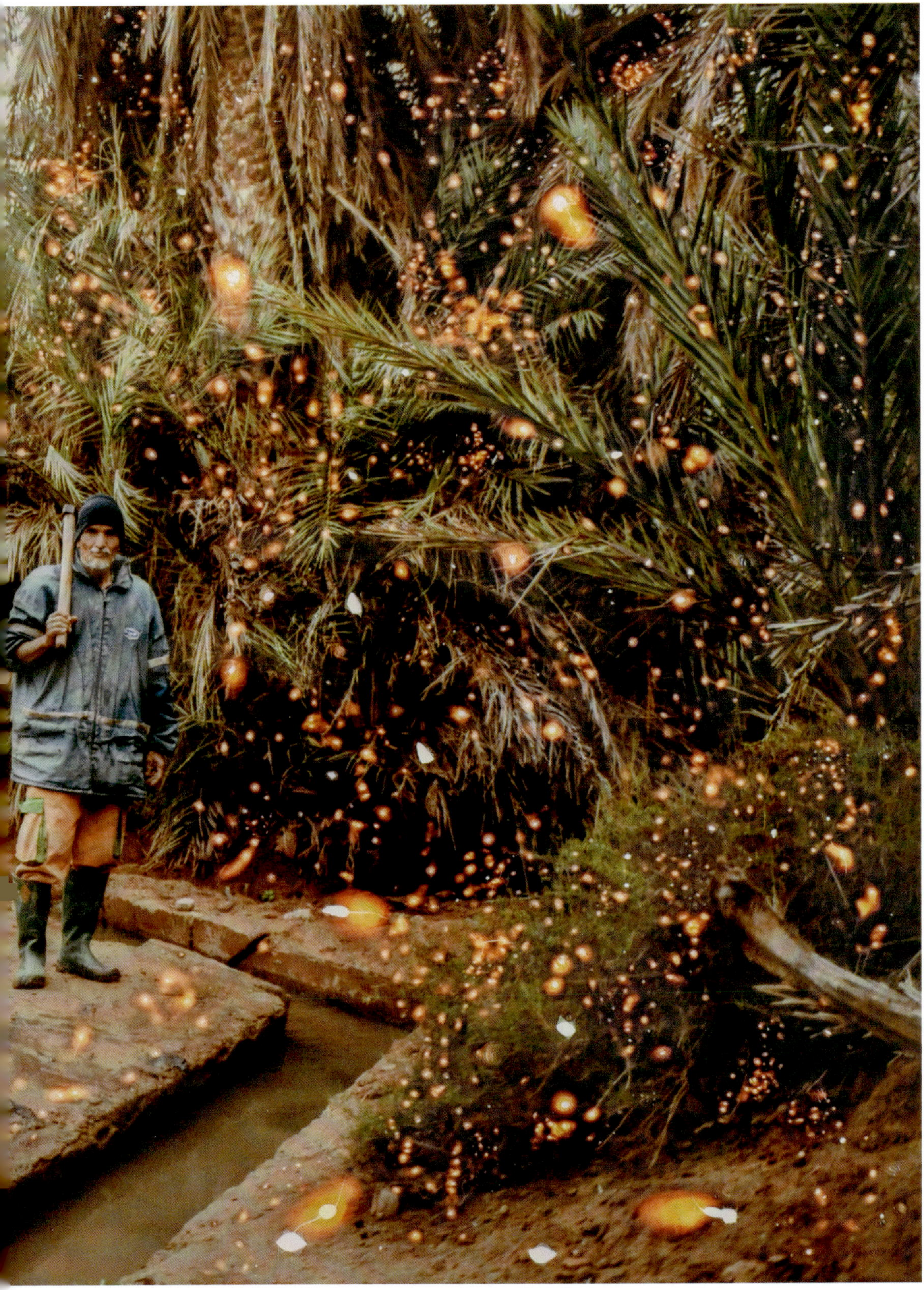

Seif Kousmate

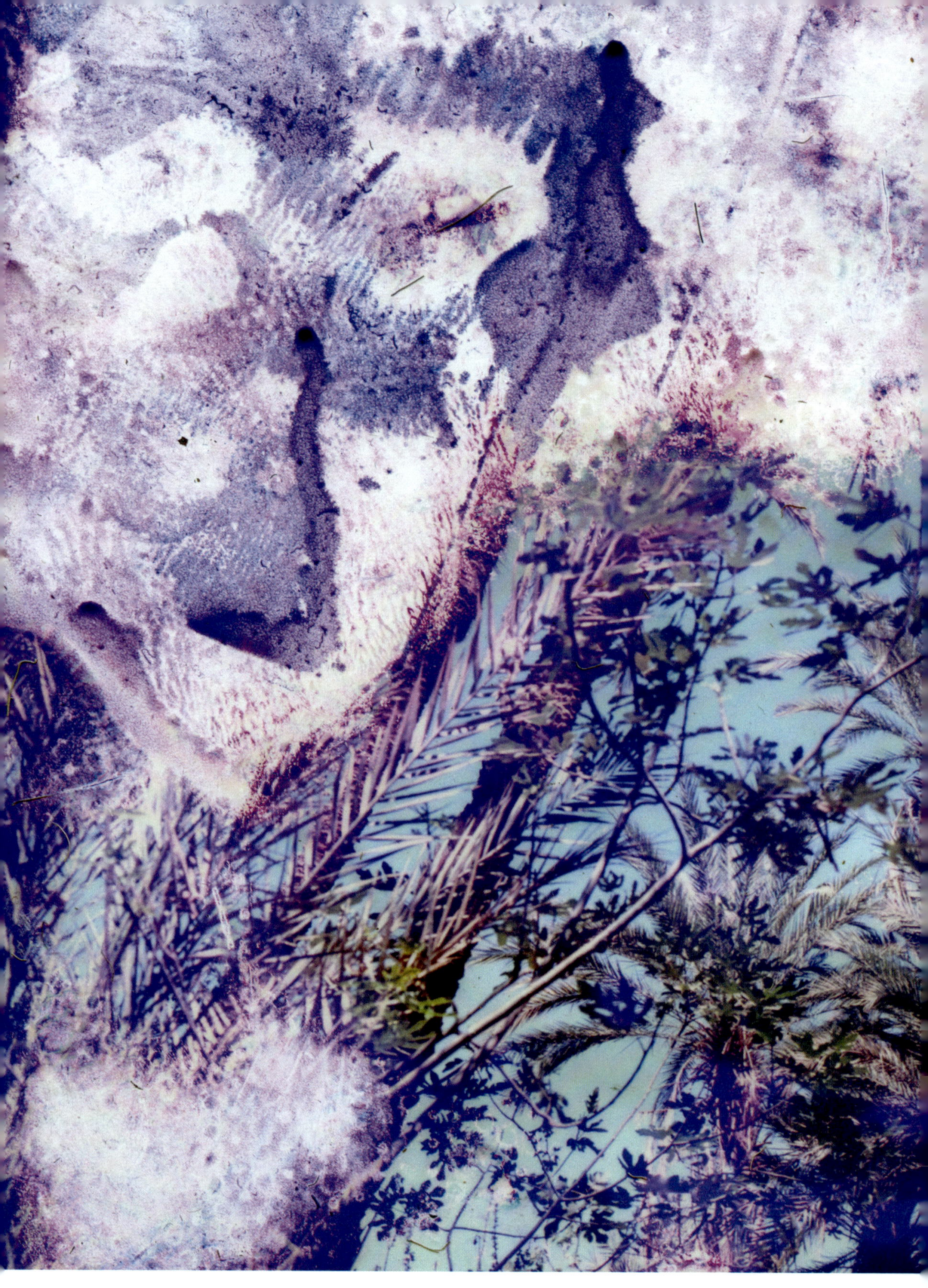

From the series *Waha*, 2020–, acid on giclée print

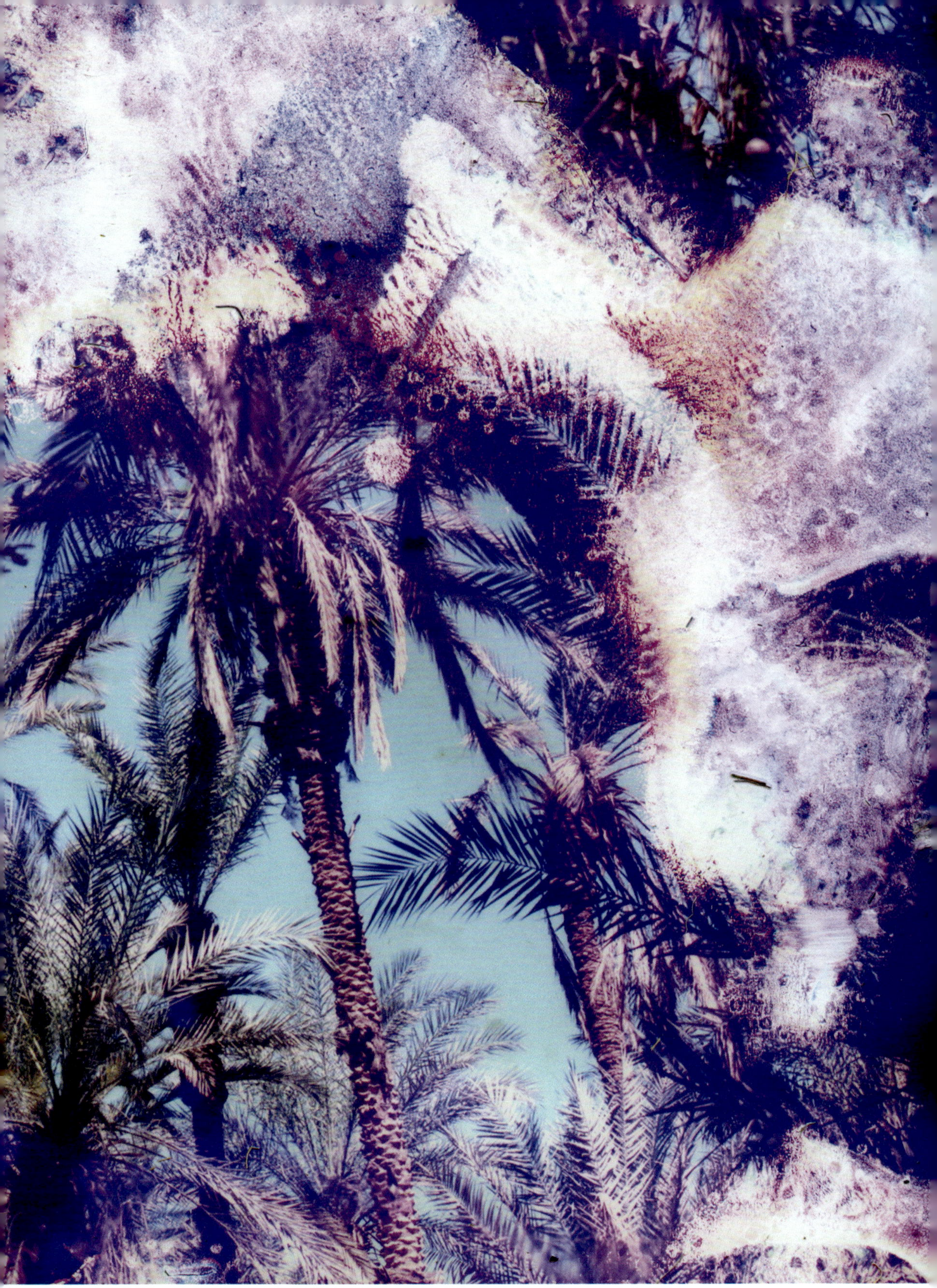

Seif Kousmate

BASIM MAGDY

Basel-based artist Basim Magdy (b. 1977 in Assiut, Egypt) **works across film, photography, installation, and painting**

Blending imaginative fiction and historical facts, Basim Magdy uses experimental photographic techniques to evoke a condition of crisis that is both dystopian and humorous. The artist chemically alters his photographic images by curing films with household solutions and exposing them to light leaks, producing color and material effects that add a layer of absurdity to their motifs. Many of his works jumble the deep time of geology with the historical past, the present, and future to imply our urgent need to recalibrate systems that are out of balance.

In the ongoing series *Someone Tried to Lock Up Time* (2018–), Magdy combines found photographs of recognized or obscure historical objects with poetic text fragments. *New Visions 2023* includes two new works made specifically for the exhibition. These clusters of images and texts are hung on walls painted in pinks and yellows, which call to mind sunrises and sunsets and hint at the passage of time. The resulting installation alludes to the human need to leave a mark on earth and to eternalize the present, and eerily displaces people from their regular environments. With the proliferation of digital social-media technologies, the work also ambiguously references the ways in which history is being recorded, stored, and written today, and the role that photography plays in constructing perceived truths about our world. Interested in time and processes of selective historicization, Magdy asks: what will be made of us when we are looked at from the future? What artefacts will remain to tell our stories?

● **Biography** MAGDY holds a BFA in painting from the Faculty of Fine Arts, Helwan University, Cairo. His work has recently appeared in solo exhibitions at Frac Bretagne, Rennes, France; KM21 Museum for Contemporary Art, The Hague; Fundació Antoni Tàpies, Barcelona; Museum of Contemporary Art (M HKA), Antwerp; Museum of Contemporary Art Chicago; MAXXI National Museum of the 21st Century Arts, Rome; and Jeu de Paume, Paris. In 2014, he won the Abraaj Art Prize and in 2016 he was selected as Deutsche Bank's Artist of the Year.

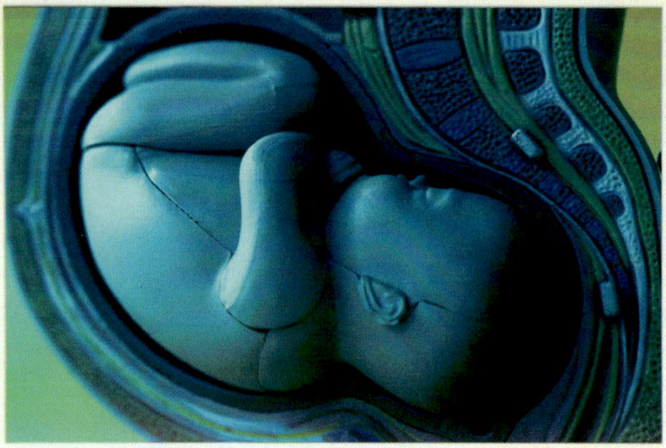

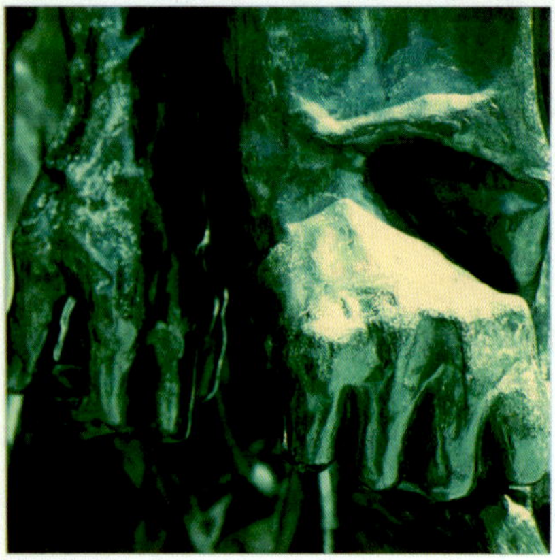

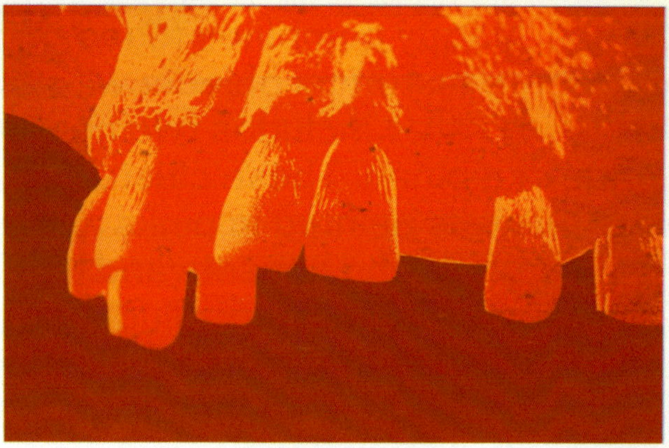

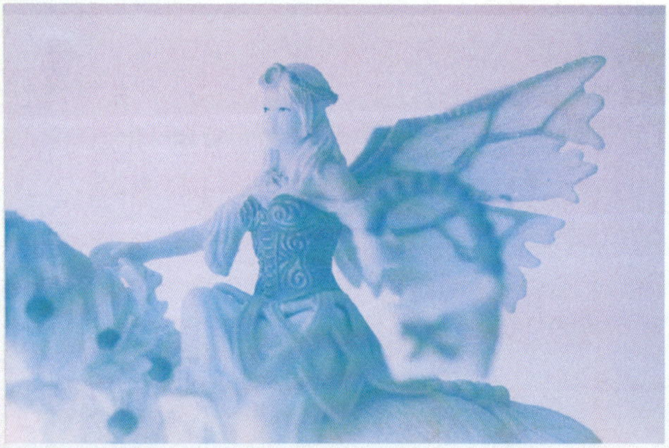

SEVEN DECADES OF PEACE, A TIME WHEN VILLAGES, CITY STATES AND MASSIVE EMPIRES BELIEVED CLOUDS WERE DREAMS, MEANT TO CHANGE SHAPE AND EVAPORATE INTO PURE LIGHT.

↑ *Someone Tried to Lock Up Time, Clouds Are Dreams*, 2018–, C-prints from chemically-altered slides
↗ *Someone Tried to Lock Up Time, Everyone Had a Drone,* 2018–, C-prints from chemically-altered slides

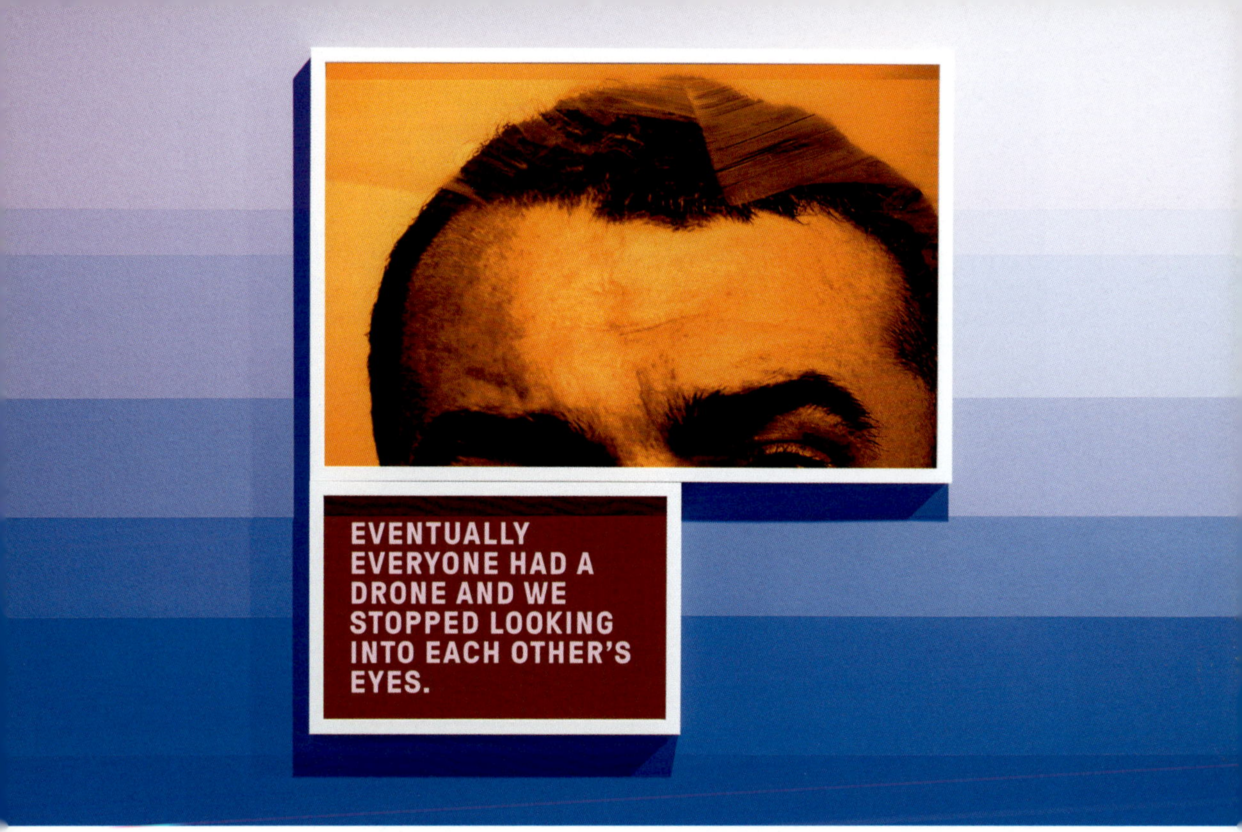
EVENTUALLY
EVERYONE HAD A
DRONE AND WE
STOPPED LOOKING
INTO EACH OTHER'S
EYES.

Basim Magdy

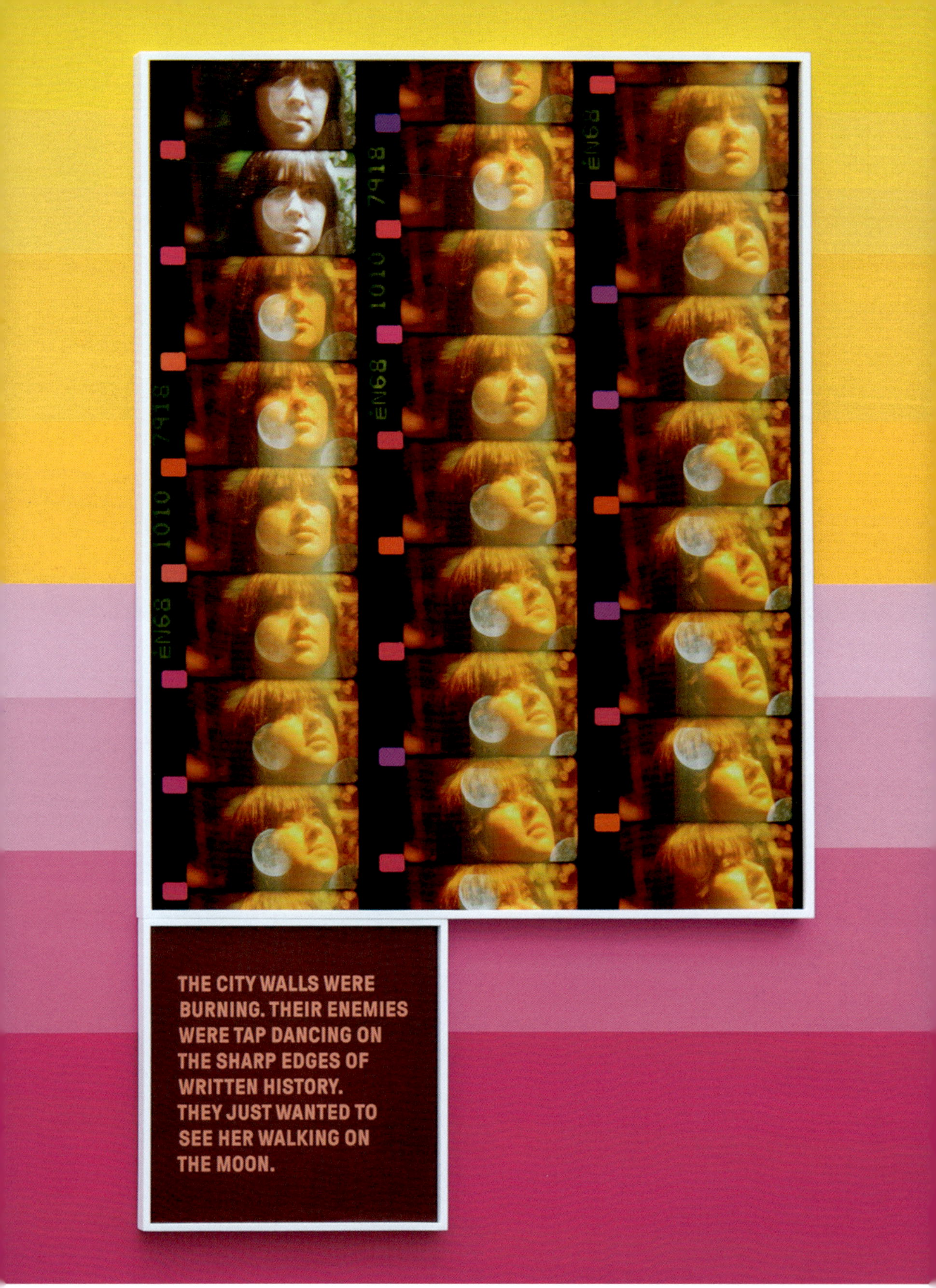

↑ *Someone Tried to Lock Up Time, Walking on the Moon*, 2018–, C-prints from chemically-altered slides
↗ *Someone Tried to Lock Up Time, Fish Tongue*, 2018–, C-prints from chemically-altered slides

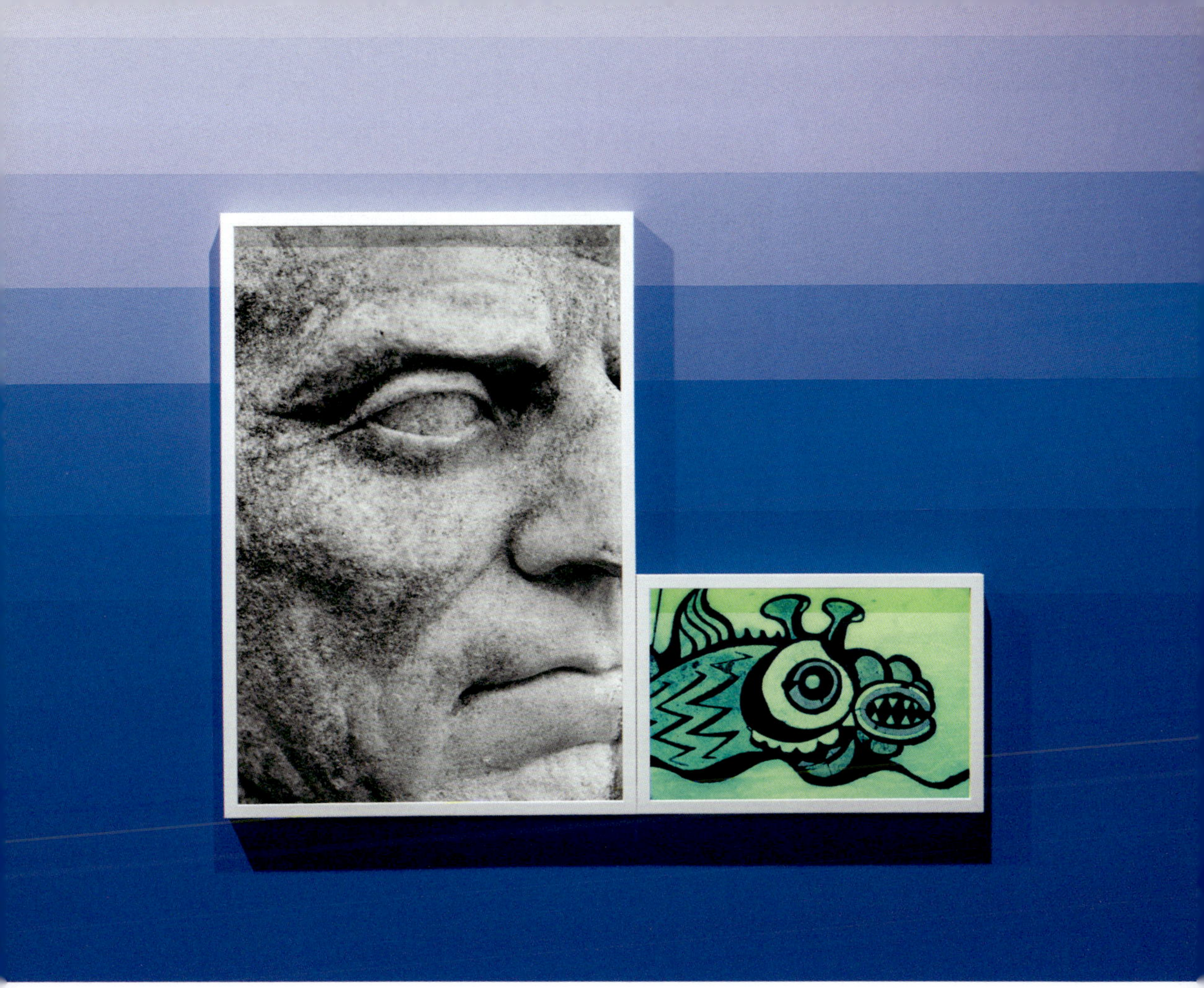

Basim Magdy

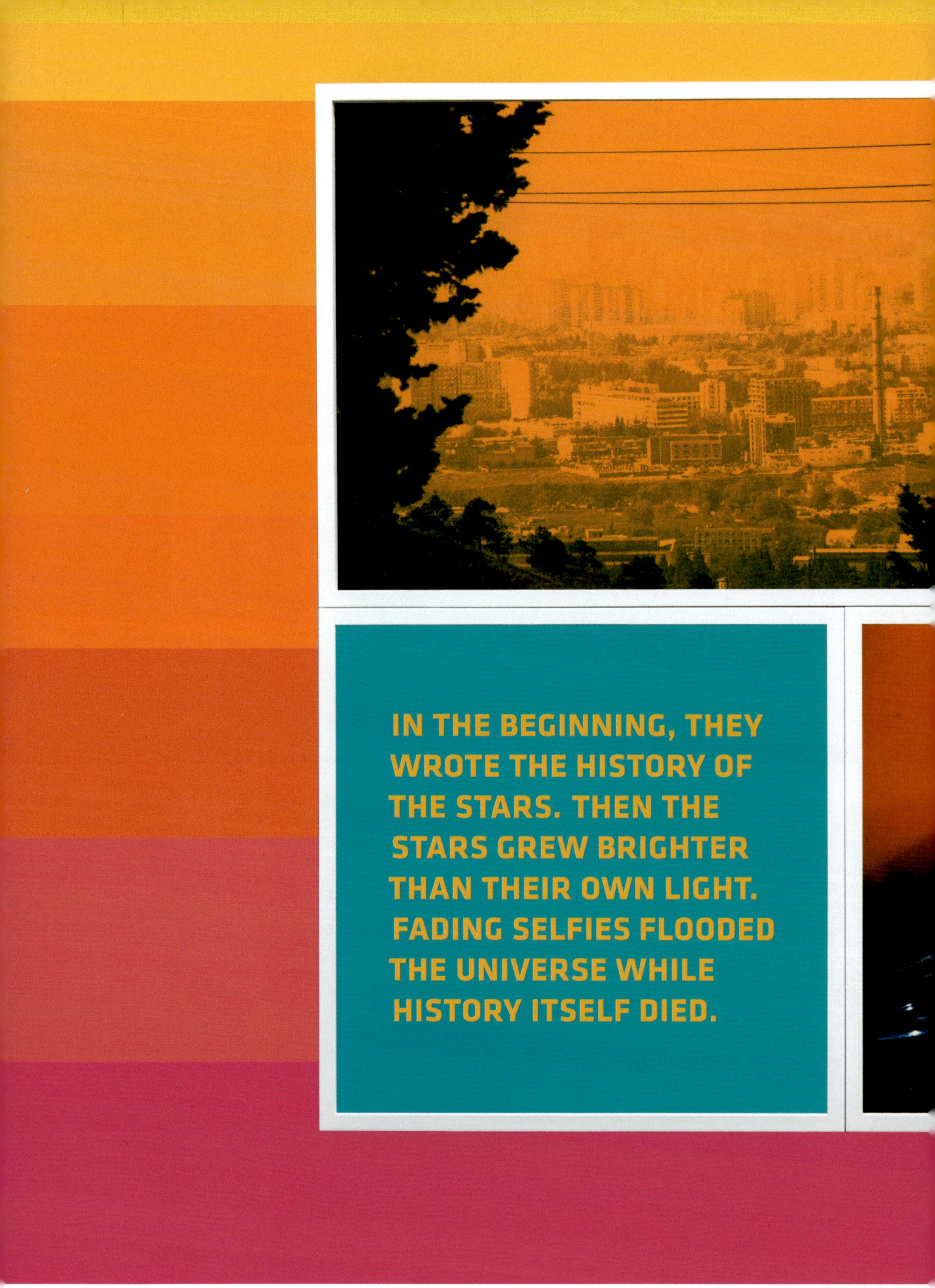

Someone Tried to Lock Up Time, History of the Stars, 2023, C-prints from chemically-altered slides

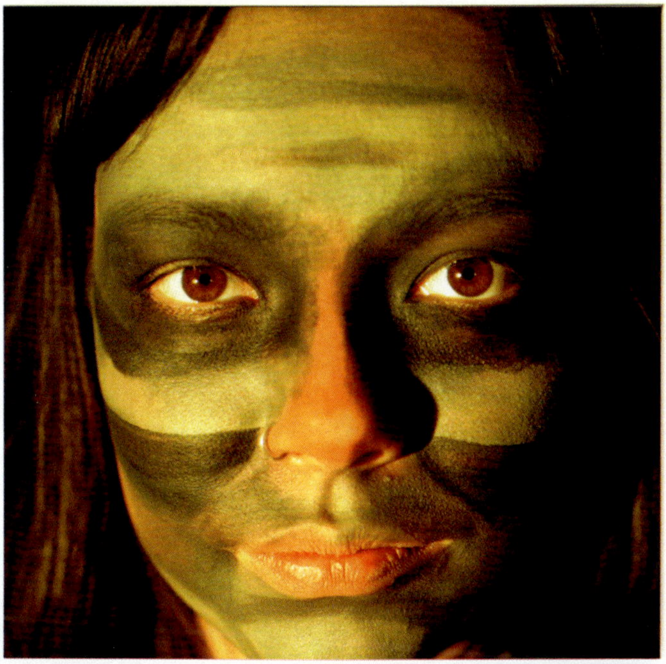
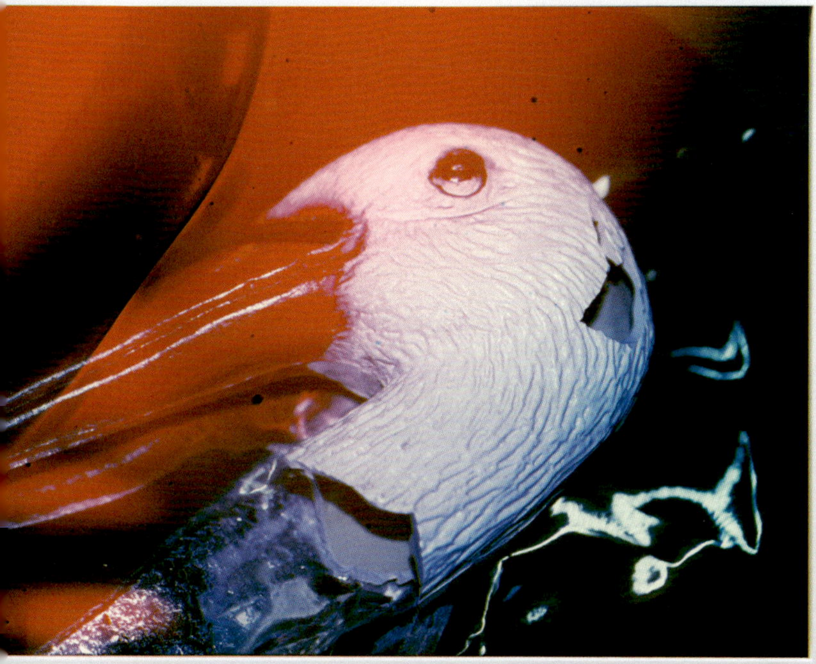

Basim Magdy

ALMAGUL MENLIBAYEVA

Almagul Menlibayeva (b. 1969 in Almaty, Kazakhstan) **is a multimedia artist who lives and works in Germany and Kazakhstan**

Almagul Menlibayeva makes photographs and site-specific multi-channel video installations that critically explore social, economic, and political transformations in post-Soviet Central Asia. Several months after the peaceful January 2022 demonstrations in Kazakhstan turned into tragic events, she made a series of prints and an animated video based on AI-generated images to depict them. What started with people protesting a rise in fuel prices soon spread across the country and evolved into a massive anti-government uprising. The government cut off internet access, leaving people without communication channels. During the information blackout, troops from the Collective Security Treaty Organization (CSTO) – a military alliance between six post-Soviet states but predominantly made up of Russian soldiers – received official permission to enter the country. Kazakhstan's only official news channel downplayed the ongoing tragedy. Menlibayeva herself was outside the country and could only gather information from the scarce sources that made it across the border.

Later collecting reports from victims and eyewitnesses, Menlibayeva used Transformer artificial intelligence algorithms to turn their words into images. The results resemble distorted realist paintings. Her work becomes a reconstruction of human memory through the synthetic memory managed by algorithms trained on Google data. With this project, she also raises questions about the power of individual voices under authoritarian regimes that suppress and manipulate media infrastructures, and how one can protect oneself in such an information environment.

● **Biography** MENLIBAYEVA studied at the Academy of Art and Theatre in Almaty. Her work has been featured internationally at the Sydney Biennale, the Venice Biennale, the Moscow Biennale, and the Gangwon International Biennale in South Korea. Her video installations and photography have been exhibited at Museum van Hedendaagse Kunst (M HKA), Antwerp; Queens Museum, New York; Herbert F. Johnson Museum, Ithaca, New York; Stenersen Museum, Oslo; and at the ZKM Museum of Contemporary Art, Karlsruhe, Germany.

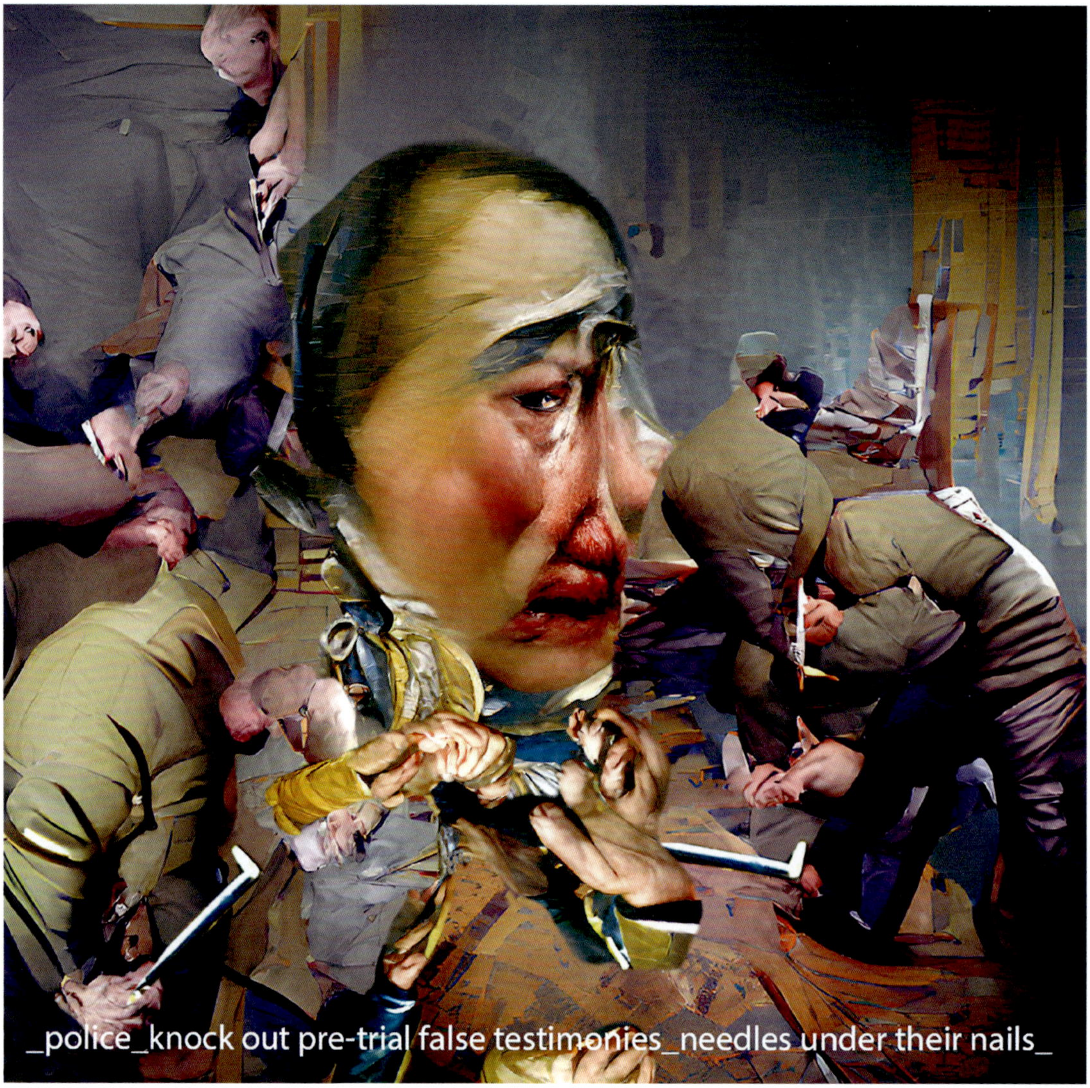

AI Realism, Qantar 2022, 2022, AI-generated image, inkjet print

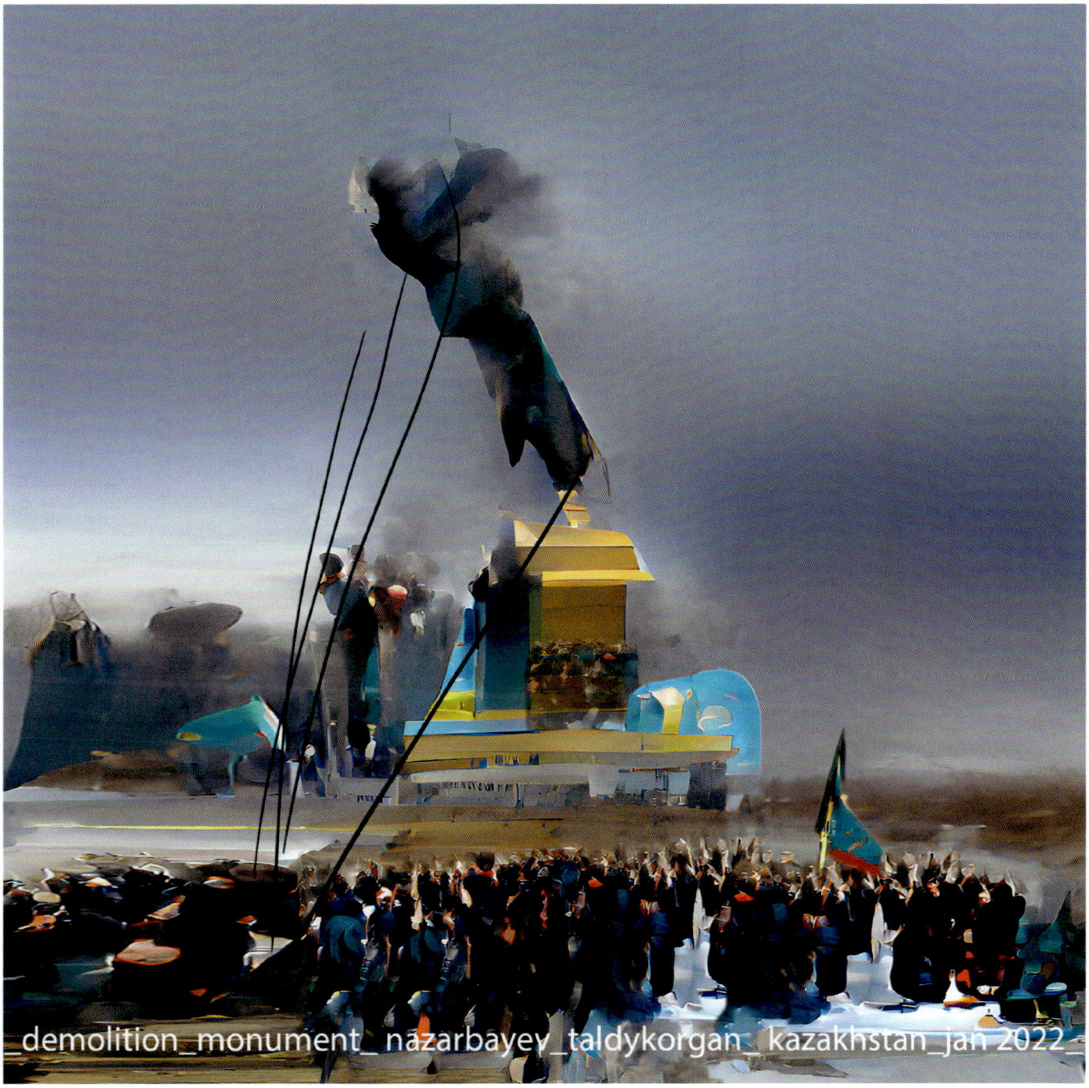

Almagul Menlibayeva

AI Realism, Qantar 2022, 2022, AI-generated image, inkjet print

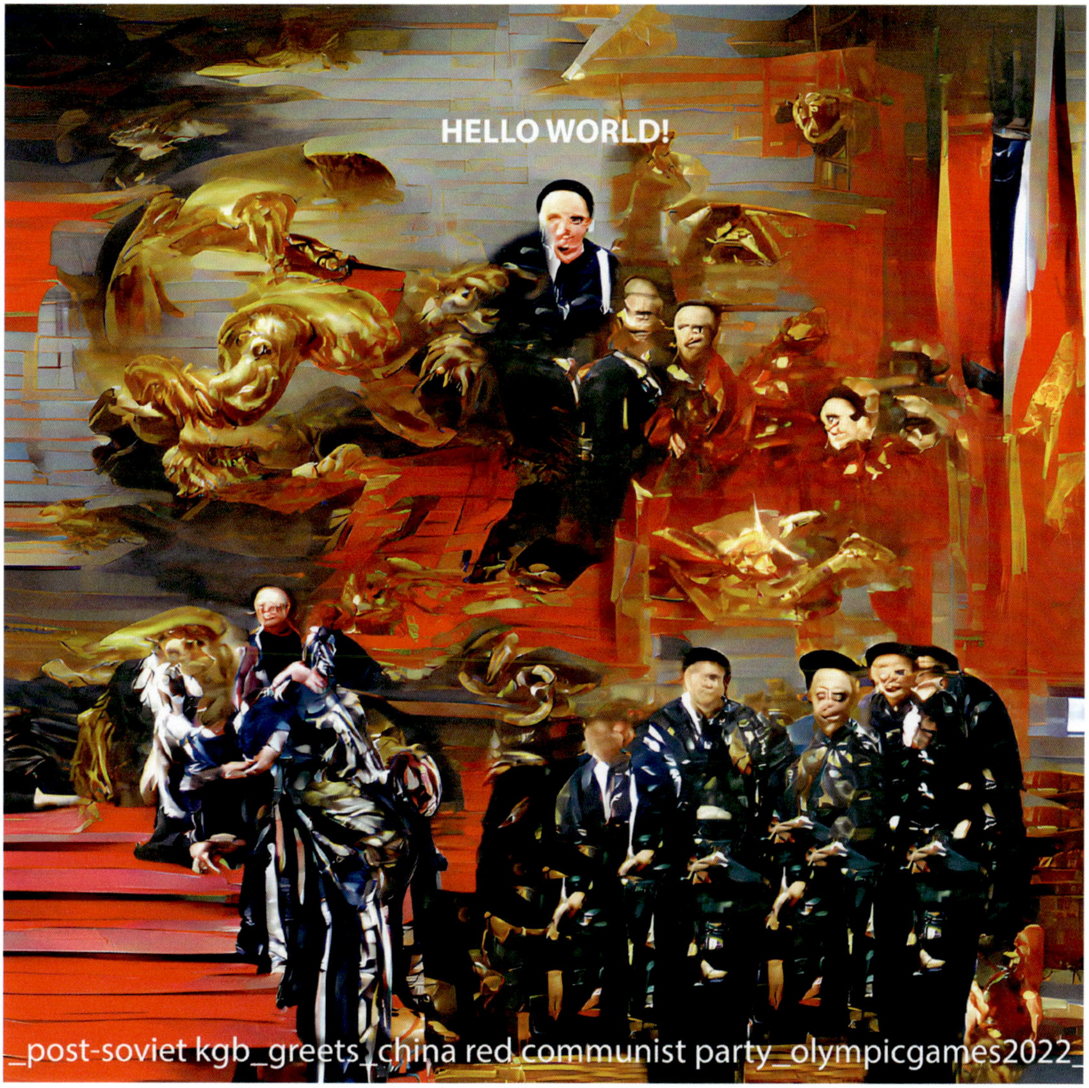

Almagul Menlibayeva

AI Realism, Qantar 2022, 2022, AI-generated image, inkjet print

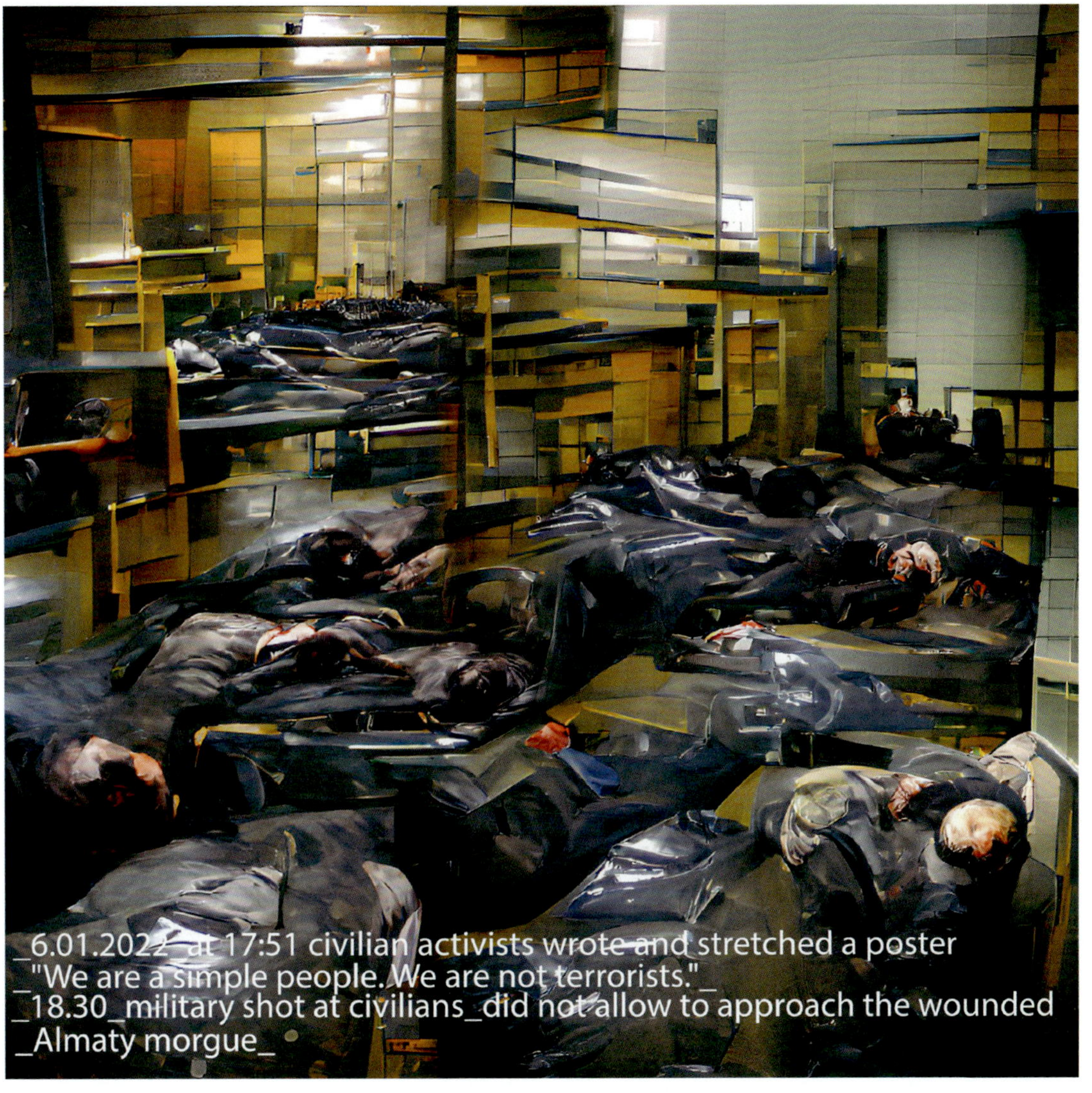

Almagul Menlibayeva

KRISTINA ÕLLEK

Kristina Õllek (b. 1989 in Tallinn, Estonia) **is an artist based in Tallinn who works with photographs, videos, and installations**

Kristina Õllek's work investigates geological matter, aquatic ecology, and human-made environments and is based on personal observations and research into the anthropocentric influences on marine ecology. In *Filtering with Cyanobacteria, Double Binds, & Other Blooms*, a recent series of manipulated photographs, Õllek focuses on cyanobacteria and the Baltic Sea. This semi-enclosed slow-moving sea is one of the most human-affected seas in the world. Its fragile ecosystem is heavily impacted by agricultural run-off, industrial chemicals, poor water management, heavy marine traffic, and underwater noise.

Many of these factors, combined with rising sea temperatures, significantly affect the cyanobacterial community and lead to an increase in the blooming of toxic blue-green algae. This creates highly depleted and oxygen-starved areas. The resulting "dead zones," together with variable ones caused by more saline-dense water remaining near the sea floor, have a major impact on marine ecology, and the sea's recovery capacity is very limited.

To highlight this often invisible issue, Õllek worked with sea salt that she grew in her studio, cyanobacteria, bioplastic, silicone, and other organic and inorganic materials, some with their own agency, to enhance her photographs with additional physical and conceptual layers. By adding chains and limestones to the installation, she "anchors" some works while allowing others to float, inviting viewers to imagine the depth of the seabed, its current conditions, and a range of future scenarios.

● **Biography** ÕLLEK graduated with a BA and an MFA from the Estonian Academy of Arts, Tallinn, and studied at Kunsthochschule Berlin-Weissensee and at the Piet Zwart Institute, Rotterdam. She won the Estonian Academy of Arts Young Artist Prize in 2013 as BA graduate and in 2016 as MA graduate. Between 2013 and 2018, she was the co-founder and a member of the artist-run space Rundum. Her works have been shown in numerous international exhibitions and are included in the collections of Kumu, Art Museum of Estonia, Tallinn; Fotomuseum Winterthur, Switzerland; European Central Bank, Frankfurt; and the New York Public Library.

Surface Accumulation no. 2, 2022, pigment-ink print on aluminum, CNC-engraved glass, beech with CNC engraving and UV silicone

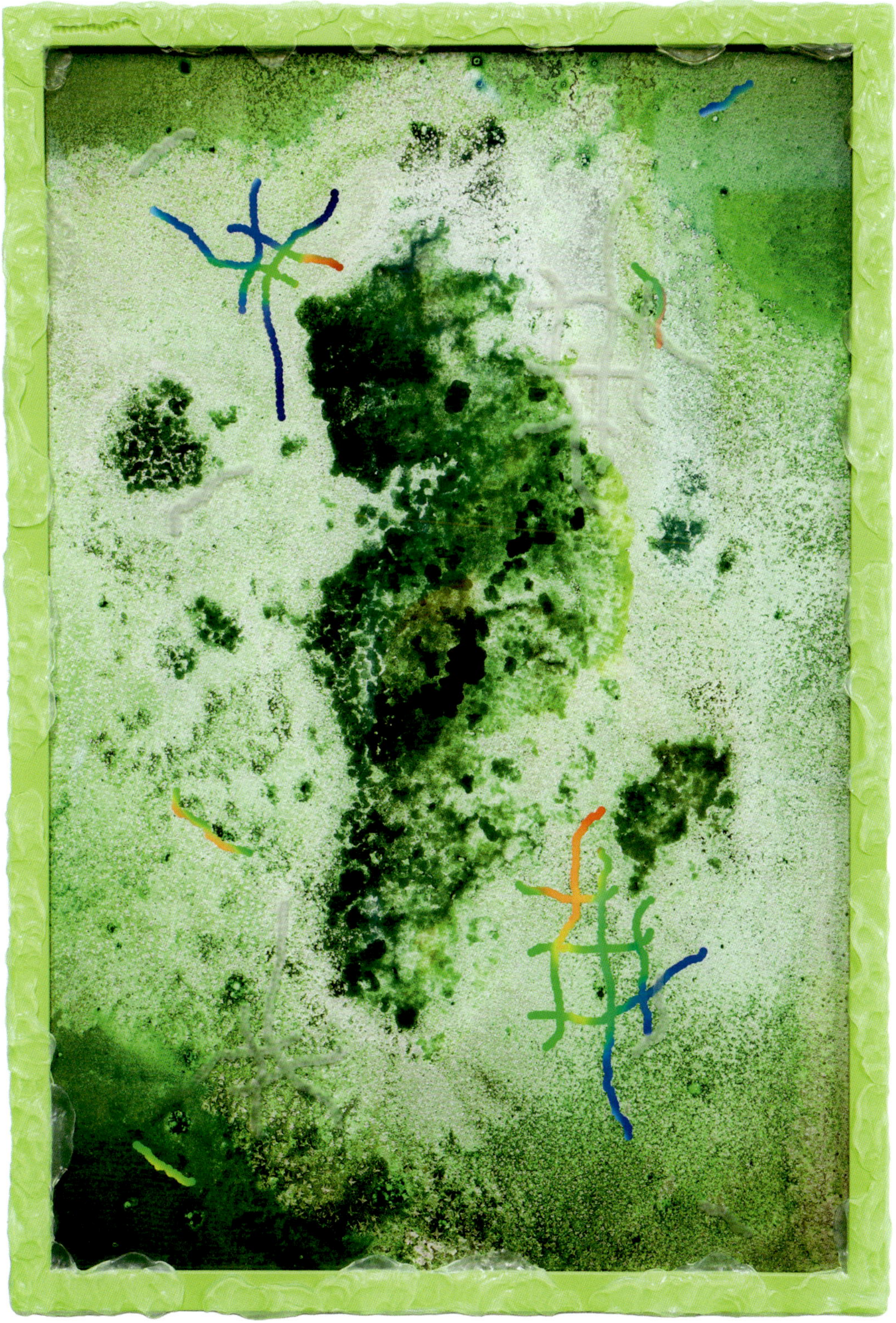

Kristina Õllek

Generous Stir, 2022, pigment-ink print with sea salt,
cyanobacteria, and green fluorescent pigment

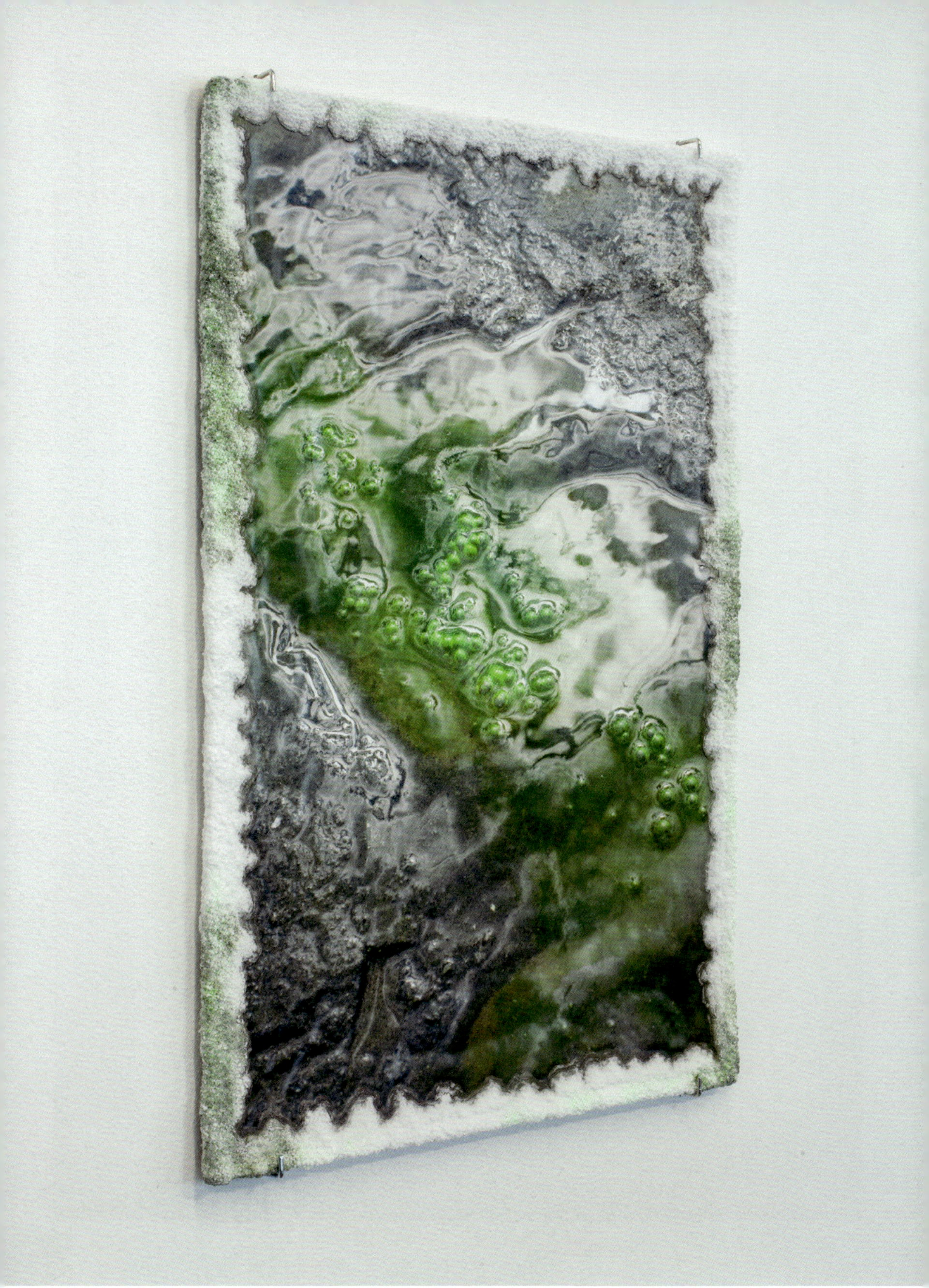

Kristina Õllek

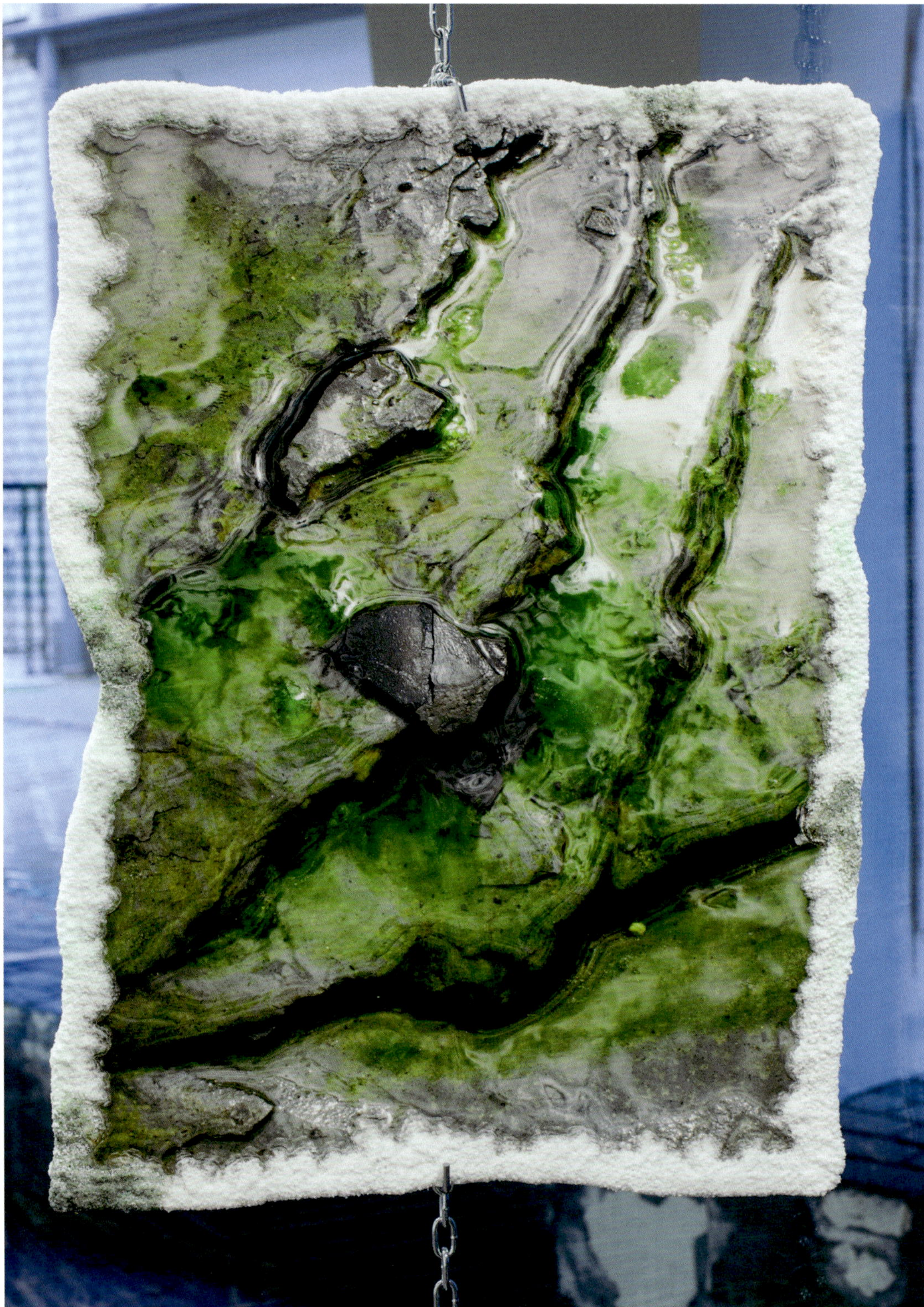

↑ *Saturated Steps*, 2022
↗ *Forming Surface no. 1*, 2022
Pigment-ink print with sea salt, cyanobacteria, and green fluorescent pigment

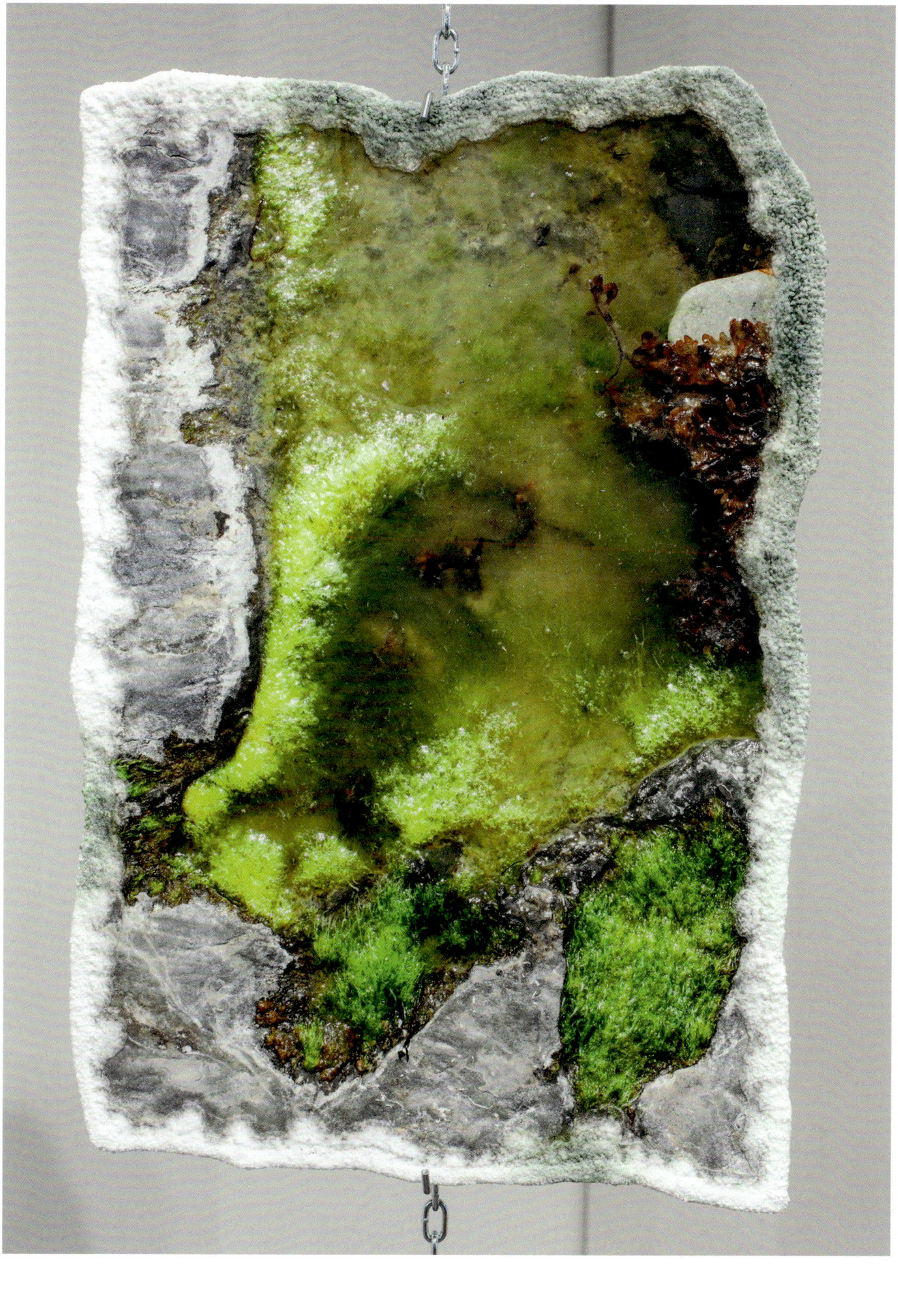

Kristina Õllek

MONIRA AL QADIRI

Monira Al Qadiri (b. 1983 in Dakar, Senegal) **is a Berlin-based artist working across mediums, including video, sculpture, and performance**

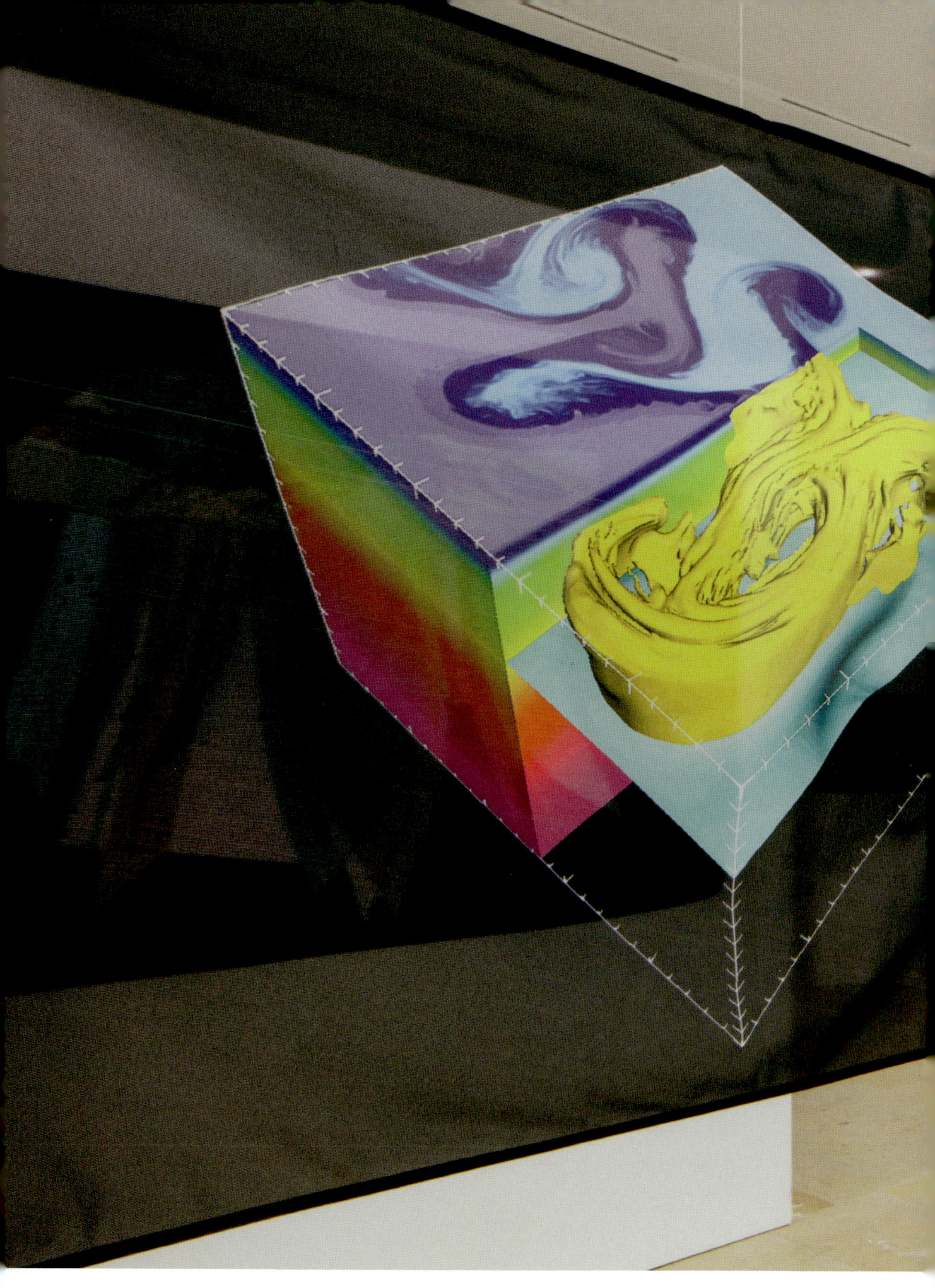

Installation view, *Reservoir Ten*, 2022, ink on polyester

Monira Al Qadiri's artworks are influenced by her upbringing in Kuwait and by living in Japan, where she studied art for a decade. She explores unconventional gender identities, petro-cultures (aspects of contemporary life founded on oil), legacies of corruption, and imagined futures.

For *New Visions 2023*, Al Qadiri presents *Reservoir Ten* (2022). Questioning the roles petrochemicals play in our daily lives, the installation includes ten printed fabrics hanging from the ceiling. The fabrics are adorned with colorful 3-D images simulating seismic surveys of oil reservoirs, which are often created during exploration periods prior to the extraction of oil. Al Qadiri imprints these images, which present phantasmagorical shapes in inviting pink, green, and pastel, onto chic black polyester fabric. The delicate and impressionable textiles are a reminder of the infiltration of petrochemicals in our lives, from the production of clothes to the sanitary products that keep our bodies and surroundings clean.

● **Biography** AL QADIRI received a PhD in inter-media art from Tokyo University of the Arts in 2010, examining the aesthetics of sadness in Middle Eastern poetry, music, art, and religious practices. She has exhibited at Guggenheim Museum Bilbao; Blaffer Art Museum, Houston; Digital Arts Resource Center (DARC), Ottawa; Art Gallery of Burlington, Ontario, Canada; Haus der Kunst, Munich; and Kunstverein Gottingen, Germany. Al Qadiri participated in the 59th Venice Biennale; the Asia Art Biennale, Taiwan; Expo 2020, Dubai; the Seoul Mediacity Biennial; the Asia Pacific Triennial, Brisbane, and in exhibitions at the Palais de Tokyo, Paris; MoMA PS1, New York; and Berlinale Forum Expanded, among other venues.

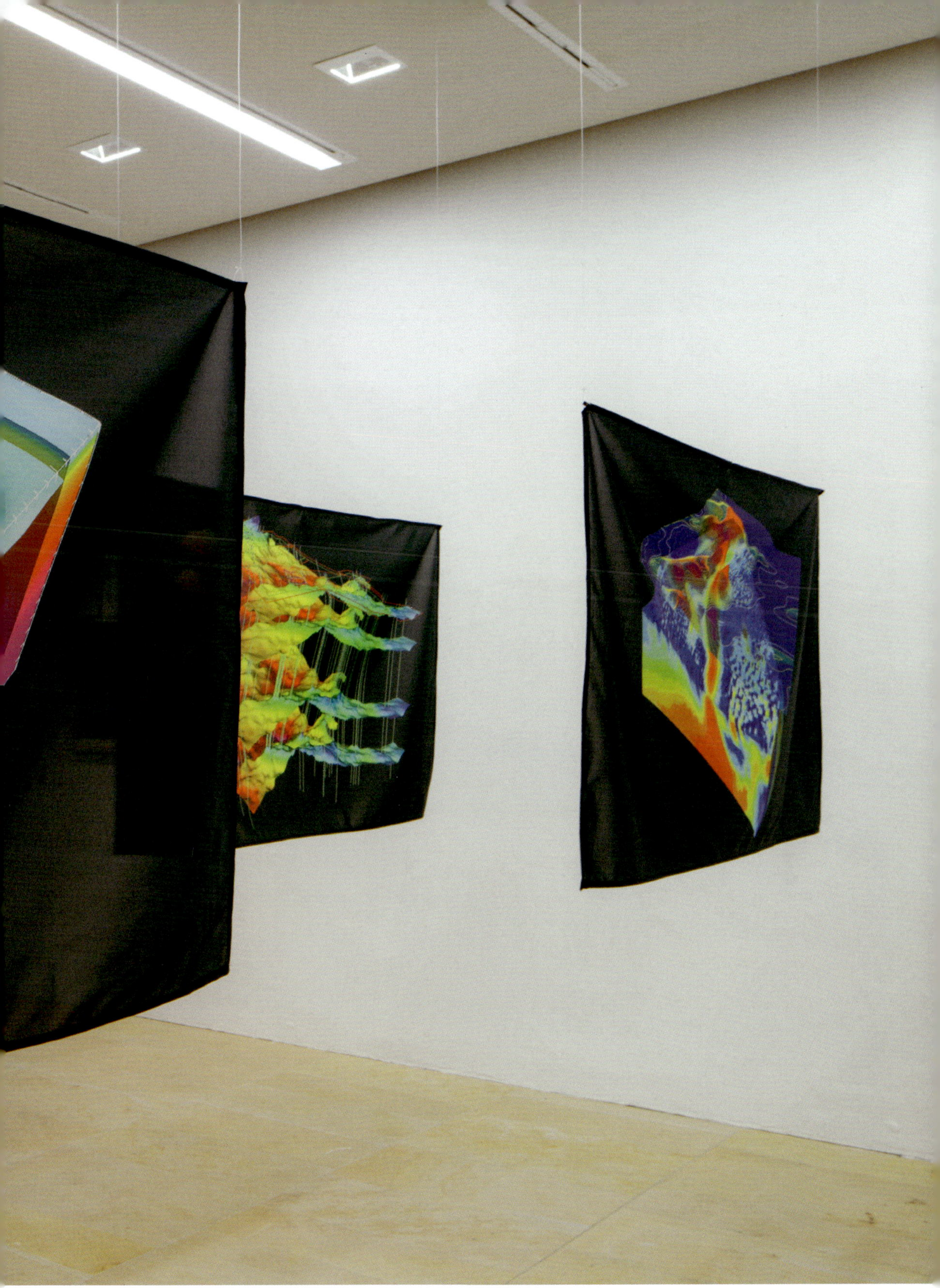

Monira Al Qadiri

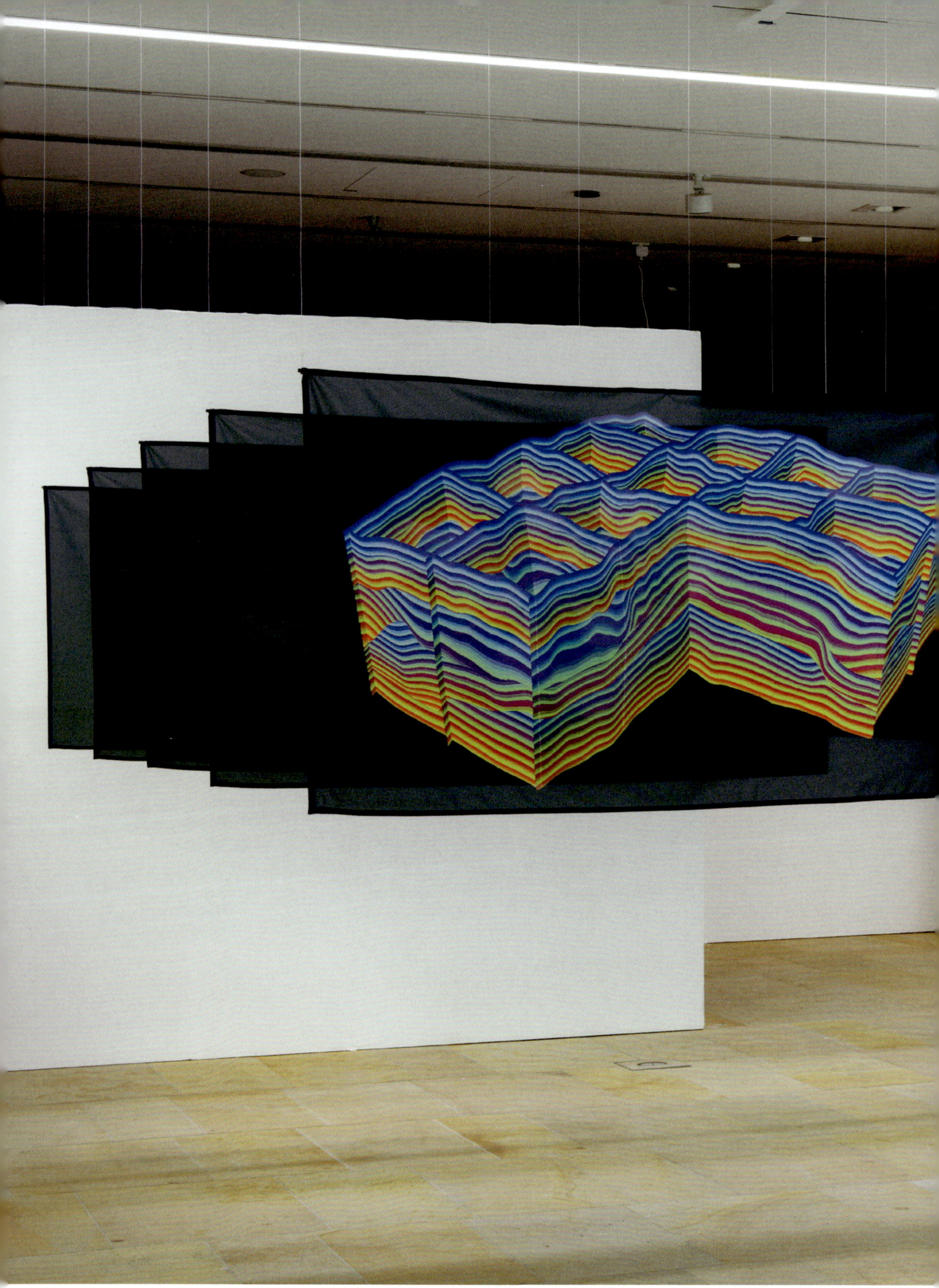

Installation view, *Reservoir Ten*, 2022, ink on polyester

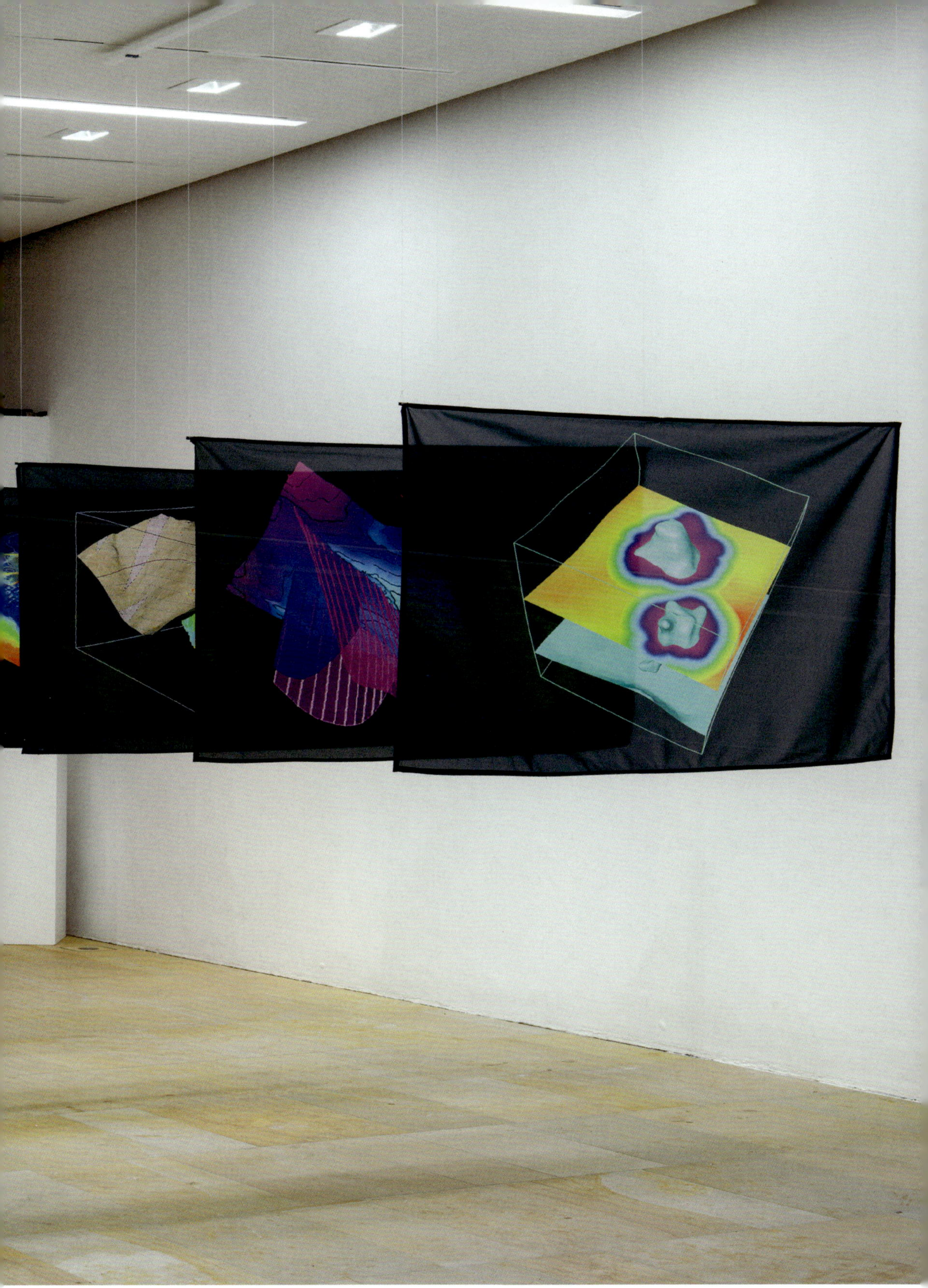

Monira Al Qadiri

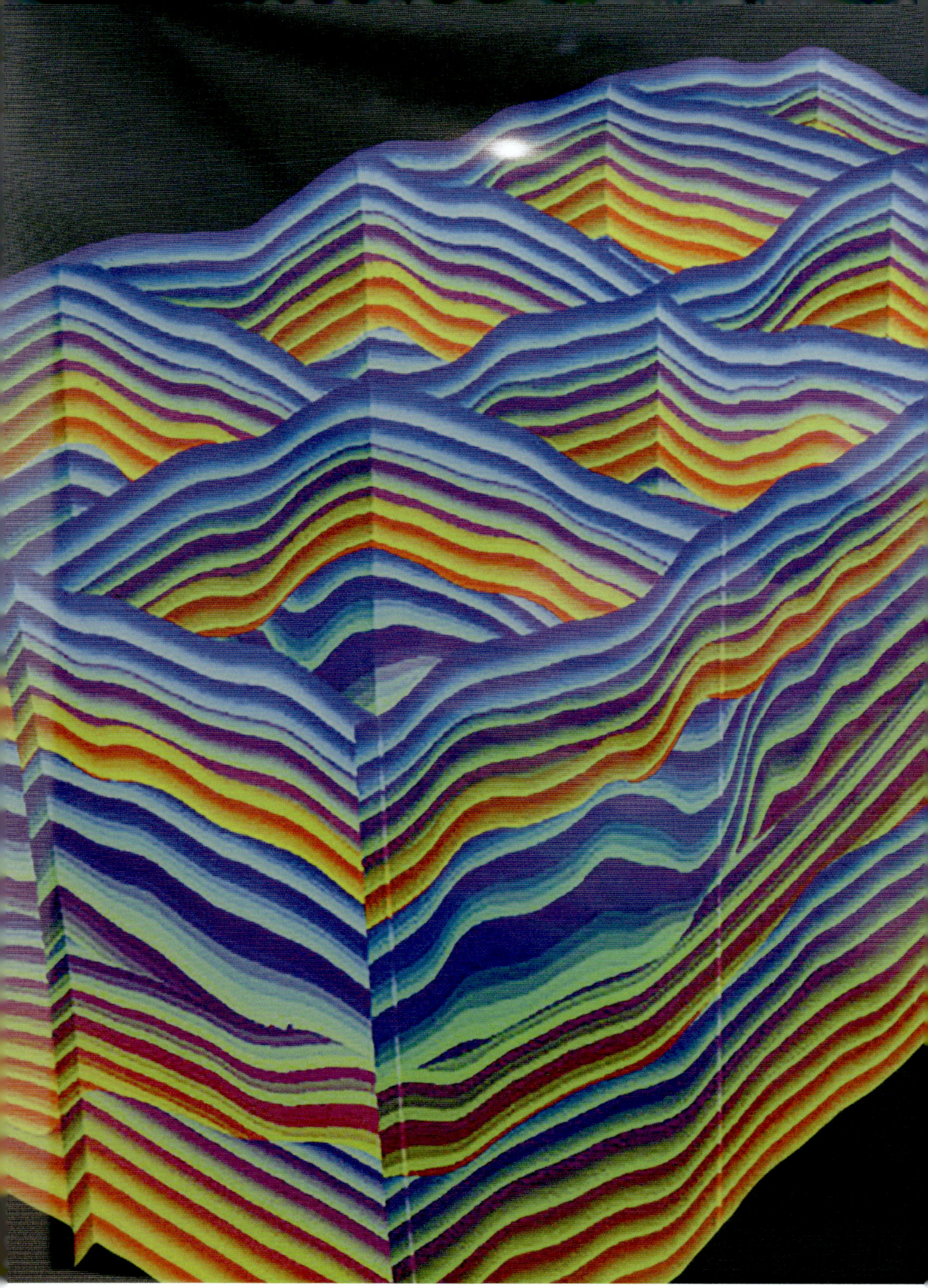

Detail, *Reservoir Ten*, 2022, ink on polyester

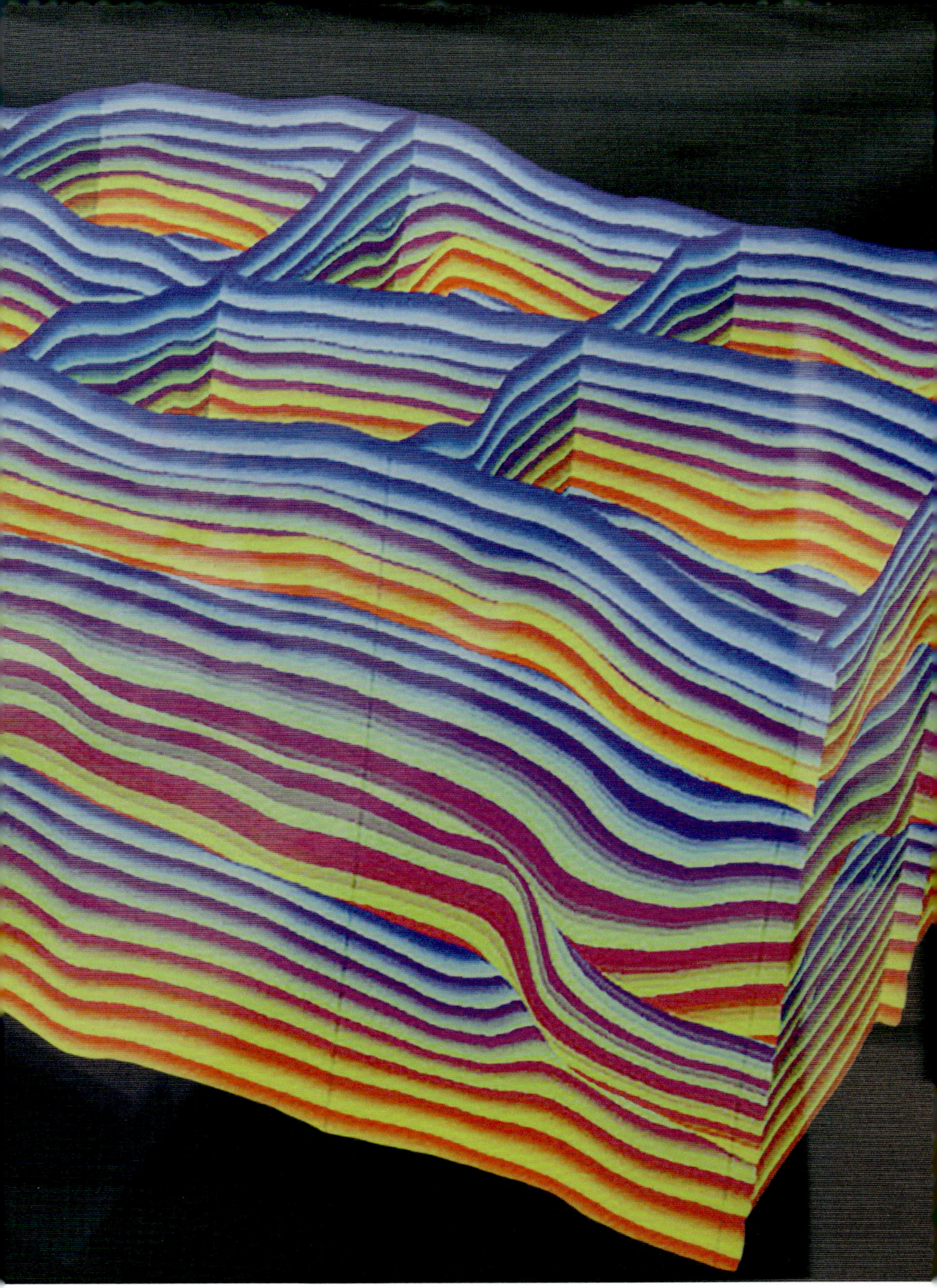

Monira Al Qadiri

FARAH AL QASIMI

Farah Al Qasimi (b. 1991 in Abu Dhabi) **is a photographer, filmmaker, performance artist, and musician who lives and works in New York and Dubai**

Farah Al Qasimi documents culture, style, taste, and interior spaces in the Gulf States. Her sumptuous, color-saturated images abound with textures and patterns found in everyday environments, such as homes and shopping malls. She is chiefly interested in questions about how these spaces and their dazzling surfaces are entangled with social norms and identities in a post-oil society. Layering is key to Al Qasimi's aesthetic, and her site-specific installations are typically constructed of framed photographs hung atop large-scale prints mounted directly to the wall. The pictures themselves often feature foreshortening, reflections, screens, picture-in-picture effects, and mirrors.

In her commission for *New Visions 2023*, Al Qasimi traces flower motifs across architecture and spaces of commerce in the Emirates. Four of the framed photographs show synthetic or digital flowers from Dragon Mart, on the outskirts of Dubai, which is the world's largest trading hub for Chinese products outside mainland China. In its various representations, the floral motif emerges as a metaphor for different kinds of extraction from the land. Particularly pertinent is the use of fresh water during water crises in the region, referenced through an image of a salt lake into which excess salt water from desalination plants is pumped. Al Qasimi's installation subtly points to the consequences of the extractive processes involved in the understanding of nature as lush, colorful, and green.

● **Biography** AL QASIMI holds an MFA from Yale School of Art and has been a student at Skowhegan School of Painting and Sculpture. She is represented in several museum collections, including the Guggenheim, New York and Abu Dhabi; Tate Modern, London; Museum of Modern Art, New York; and the Museum of Contemporary Art Chicago. Her work has been featured in exhibitions at institutions such as the Sharjah Biennial, Jameel Arts Centre, Dubai; the San Francisco Arts Commission; and Helena Anrather, New York.

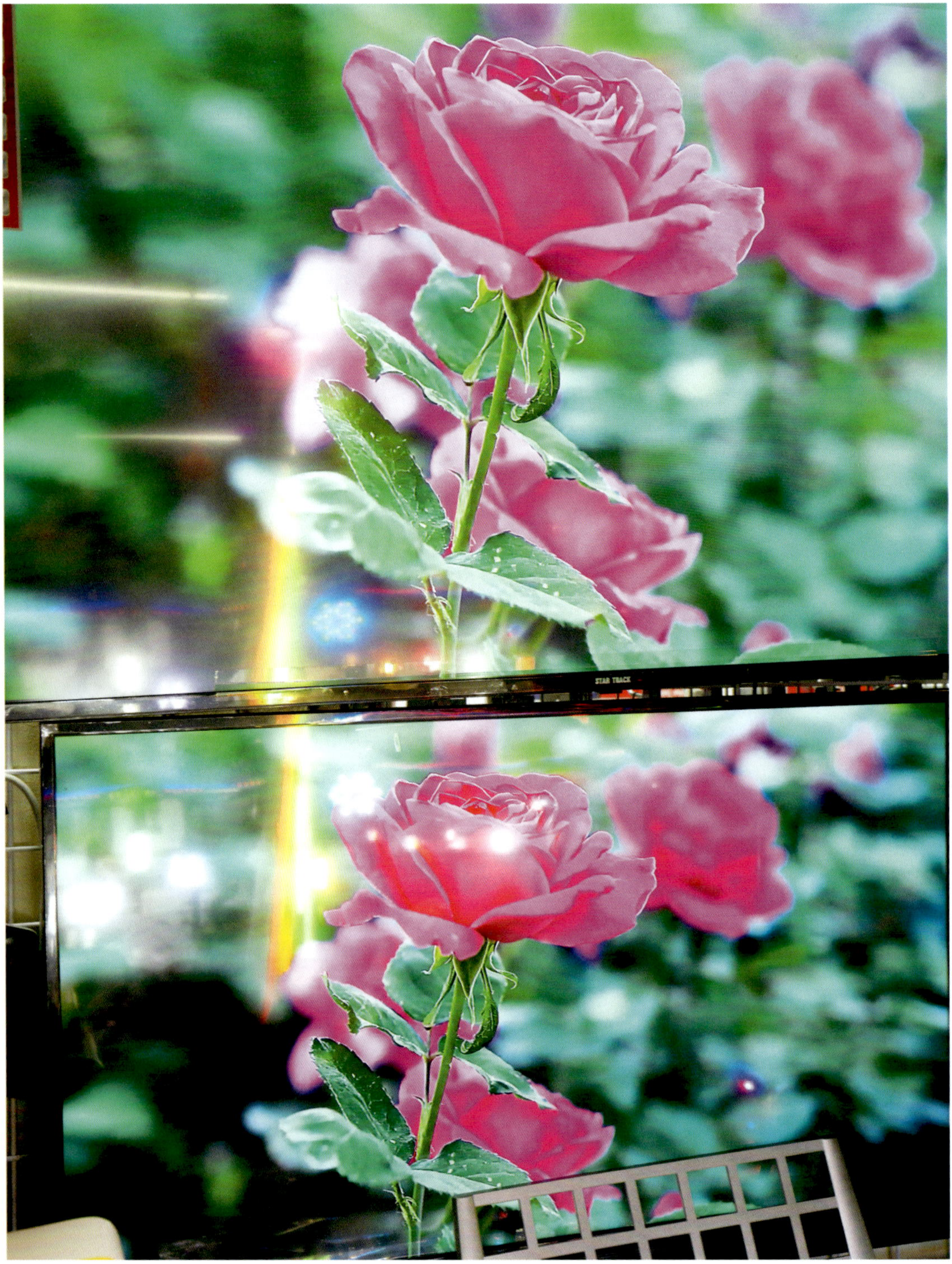

↑ *LED Rose*, 2023, inkjet print
↗ *Baba, Shadow*, 2023, inkjet print

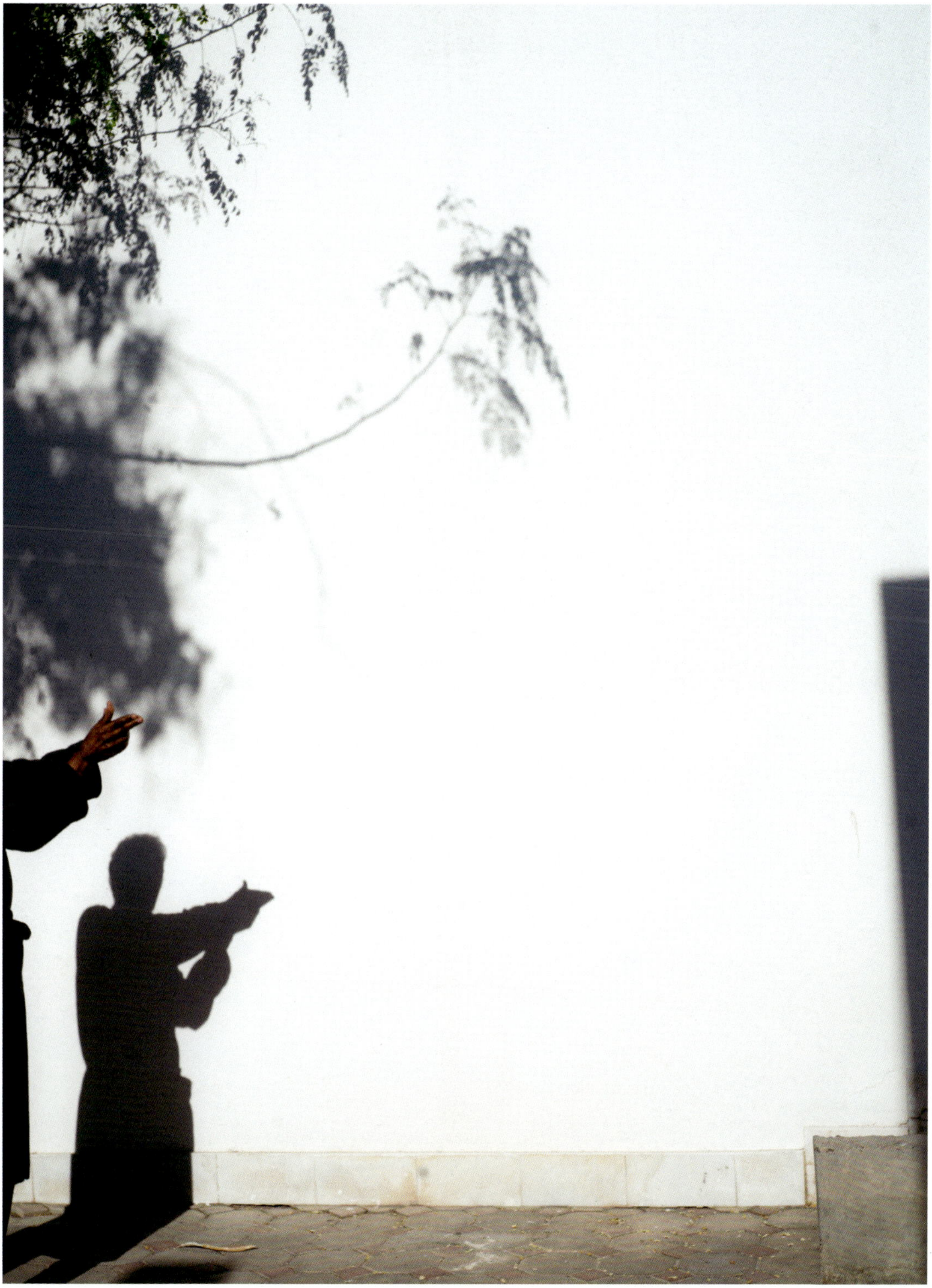

Farah Al Qasimi

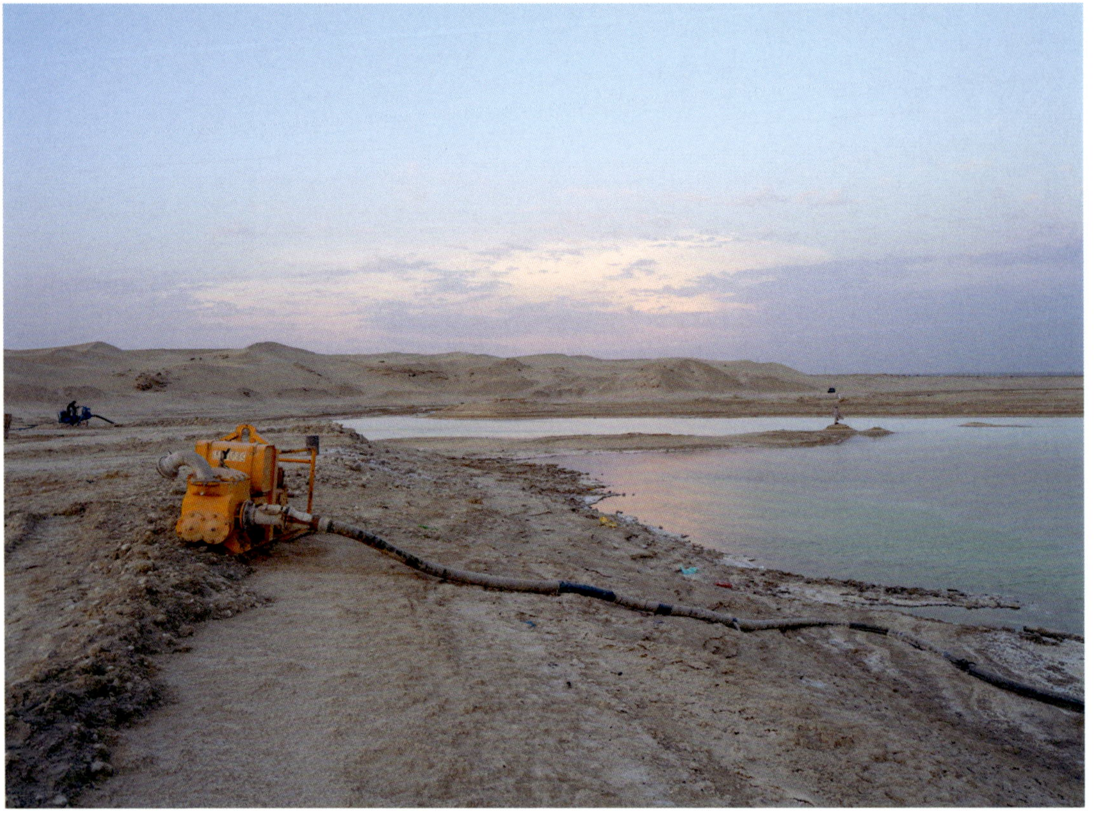

↑ *Salt Lake Sunset*, 2023, inkjet print
↗ *Dragon Mart Still Life 6,* 2022, inkjet print

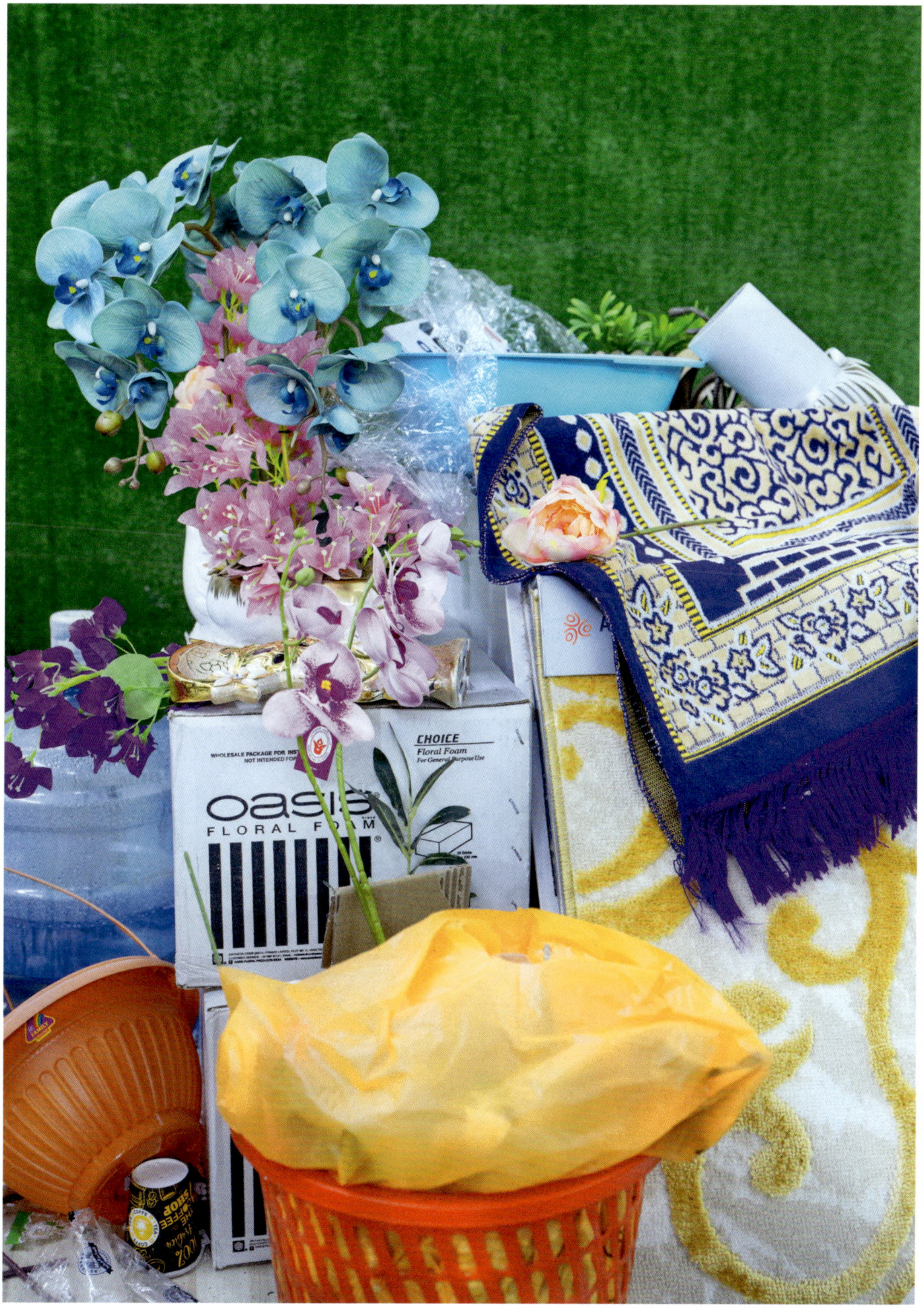

Farah Al Qasimi

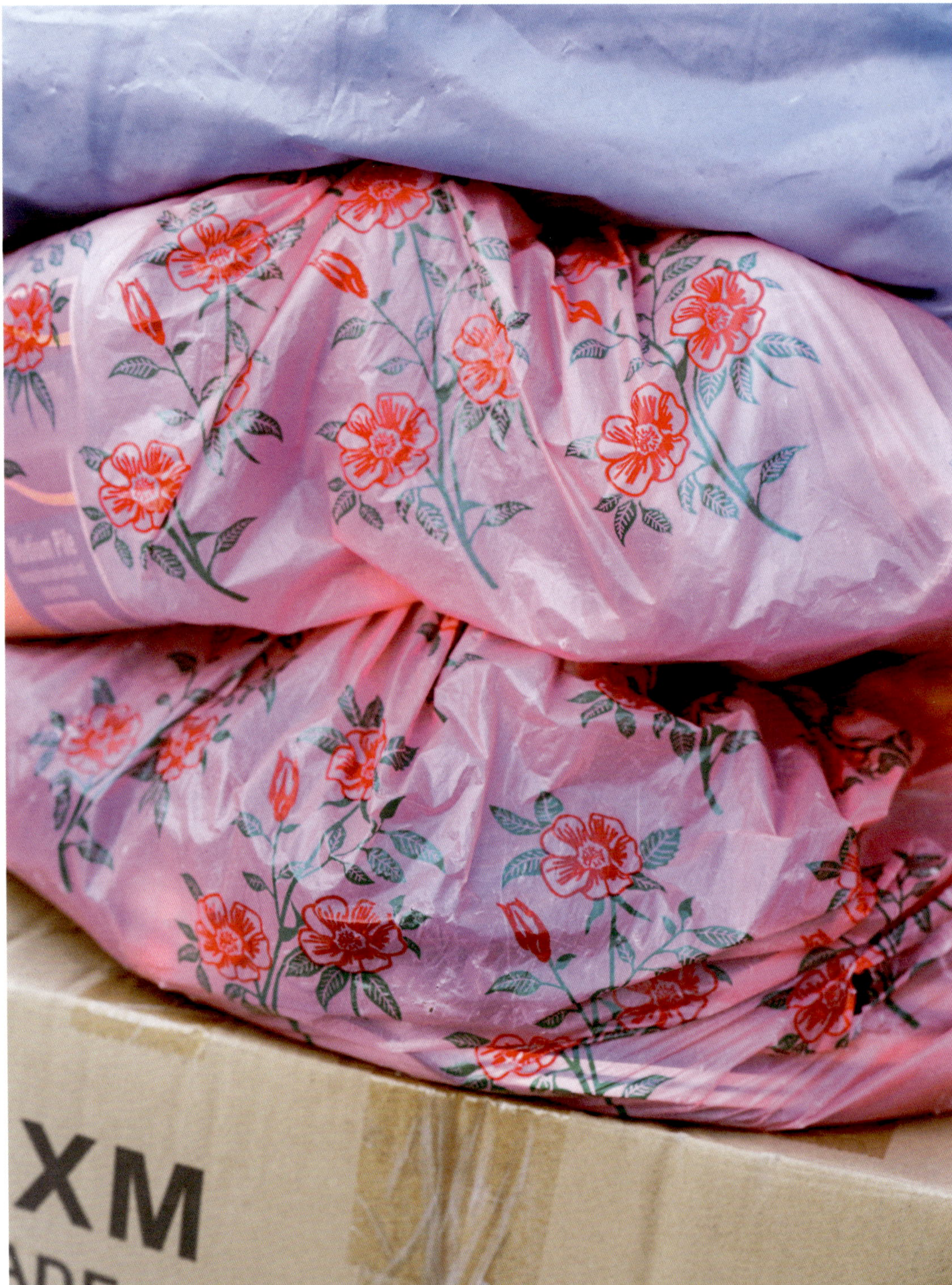

↑ *Shopping Bags*, 2023, inkjet print
↗ *Dragon Mart Still Life 2,* 2022, inkjet print

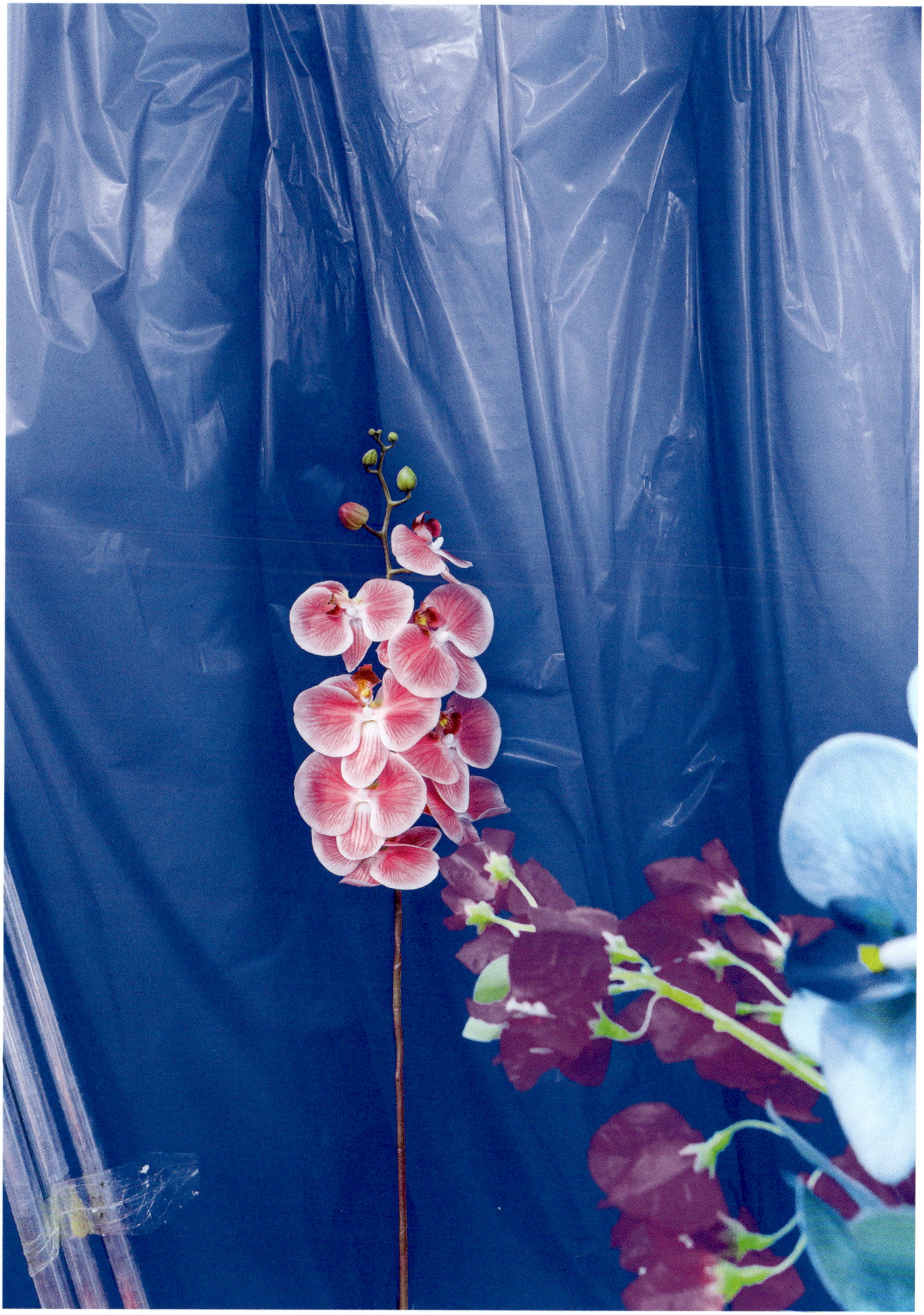

Farah Al Qasimi

EMILIJA ŠKARNULYTĖ

Emilija Škarnulytė (b. 1987 in Vilnius) **is a nomadic artist and filmmaker**

Emilija Škarnulytė blends fiction with documentary in her site-specific video installations, which explore deep time and invisible structures – from the cosmic and geologic to the ecological and political. In *RAKHNE* (2023), her commission for *New Visions 2023*, she deploys computer-generated imagery to envision an undersea data-storage infrastructure. Due to the exponential growth of data, entities that control cloud servers continually seek novel means of storage. The deep oceanic environment offers temperature control and insulation from both human error and seasonal vicissitudes. At the same time, this environment presents new vulnerabilities, ranging from marine fouling by invertebrate lifeforms and chemical reactions to unpredictable seismic events.

As we generate more and more data, the corporations that control it place these files and databases in environments increasingly remote from those who author or are represented by it. The materiality of that data – in the form of large-scale servers and the electrical and cable networks that connect them to the power grid – is kept hidden from the general public. In *RAKHNE*, Škarnulytė speculates that these sites may, in decrepit form, one day be subject to archaeological research and to the myths and codices of a forgotten era.

● **Biography** ŠKARNULYTĖ won the 2019 Future Generation Art Prize. She has had solo exhibitions at Tate Modern, London; Kunsthaus Pasquart, Biel, Switzerland; Den Frie, Copenhagen; and the National Gallery of Art, Vilnius and has participated in numerous group shows. She holds an undergraduate degree from the Brera Academy of Art in Milan and a MA from the Tromsø Academy of Contemporary Art. Her films are in the IFA, Kadist Foundation, and Centre Pompidou collections and have been screened at The Museum of Modern Art, New York. She is a founder and currently co-directs Polar Film Lab, a collective for analogue film practice located in Tromsø, Norway and is a member of the artist duo New Mineral Collective.

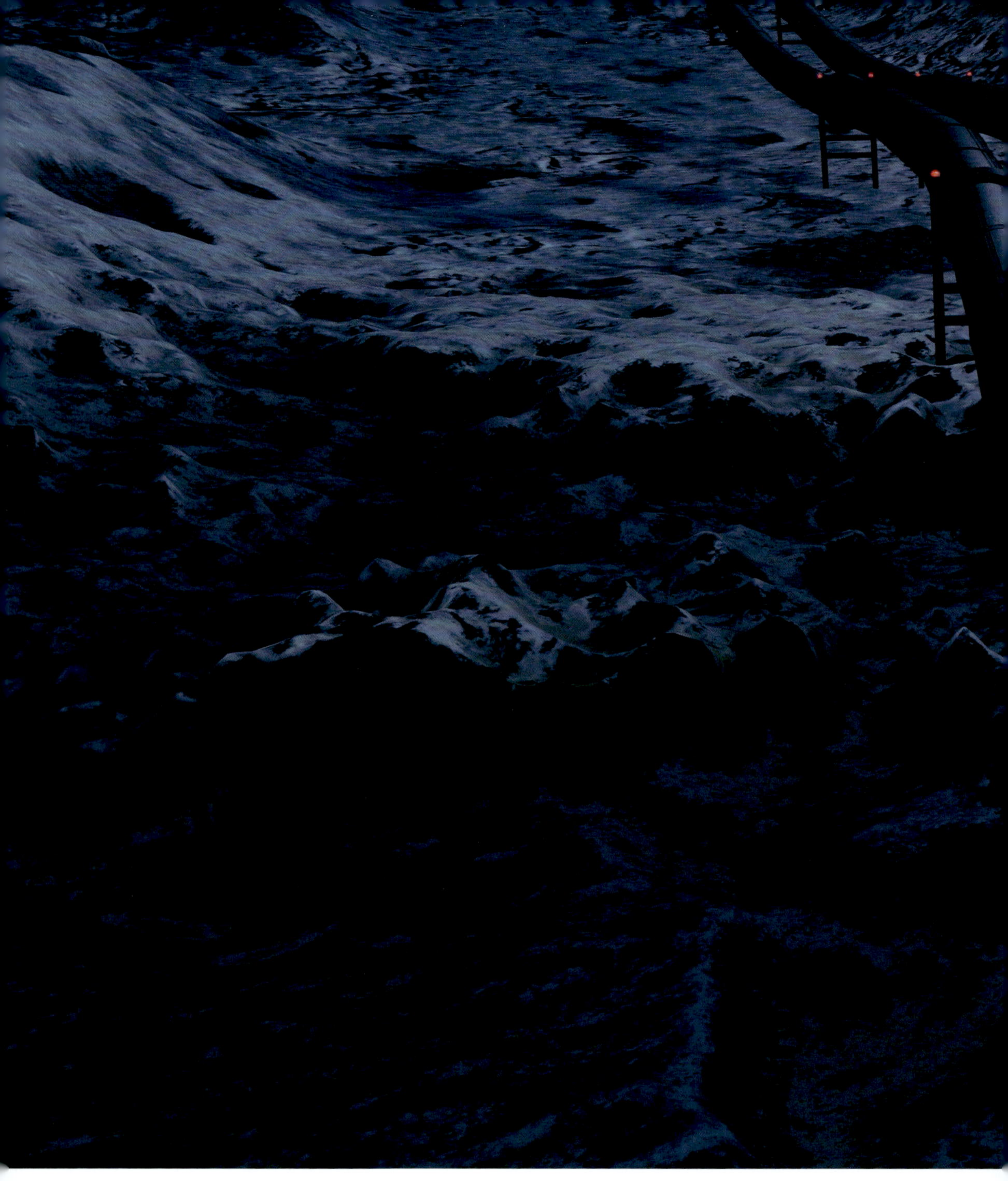

Still from *RAKHNE*, 2023, 4K singel-channel video installation

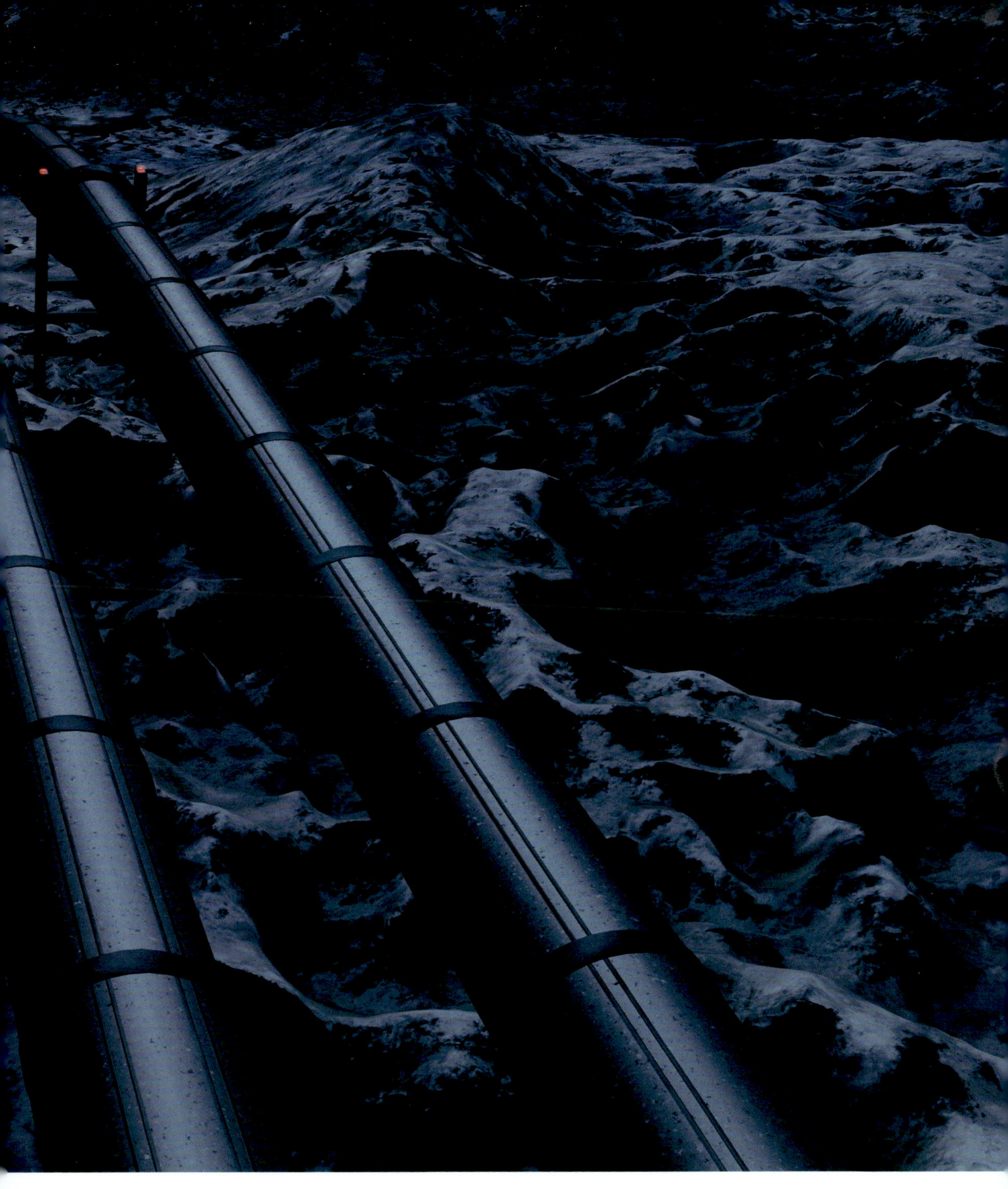

Emilija Škarnulytė

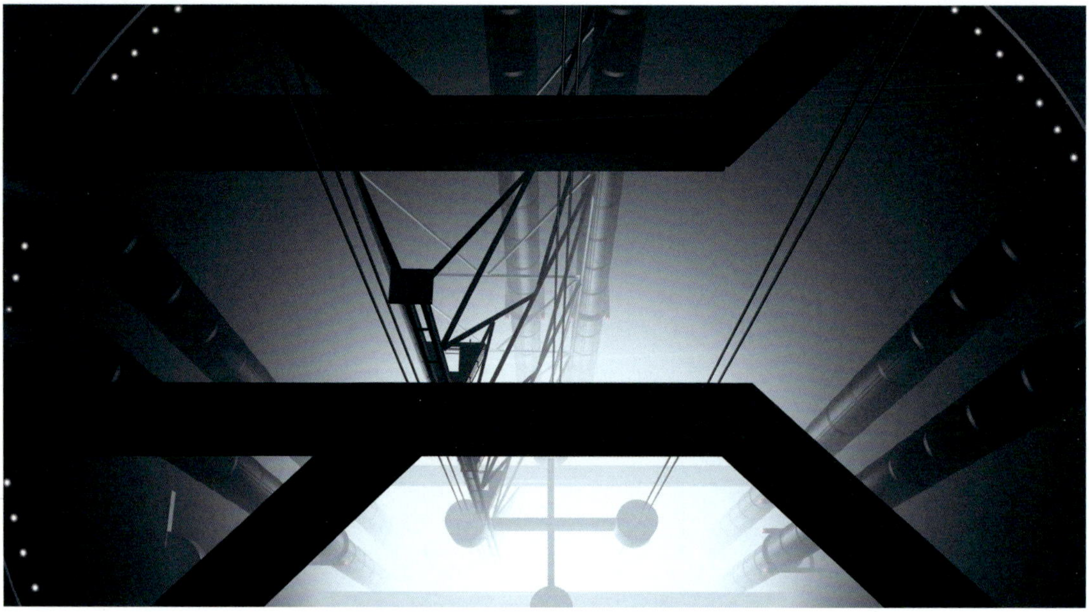

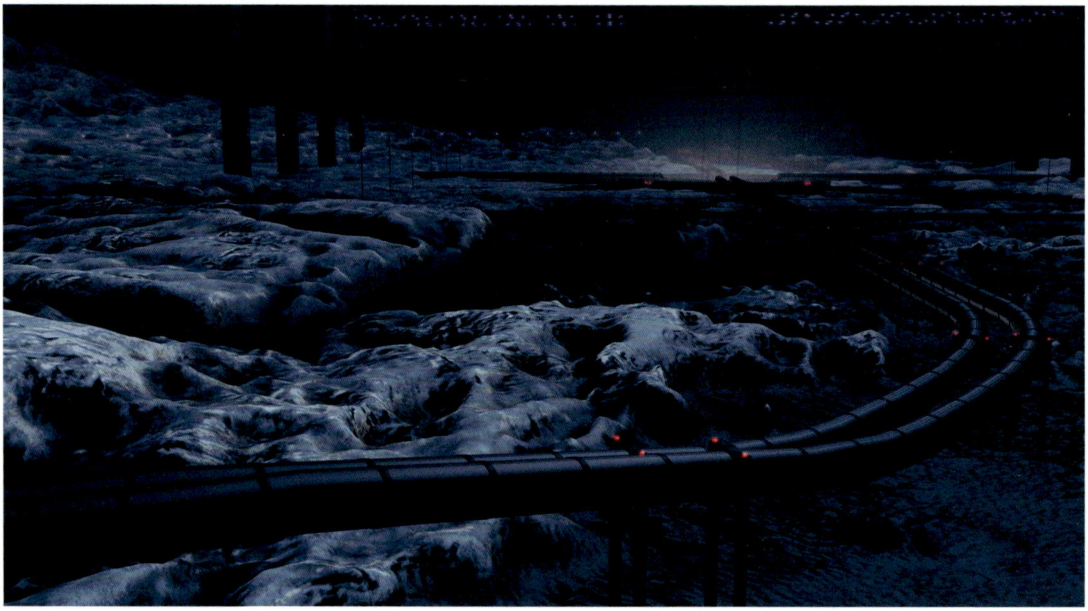

Stills from *RAKHNE*, 2023, 4K singel-channel video installation

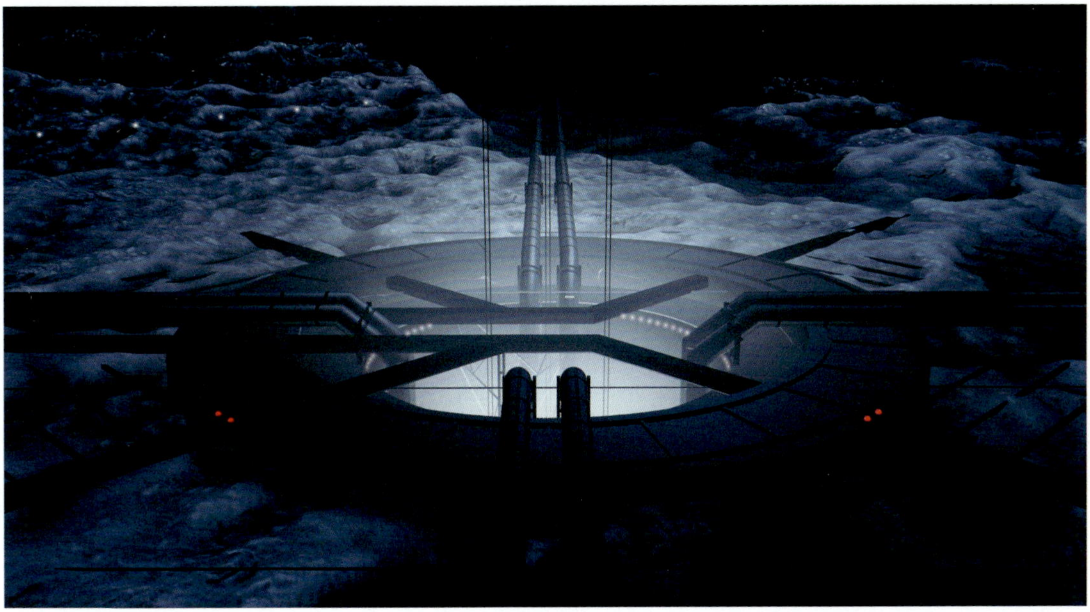

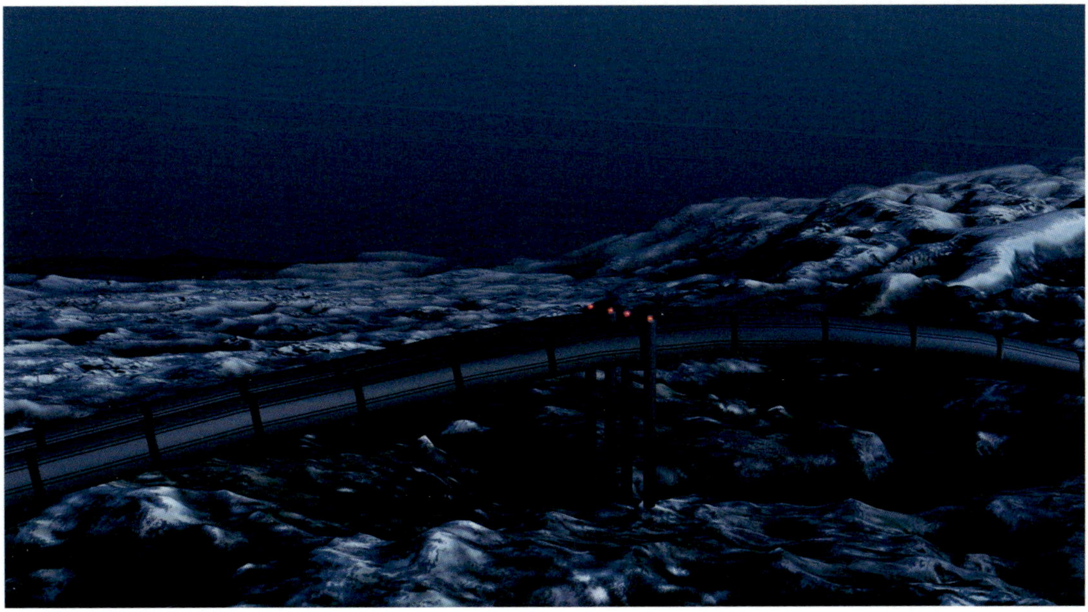

Emilija Škarnulytė

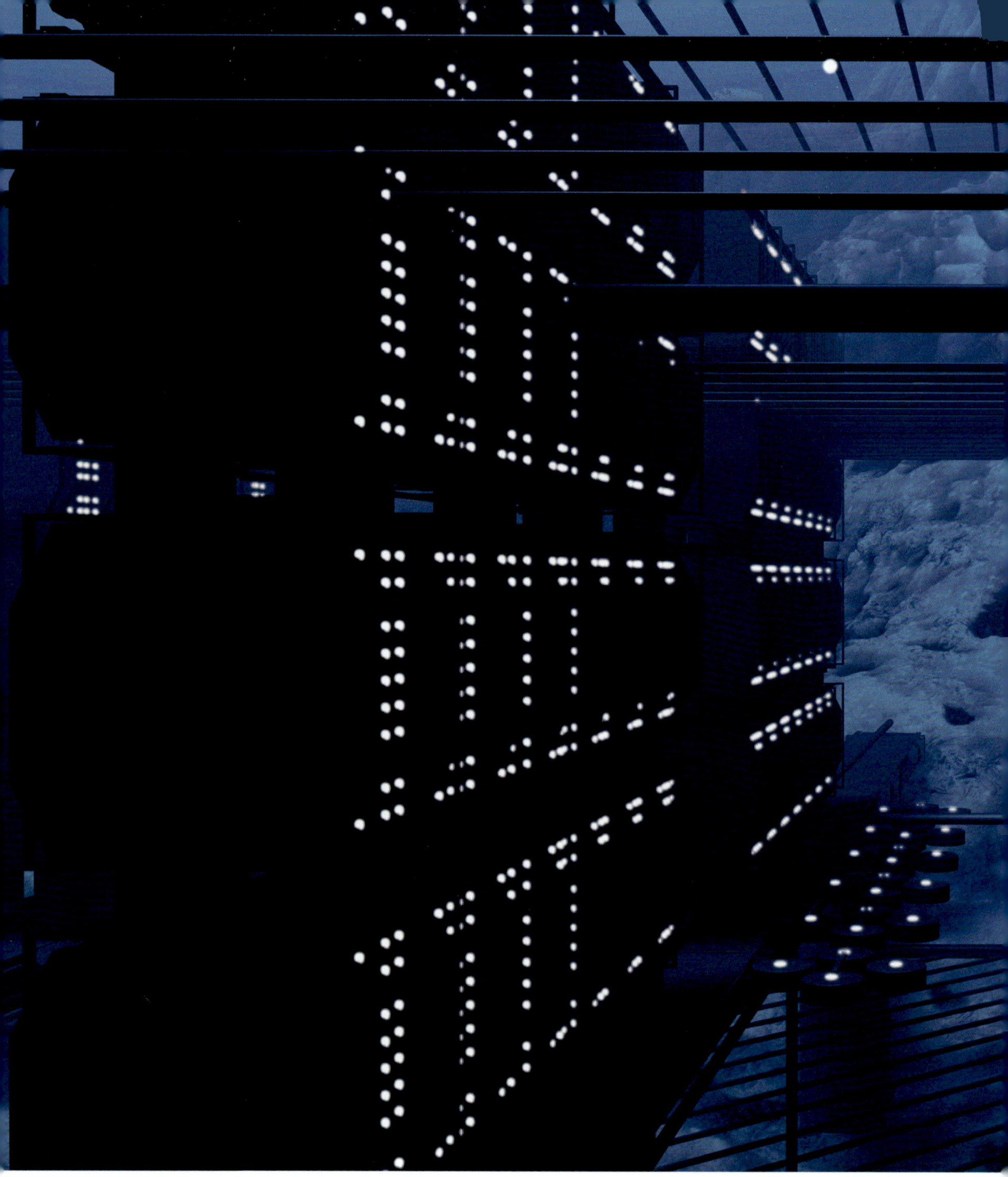

Still from *RAKHNE*, 2023, 4K singel-channel video installation

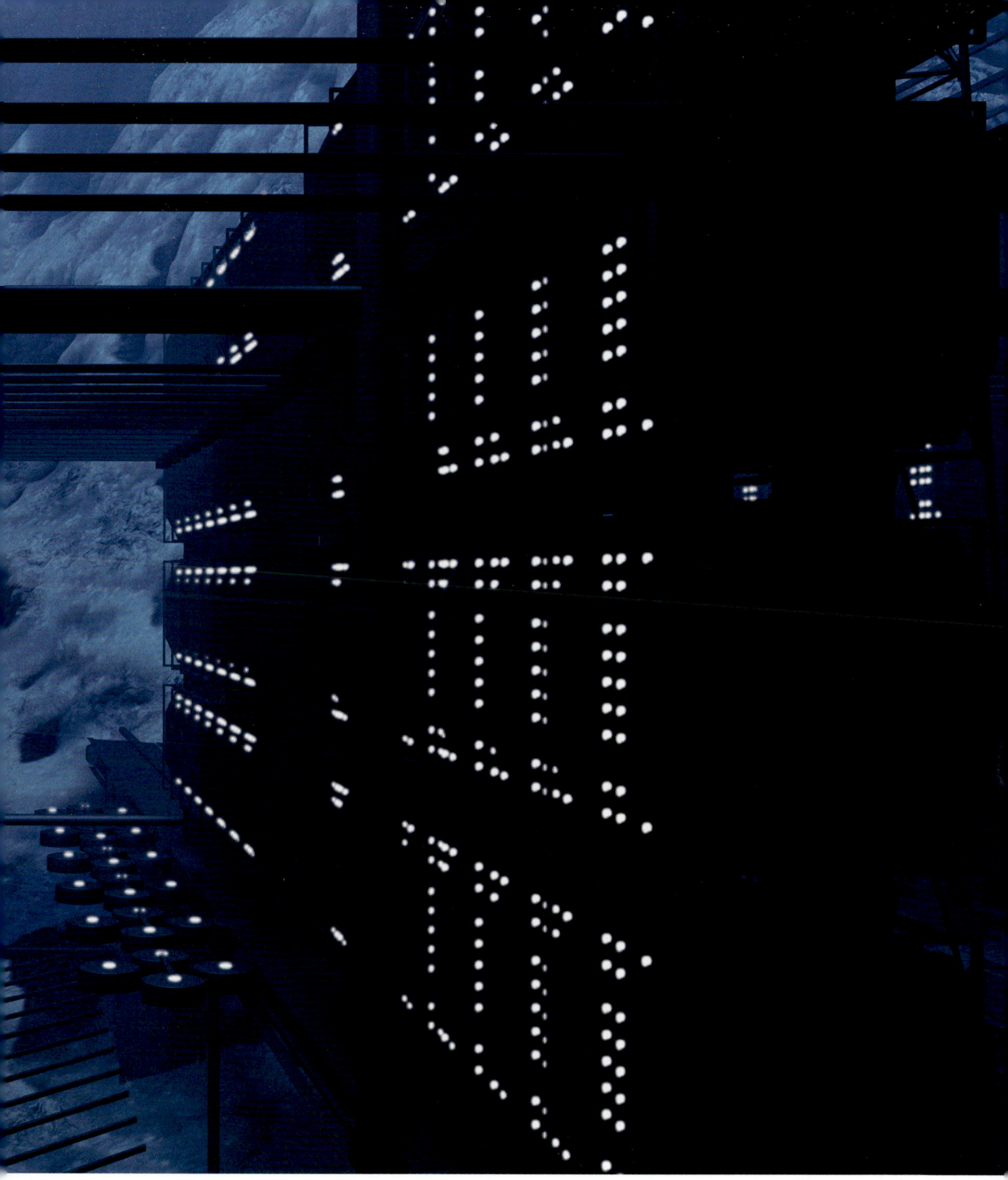

Emilija Škarnulytė

LESIA VASYLCHENKO

Lesia Vasylchenko (b. 1990 in Kyiv) **is an artist and curator based in Oslo who works across photography, video, and sculpture**

The sculptural video installation *Sensing the Near Real-Time (SNRT)* (2023) continues Lesia Vasylchenko's interest in remote-sensing technologies and the different temporalities they register and construct. Four screens display images that portray the temporal scales of our planet's geological changes: the deep time of melting glaciers at Spitsbergen; earthquakes in Ethiopia; expanding nuclear capabilities in China; and nuclear terrorism in Ukraine, where, at the time of writing, Russian forces occupy the Zaporizhia Nuclear Power Plant. The videos are based on images produced by satellites from low earth orbit through Synthetic Aperture Radar (SAR) and are obtained in collaboration with the Department of Geosciences at University of Oslo, the National Institute of Geophysics and Volcanology in Rome, Italy, and the Open Nuclear Network in Vienna. SAR images are not captured by photographic lenses, but by radar signals bouncing off a surface. These signals can "see" through darkness, clouds, smoke, vegetation, snow, or sand to reveal what is underneath.

This commission also entails simulated nuclear-waste glass. Vitrification, the process through which melted materials are solidified into glass, is currently the leading method for the long-term storage and disposal of nuclear waste arising from spent fuel. By juxtaposing simulations of this material with soil from a war-damaged Ukrainian grain field, and images of planetary surfaces, Vasylchenko engages with geological and human timescales and points to how data is extracted from above and below.

● **Biography** VASYLCHENKO is a co-curator of the artist-run gallery Podium in Oslo and a founder of *STRUKTURA. Time*, a platform for research in art and media archaeology. She holds a degree in journalism from the Taras Shevchenko National University of Kyiv and a degree in fine arts from the Oslo National Academy of the Arts. Her work was included in the MUNCH Triennale in Oslo and has been shown at the Louvre Museum, Paris; Haus der Kulturen der Welt, Berlin; Oslo Kunstforening; and The Wrong New Digital Art Biennale. Her work is part of the collection of Museum of Contemporary Art KIASMA, Helsinki.

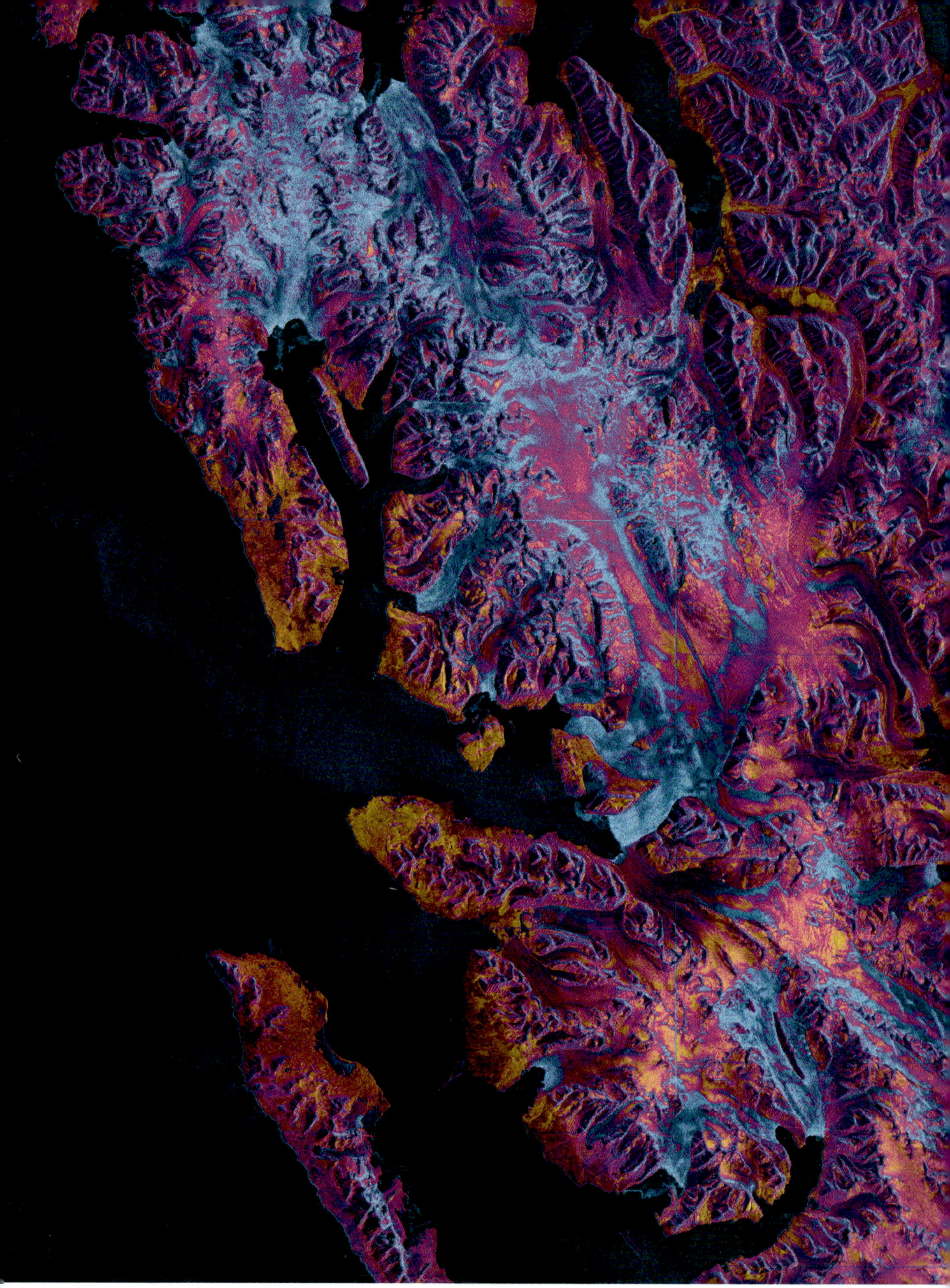

InSAR-image from *SNRT,* 2023, video sculpture, mixed media
Image: Andreas Kääb and Thomas Schellenberger, Department of Geosciences, University of Oslo
Copernicus Sentinel-1 data / European Space Agency (ESA)

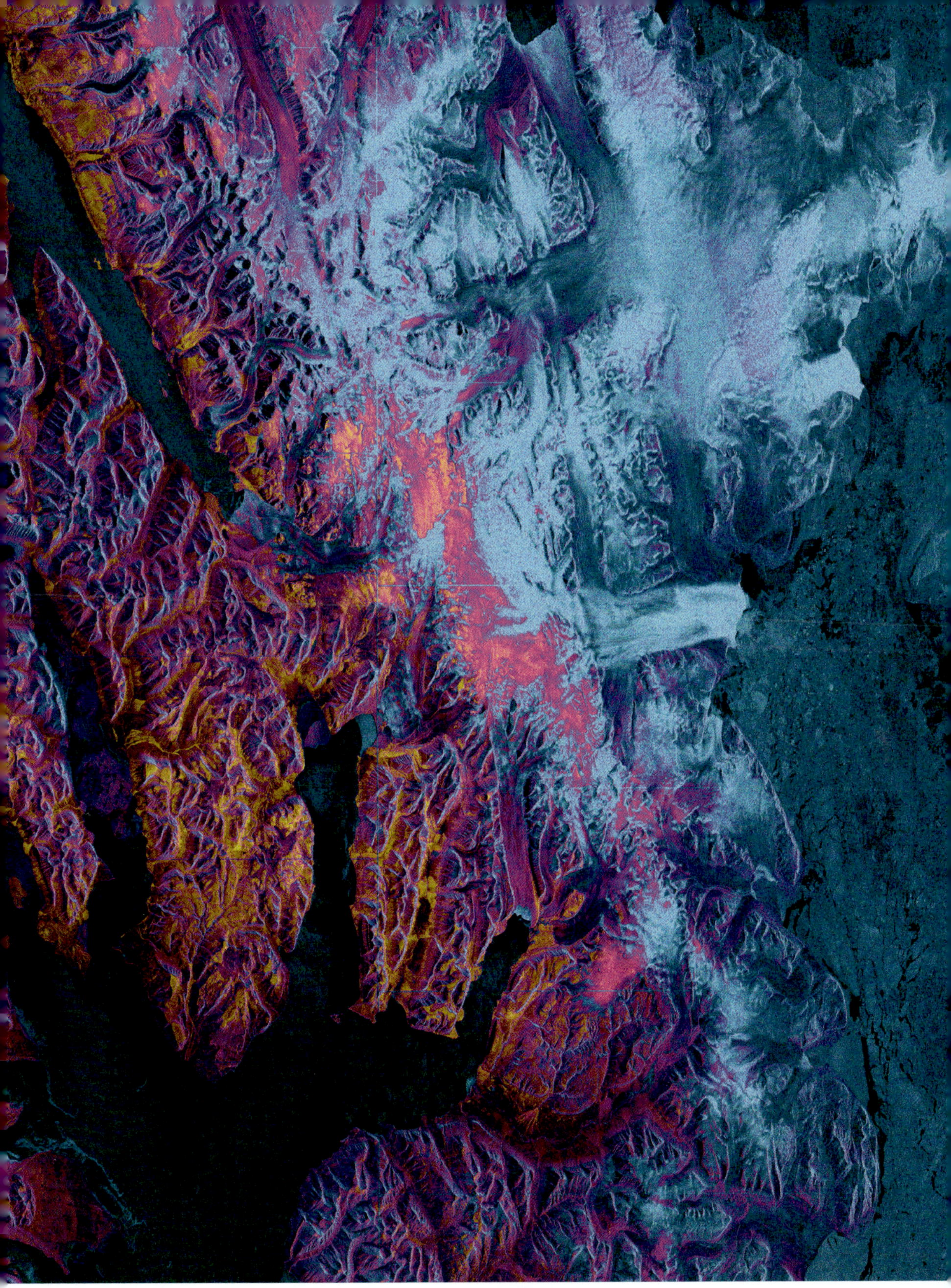

Lesia Vasylchenko

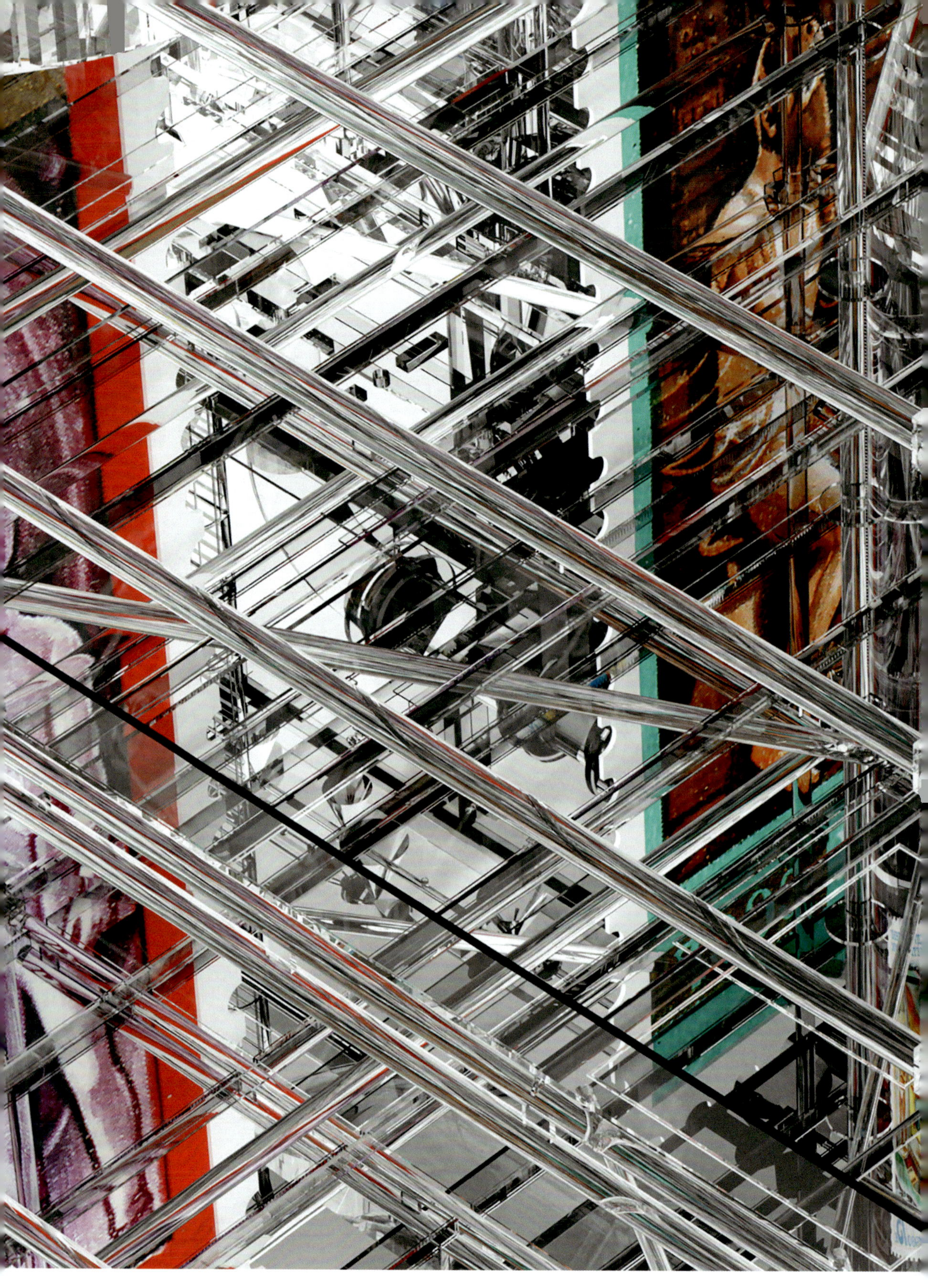

Still from *Postcard From Non Existing City*, 2021, single-channel color video with sound

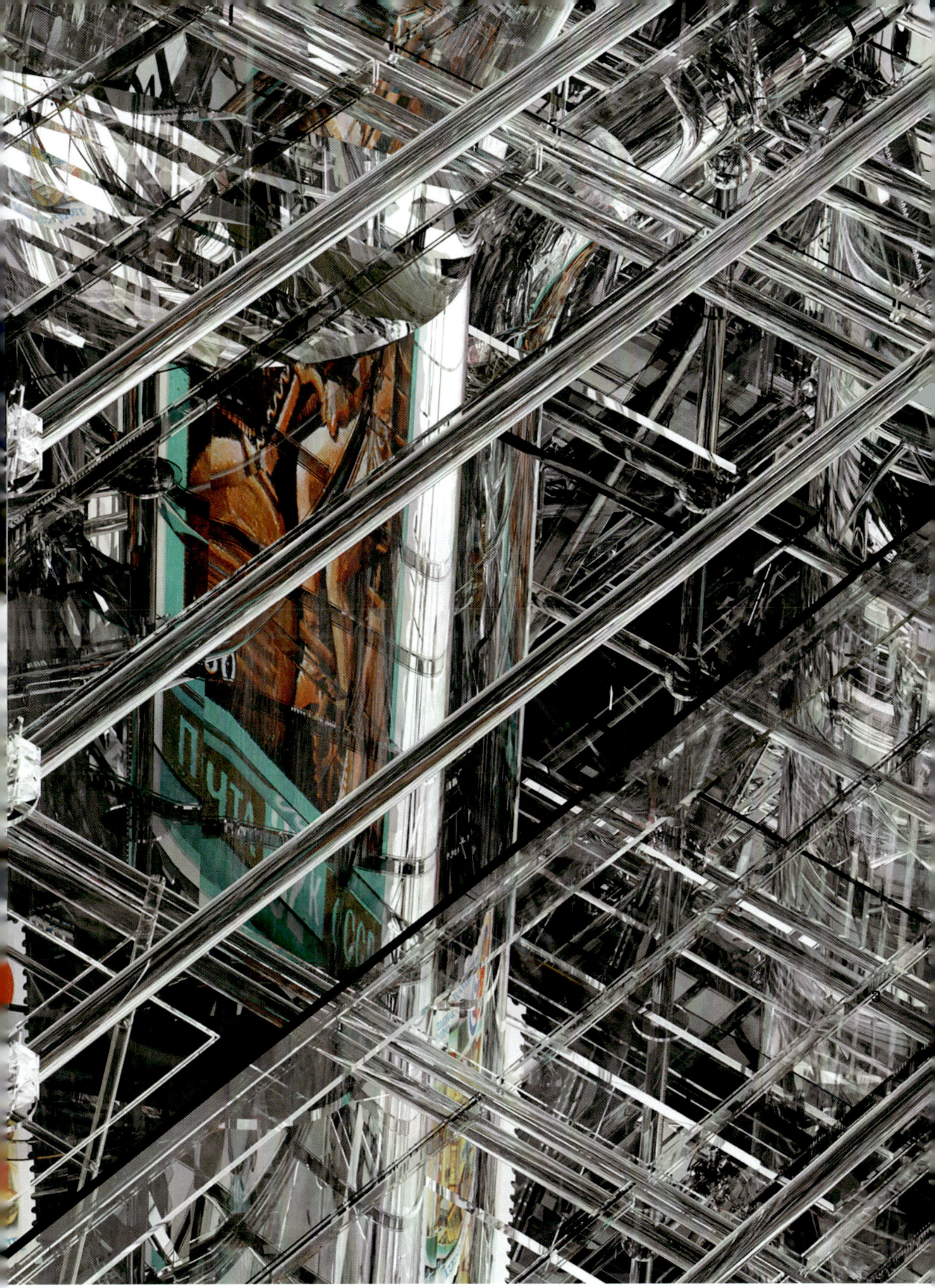

Lesia Vasylchenko

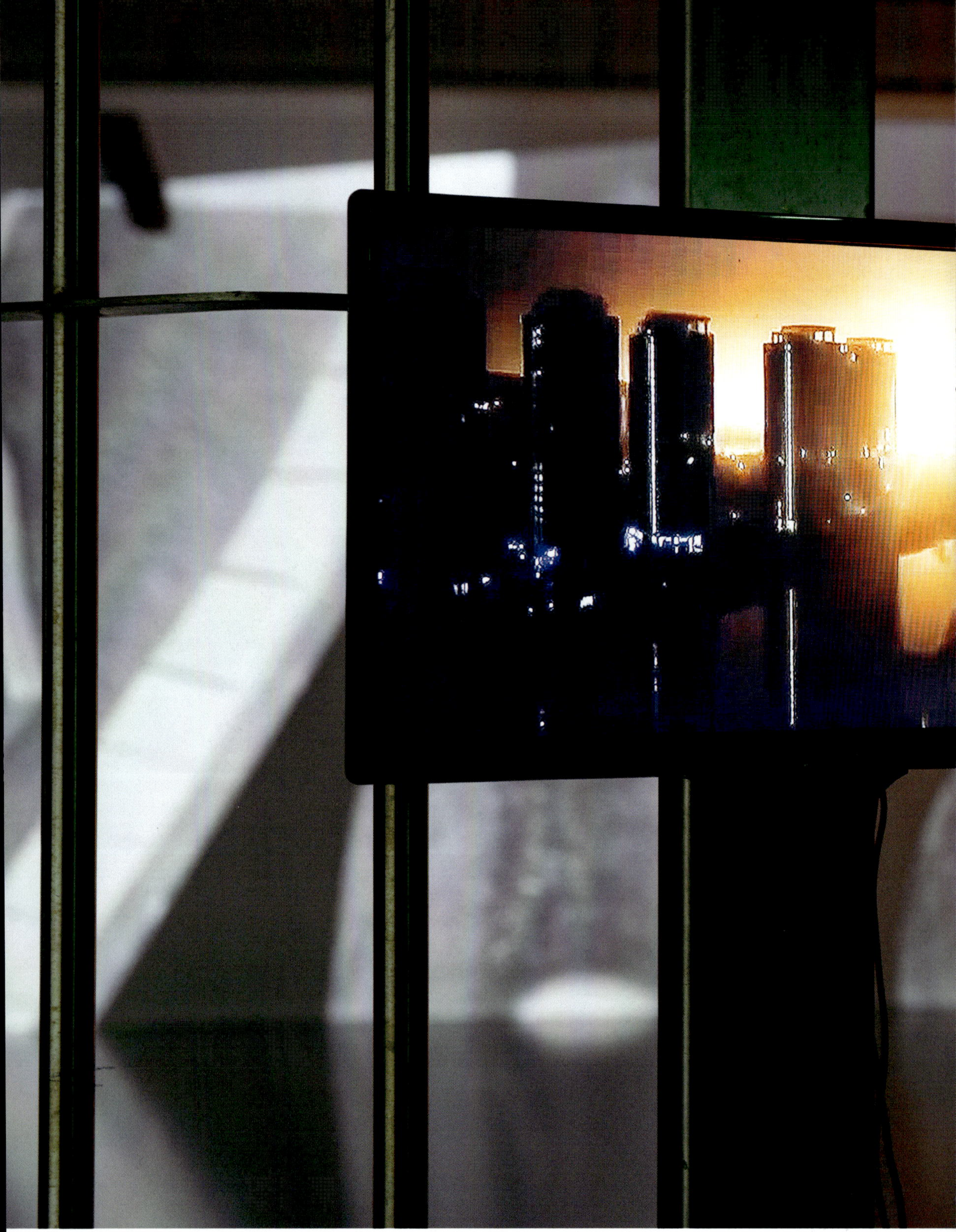

Installation view, *Tachyoness*, 2022, multi-channel video installation

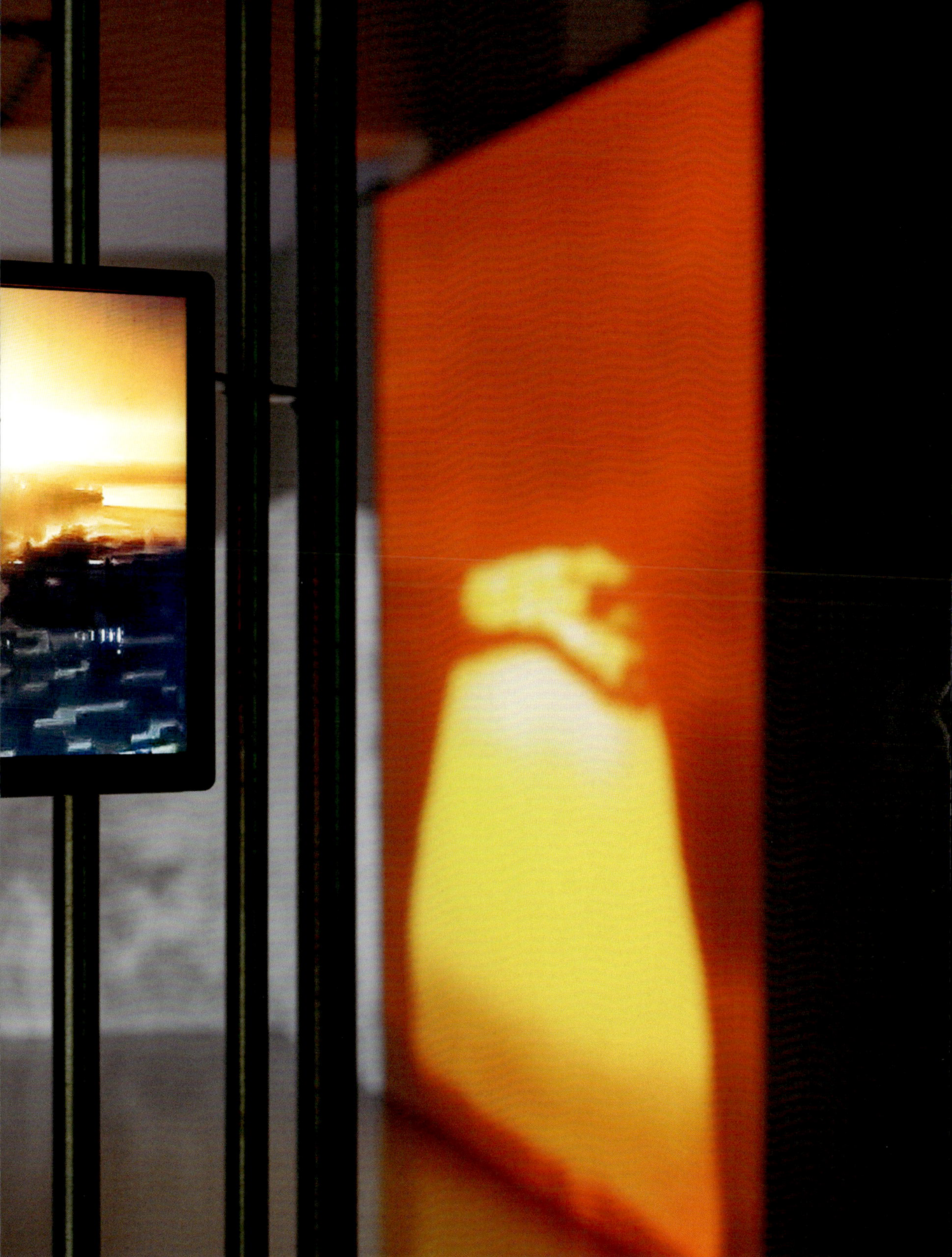

Lesia Vasylchenko

ISTVAN VIRAG

Istvan Virag (b. 1982 in Oroshaza, Hungary) **is a photographer and artist living and working in Oslo**

Commissioned for *New Visions 2023*, Istvan Virag's *Pixel Pitch vol. 4* is the latest in a series of research-based videos exploring the relations between economics, the overconsumption of energy, and our environment. The videos are displayed on low-resolution outdoor LED-screen modules with a pixel pitch of 12 mm. "Pixel pitch" designates the distance between the pixels and indicates the resolution of the screen. Depending on one's distance to a screen, the pixels fluctuate between being legible as a coherent image and appearing as pure source of artificial light. These screens, which are approximately human height and lean against the wall, could also serve as building blocks in large-scale advertising boards – and therefore reference their role in the continuous, global flow of capital.

In *Pixel Pitch vol. 4*, Virag comments specifically on the current state and uncertain trajectories of the energy economy. Through a montage of documentary and digitally rendered video clips that he has sourced online as well as captured himself, Virag conducts a meditative visual examination of the oil industry and of alternative energy futures beyond fossil fuels. The video interlaces image sequences pertaining to the abstract mechanics of energy production, such as industrial landscapes and extraction infrastructure, with clips of organic motifs related to the ecosystems and species that are affected by fossil-fuel extraction, including plankton and humans. *Pixel Pitch vol. 4* explores associative relations between the dark-colored, viscous oil fueling capital flows and the hundreds of millions of years of sun-powered, compressed life that comprise it.

● **Biography** VIRAG studied photography at Bilder Nordic School of Photography, Oslo and holds a BFA from Oslo National Academy of the Arts, an MSc in economics from University of Pécs, Hungary, and a BSc in economics from Budapest Business School. He has presented solo exhibitions at Podium, Oslo; White Box Gallery, Oslo National Academy of the Arts; and the School of Visual Arts, New York. Virag's work has also been displayed at Greenlightdistrict 2021, Skiens Kunstforening, Skien, Norway; Oslo Negative; Studio 17, Stavanger, Norway; Kunsthall Oslo (in collaboration with the artist group Infopsin); and Statens 131. Kunstutstilling at Kunstnernes Hus, Oslo.

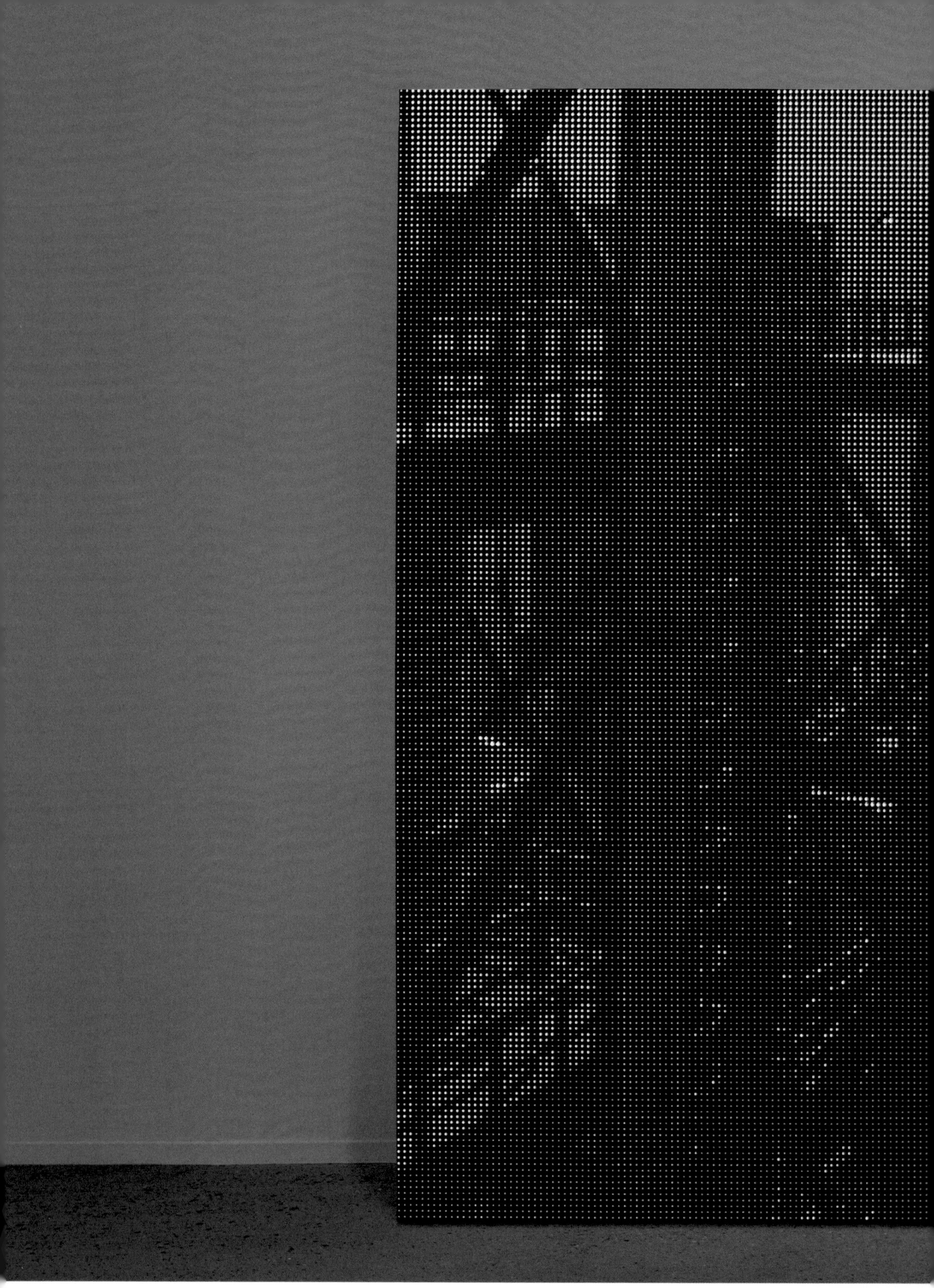

Pixel Pitch vol. 4, 2023, video on LED display

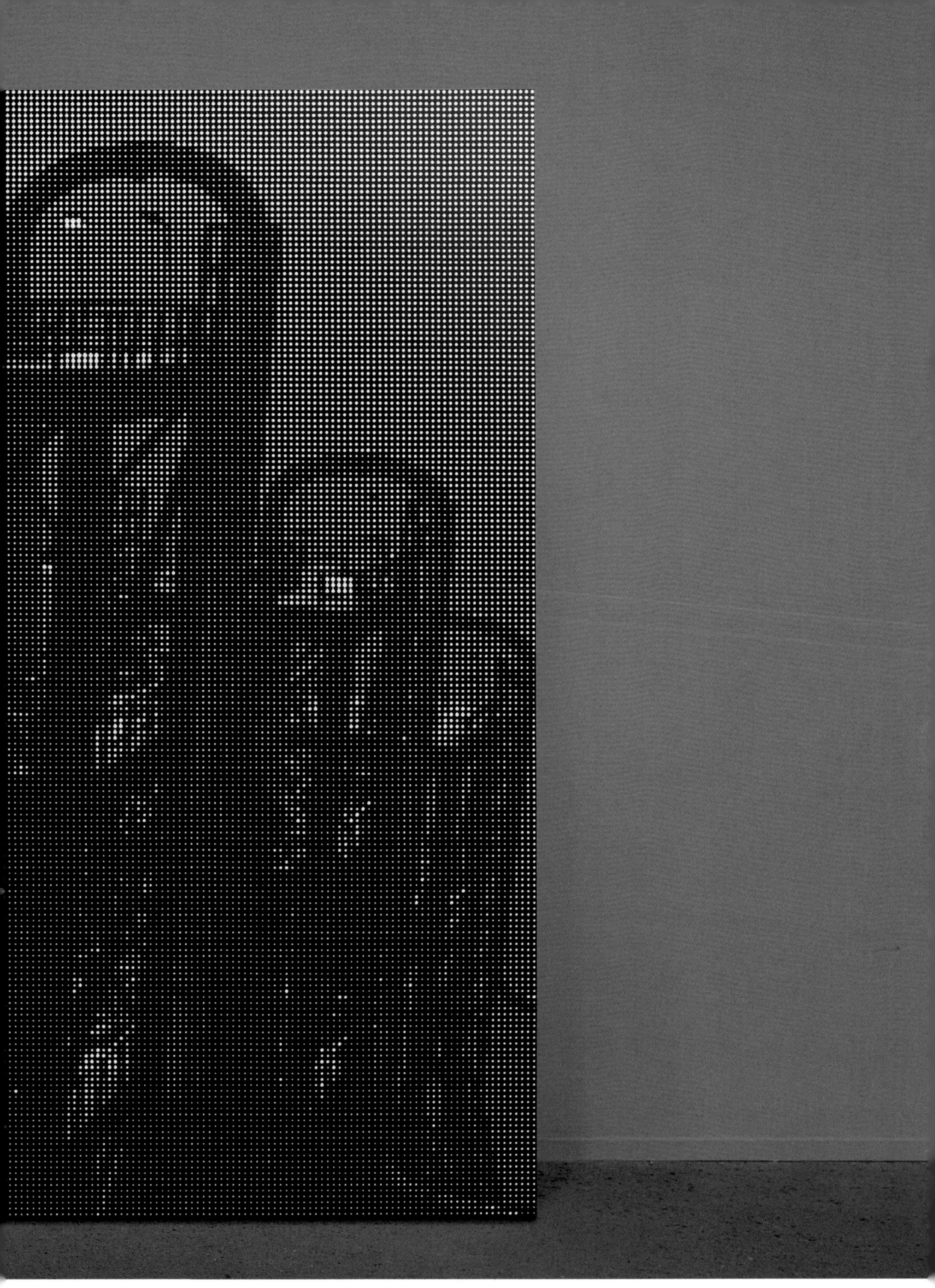

Istvan Virag

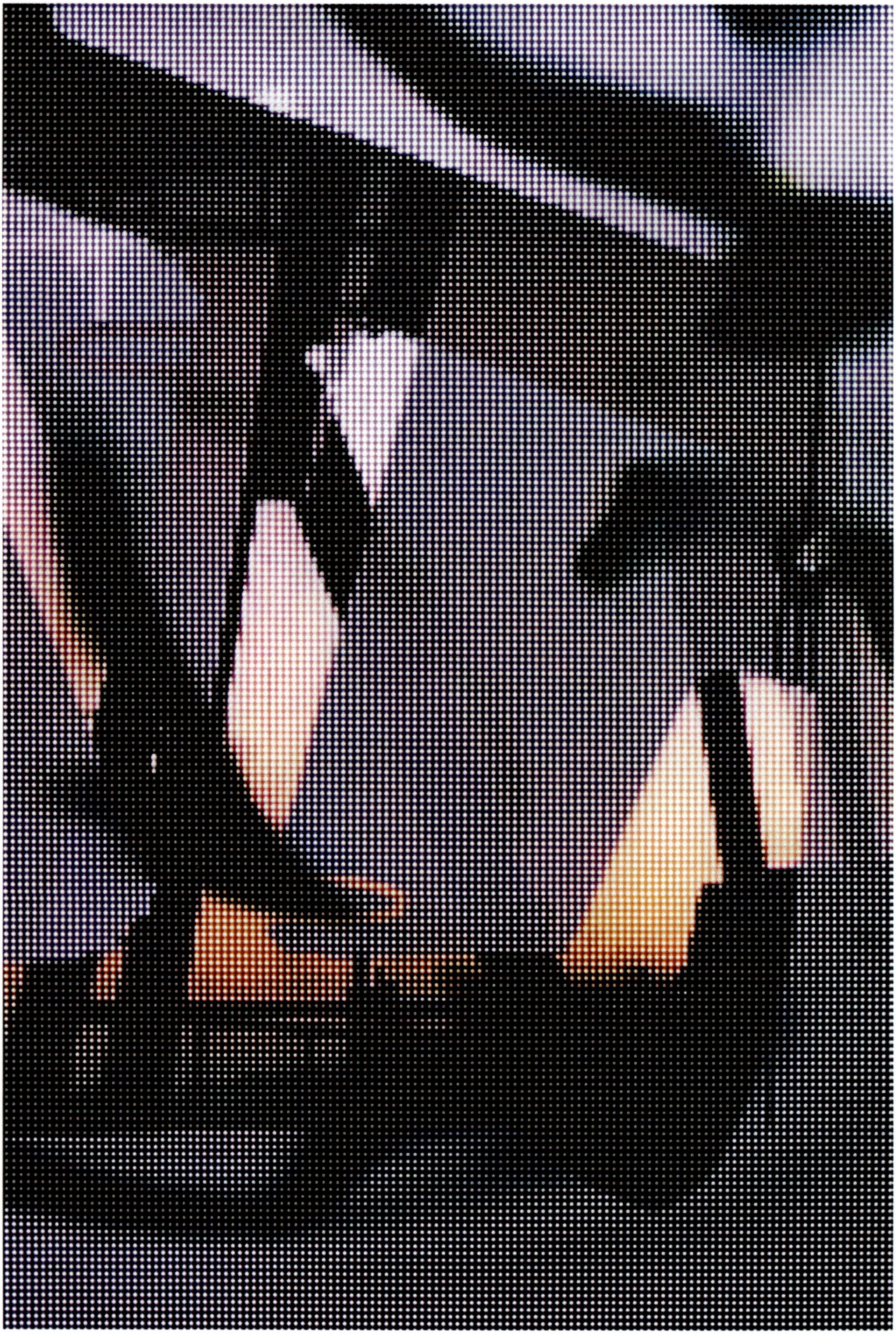

Details of *Pixel Pitch vol. 4*, 2023, video on LED display

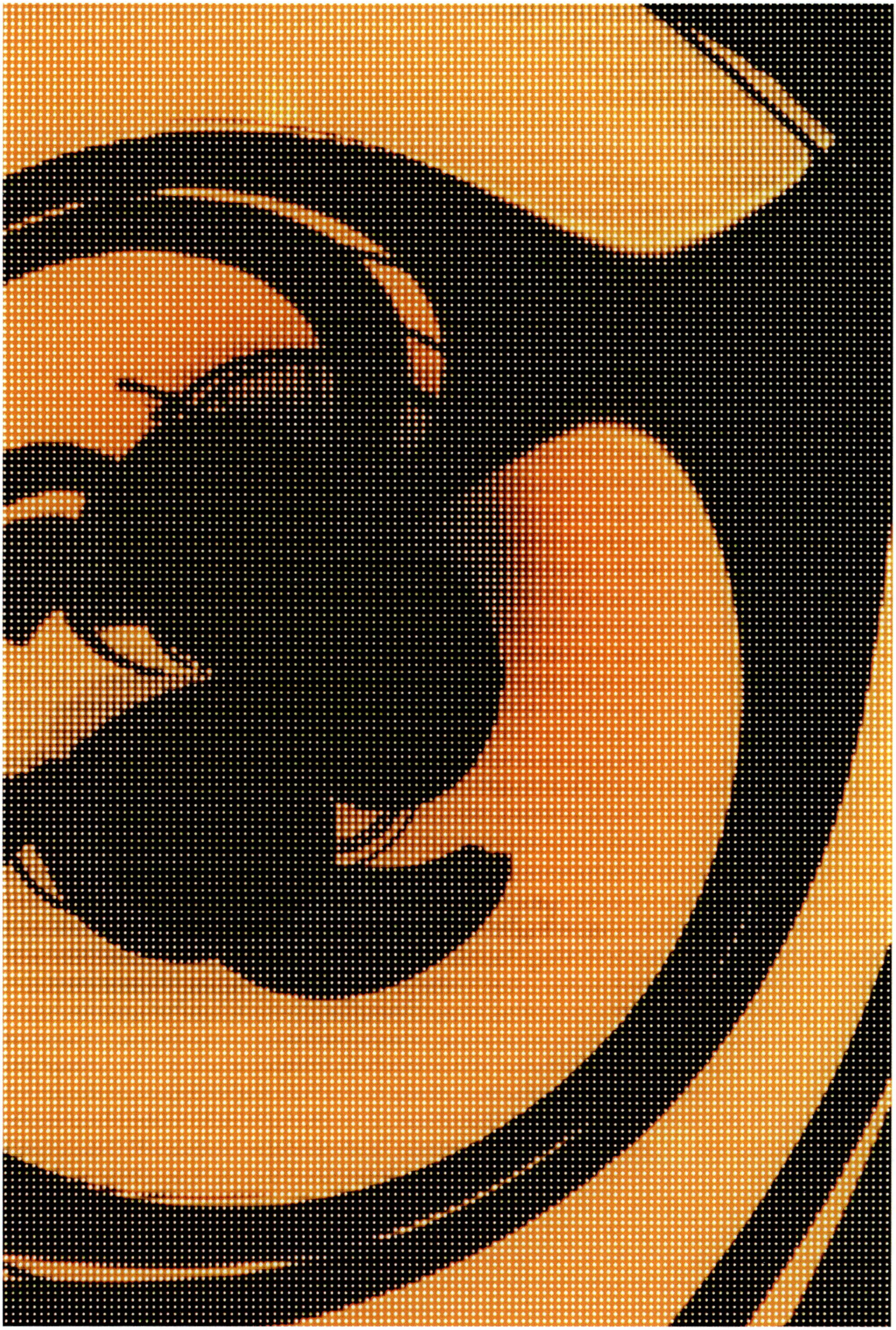

Istvan Virag

Detail of *Pixel Pitch vol. 4*, 2023, video on LED display

Istvan Virag